Christina Nob [illegible]
Liberties, shor [illegible] up in severe poverty in Ireland she later moved to England where she was married twice. She has three children from her first marriage. She now runs the Christina Noble Foundation in Vietnam, caring for orphaned street children.

The sequel to *Bridge Across My Sorrows*, *Mama Tina*, is also published by Corgi Books.

Robert Coram is a former journalist who has been twice nominated for the Pulitzer Prize. He is now a part-time writing instructor at Emory University, Georgia, and writes novels and works of non-fiction.

www.**booksattransworld**.co.uk

Also by Christina Noble

MAMA TINA

and published by Corgi Books

Bridge Across My Sorrows

THE CHRISTINA NOBLE STORY

Christina Noble
with Robert Coram

CORGI BOOKS

BRIDGE ACROSS MY SORROWS

A CORGI BOOK : 0 552 14288 3

Originally published in Great Britain by
John Murray (Publishers) Ltd

PRINTING HISTORY
John Murray edition published 1994
Corgi edition published 1995

17 19 20 18 16

Set in 10pt Plantin by
Phoenix Typesetting, Ilkley, West Yorkshire.

Corgi Books are published by Transworld Publishers,
61-63 Uxbridge Road, London W5 5SA,
a division of The Random House Group Ltd,
in Australia by Random House Australia (Pty) Ltd,
20 Alfred Street, Milsons Point, Sydney, NSW 2061, Australia,
in New Zealand by Random House New Zealand Ltd,
18 Poland Road, Glenfield, Auckland 10, New Zealand
and in South Africa by Random House (Pty) Ltd,
Endulini, 5a Jubilee Road, Parktown 2193, South Africa.

Printed and bound in Great Britain by
Cox & Wyman Ltd, Reading, Berkshire

To my mother. I made it because you were my beginning, and a mother to the end.

To my children, Helen, Androula and Nicolas. Without you, my dream could never have been realized. I love you.

To my son, Thomas, never forgotten.

To my sisters and brothers. I love you.

To Madame Nguyen Thi Man for believing in me.

To the Sunshine Children of Ho Chi Minh City and to the children of the world.

Contents

List of Illustrations

The author and publishers would like to thank the following for giving their permission to reproduce illustrations: 1: Radhika Chalasani/Gamma-Liaison; 15 (top): Gail Fisher/*LA Times*

Acknowledgements

The success of my work is due in large part to all of those wonderful people in the Christina Noble Foundation International. There are so many of them that it would be impossible to mention all the names. But I am deeply grateful to each and every one. Thanks also to the selfless staff at the Children's Medical and Social Centre in Ho Chi Minh City and to the dedicated people in my office.

There are a number of people, however, whom I must single out. Peter Williams, British Ambassador in Vietnam, has been a great supporter and friend. At Enterprise Oil in London there are: Graham Hearne, Chairman and Chief Executive, John Walmsley, Managing Director, Ray Dafter, Director of Corporate Affairs, Joe Woolf, Director of Human Resources, and John Shute, Operations Manager. Tom Newman, Manager of Enterprise Oil in Vietnam, was there at the beginning. For her enthusiasm, my thanks to Mary Riddell, Women's Deputy Editor, *Today*.

The support of Les Blair, Manager of British Gas in Vietnam, Neil Rigden and the *Vietnam Investment Review*, has been of long duration.

Dr John McCusker, surgeon of St Margaret's Hospital in Sydney, and Professor Michael Bennet, Head of Gynaecology and Obstetrics at the Royal Women's Hospital, Sydney, saved my life in the summer of 1993.

For their support and hard work, I thank Lloyd and

Lois Jones, Leigh Hatcher, Janete Davenport, Dr Sandra Short, Jill Death and Pauline Barton, Sylvestre Poulain, Director of the Laboratoires Biogaleniques, Jean Antoine Bouchez, President of Association Christina Noble, France, Martine Sonneville, Raymond Laas, Albert Pinay and Ecoles Sans Frontières. Also, Jacques Thai Son, Miss Oanh, Mama and family, and Dominique Torres, of Antenne 2. The interest expressed by UNESCO in Paris has been of immense help.

I would also like to thank Tom Ward, Peter Banham of Banham Security, Joanna Pyner and her mam, Aideen Naughton, Senior Paediatrician, Royal Leicester Infirmary, for her help both in and out of Vietnam, Audrey Kenrick, for her generous help, the West Midlands Health Authority, and Catherine Mylofski.

Thanks to the Eye and Ear Hospital in Dublin; Doctor Vincent Kenny and the three doctors he sent to Vietnam from the Institute of Tropical Medicine, Dublin, Bridget Ruean, Gay Byrne, and the people of Ireland.

In America, I would like to thank in particular Glenn Meisenheimer and the Board of the Christina Noble Foundation, Bill Kimball of Vets with a Mission, Gene Spanos, and March Schwartz .

I must offer my special thanks to the Government of Vietnam, especially Mr Nghiem Xuan Tue and Ms Thien Huong at the Ministry of Labour, Invalids and Social Affairs, Dr Phuong, Tu Du Hospital, Mr Tran Van Viet and Mr Luong Van Ly, Department of Foreign Affairs, the People's Committee of Ho Chi Minh City, Mr Hanh, Mr Ngo Trung, and Tran Quynh Dan. Also to Federico Mayor of UNESCO, a big thank you from the street children of Ho Chi Minh City.

Finally, Robert Coram showed immense tolerance and humour during the writing of this book, for which I am grateful.

Prologue

I came to Vietnam because of a dream I had almost twenty years ago. The dream told me to work with the street children of this poor, jangled, disease-ridden country. You might laugh at that. You might say it was nothing but a dream and that only someone who is Irish would act on a dream as if it were a message from God. And you could be right. After all, my coming here was not anything I could explain then or anything I can explain today. I had a dream – a vision, if you will – that ordered me to Vietnam. That is all.

My eyes were wide with anticipation that day as the aircraft dropped low over the flat fields and prepared to land at Ho Chi Minh City. The fields were as green as in my native Ireland. But the sun was of a blinding brilliance that I rarely saw as a child. As we approached Tan Son Nhat airport, I saw clusters of small circular lakes. 'That's where the Americans dropped bombs,' said the man sitting beside me. Now the ground was close and rushing past with such speed that the green fields, laid out in almost geometric patterns, were blurred. I sat back, tightened my seat belt, and took a deep breath.

It was September 1989, and I was a middle-aged woman with no education, no money, and no real idea of what I was going to do in Vietnam. Behind me was a life that – except for the birth of three beautiful children – I considered devoid of accomplishment.

When I stepped off the aeroplane I thought I had entered a creaky old picture set. This could not be a real place. Grassy areas along the runways were still pockmarked with bomb and rocket craters from a war that had ended almost fifteen years earlier. Revetments and bunkers, burned by years of hot sun and washed by years of monsoon rains, stood grey and bleak across the runway, reminders that this was the Americans' centre of air operations during the war. Aircraft hangars lined the taxiway, and behind the hangars, some of which still contained old American military aircraft, was a tall fence topped by rusty barbed wire. Machine-gun emplacements and security guard posts stood empty.

Small, slender, stern-faced soldiers surrounded the aircraft. Their faded and tattered green uniforms were emblazoned with the yellow star of this communist country. They wore sandals, a touch that, were it not for their reputation in war and for their unsmiling faces, might have been almost comical. But there was nothing at all humorous in the brisk no-nonsense fashion in which they loaded us aboard a rickety old bus and drove us across the tarmac to the terminal. The bus had curtains in the windows.

Inside the terminal I felt assaulted by the high, tinny, wailing dissonance of martial music blaring over the public address system, and by the heat and humidity that seemed to wrap me in a steamy blanket.

I was gripped with fear as I waited to be processed by customs and immigration. All I could think of was what the nuns drilled into us when I was a child in Ireland.

'Tell me, children,' the nun would say as she raised her eyebrows expectantly, 'who are the communists?'

'The communists torture Catholics, Sister,' we would respond in our high and obedient young voices.

'Why do the communists torture Catholics, children?'

'To make them give up their faith, Sister.'

'Would you give up your faith, children?'

'No, Sister.'

Then the nun would lower her voice, narrow her eyes, and in dramatic tones ask, 'What if the communists lined your mothers and your fathers up against a wall and gunned them down? Would you give up your faith then, children?'

'No, Sister.'

The nun would nod in approval. Her eyes would rove over us seeking out the faint of heart. 'Beware of the communists, children.'

I trembled as I picked up my luggage and prepared to go through customs. There was nothing welcoming or even remotely friendly about the interview. It was more of an interrogation. Why was I in Vietnam? How much money did I have? Who would I see? Did I know anyone in the government? One of the officials took my watch and my jewellery and weighed each piece in his hand before returning it to me.

It was more than three hours before I came out of the terminal and caught a cab into Ho Chi Minh City. Already I was beginning to wonder if I had made the right decision in coming here. My dream of working with the street children was beginning to seem rather silly. I had never been to South-east Asia. I knew nothing of this country. I was frightened of the communists. I did not speak Vietnamese. I had no idea of how to get government approval to work with children. And everywhere I looked I saw another reminder that I was a stranger in a strange land.

The wide avenue into town was littered with wrecks; all of the cars and lorries were very old and they coughed and roared and rattled and raced through crowds of people. Motorbikes zipped about like frenetic ants. Horns beeped. Brakes squealed. Bicycles by the hundred flowed through the intersections, guided, it seemed, by some arcane set of metaphysical rules as they mixed with cars and cyclos and monstrous lorries. Men in pyjamas and conical hats hunkered down beside the road while countless others roamed aimlessly, their eyes glazed and their shoulders hunched. Many were young men who wore the faces of their fathers. Women talked while, at their feet, children defecated. Everywhere I looked, men and children were urinating. I rolled down the window of the cab and was slammed with the foul stench of human waste that was heaped high in the gutters. I could hardly breathe the thick, hot, humid air. The place was mad. Orderless.

How could the customs and immigration officers be so slow and meticulous and controlled when the city seemed so out of control?

I arrived at the Rex Hotel hot, covered with perspiration, and very frazzled. I tossed my clothes on the bed and rushed straight into the shower where I encountered the largest cockroach I had ever seen. Spiders and ants crawled across the floor. I whirled and almost leapt from the room.

'Jesus, God,' I said aloud. 'I can't handle this. I'm going to die.' Was I wrong in coming to Vietnam? Could I ever get used to this place?

And then I remembered the dream of almost twenty years earlier and knew that I had to stay, at least until I decided if the dream was a vision that directed my life, or if it was only a dream. In my dream I had seen a little girl reaching towards me for help. Somehow I knew she was hungry and frightened and that she had no family. Behind her were many other children, all rushing towards me and all crying for me to help. But I couldn't reach her. Then she was gone and all that was left was grey smoke that twirled and twirled as the wind moaned. Through the smoke appeared a light, a great white light, and within seconds the light evolved into letters. Then the word 'Vietnam' was burning across the sky in brilliant, almost blinding lights.

When I had awakened that night, I wondered if children were truly suffering as they seemed to be in the dream. And I knew then I must go to Vietnam. It was my destiny. But I had three children and a business to run. So why did I have such a dream when I could do nothing?

Now I was here. But why? What could I do?

During the next few weeks I ventured further and further from the hotel. I met a few Vietnamese people and knew we would become friends. One was a lovely woman named My Loc whom I met at the Ben Thanh market. She sold children's clothes from her little stall. I remembered as I stopped there that shoppers drove their motorbikes into the stall and that a dog chased a rat through the market filled with people and everyone ignored the chase.

Once I stopped at a little kerbside vendor and ordered a special treat, a banana leaf in which was packed a nut-filled ball of rice. As I accepted the delicacy I saw an enormous black and very fat rat run through the vendor's stand. No-one paid any attention. But I couldn't eat the rice.

Everywhere I saw ragged children. Someone told me as many as fifty thousand of them roamed the streets of Ho Chi Minh City. They are called *bui doi,* a harsh, dismissive term meaning 'the dust of life'. They are terribly poor. They are covered with lice and fleas and infected with numerous diseases. No-one will touch the *bui doi.* No-one wants to be close to them. No-one speaks kindly to them. They are treated like vermin.

I was reminded then of my growing up on the streets of Dublin and how I was treated by others.

One night I was feeling very sad and walked down to the market to visit my new friend, My Loc. Her brother, Tien, was there and he was holding a guitar.

'Do you play the guitar?' I asked.

He nodded shyly.

'Sit here beside me and I'll sing a song for you,' I said to him.

I began singing. A few moments later the street children began sliding from the shadows, drawn by the sound of my voice. Soon there were dozens of them. As do most children when they hear music, these children listened enraptured. They stared at me as I sang 'Yesterday Once More' and 'Sad Movies'. I started to sing 'Danny Boy' but I stopped after the first few words. It was too painful for me. My mam had sung that song around the house in Dublin. My dad had sung that song to me when I was a child. And I used to sing that song to my little brother when I was putting him to sleep. Every Irish person loves that song but I could not sing it that night.

I stared at the children, my gaze lingering on each of them. Beyond the filth and the lice and disease they were beautiful children. I was being forced towards a decision. I was being forced to confront my dream. I got up and ran for the hotel.

Several days later, late in the afternoon, I stepped from the lobby of the Rex Hotel and stood on the top step talking to the doorman about the shops around the corner. The Rex then was a hotel only for foreigners. It is at the intersection of Nguyen Hue and Le Loi, two of the most famous streets in Ho Chi Minh City, and dozens of street children hang out in the small park across the street. As I talked to the doorman, I noticed two little girls sitting on the ground across the street, *bui doi* playing in the dirt.

I stared through them, not wanting to see them. But one of the little girls caught my eye and smiled. She had only two teeth. She held out her hand towards me, palm up, begging. Very faintly I heard her say, 'Give me. Give me.' The two girls were very dirty and their clothes were old and ragged.

Suddenly the memories of Ireland were very strong. The condition of the little girls, the state they were in, brought back painful memories. I did not want that pain again. I walked down the steps and tried to talk with a woman who was selling cigarettes. But the only English she knew was 'No money, no honey.' I didn't know what she meant. Later I discovered it was an expression left over from the Americans.

I walked on. At the corner I paused. An impulse I can't explain caused me to turn and look again at the little girls across the street.

The air was filled with the beep-beep cacophony from the horns of thousands of motorbikes. Blue exhaust smoke lingering in the calm late-afternoon air was disturbing and ominous. I felt that something was about to happen but I didn't know what.

I stared at the two girls. Even with her gap-toothed smile, the one who had reached towards me was a child of uncommon beauty. She had long dark hair and enormous eyes and delicate features. As she looked into my eyes, I imagined I could read her mind: 'I thought you were coming to us and now you've gone away.'

I wanted to turn to the right and go round the corner and walk down Le Loi and look at the shops, but I simply could not walk away. I slowly crossed the street towards the two girls.

One of them was about five and the other perhaps three. As I approached, the younger one looked up and her eyes told me what she saw: a wealthy white European, a person far superior to her. They did not see my fears and doubts, they did not see me as I saw myself, a foreigner in a strange land, and they did not sense my insecurities. All they saw was a person of importance.

But I wasn't important. I was one of them. I was like those little girls. But could I admit that? Did I have the ability, the strength, the courage, to say, 'Yes, I am one of them.'

The girl's eyes were locked on mine. An ant ran across her face. Without breaking her stare, she slapped at the ant then pulled it into her mouth. I thought the girls were playing in the dirt, but they were grubbing for ants.

They lived like animals in the gutter. They crawled like animals. But I knew what was going on inside them. Beyond dirt, beyond filth, beyond the knowing that nobody cares or notices whether you are dead or alive, I knew. They had all the organs of human beings, all the feelings of human beings, but most people would look at them and see only filth.

This was *bui doi*.

This was the dust of life.

This was a bloody nuisance.

This was nothing.

And there I was, a white woman with blonde hair, nice white trousers, white shirt, and a blue cravat, and for the first time in her life, someone was looking at her as someone important.

I stared at the girls and said to myself, 'God, I could latch on to this. God, I could feel good about this. Isn't this what I've wanted all my life? To be important? To be tall? To tower? To be a part of society? And right here, right now, I am important. I am respectable. I am clean. I am a part of society. I've suffered enough in my life. I've been in the gutter and I crawled out. Sure, it was an Irish gutter. But there's no difference between an Irish gutter and a Vietnamese gutter. At the end of the day they are the same.'

My years as a street child in Dublin washed over me in a great tidal wave, and for a moment I almost fainted. Tears cascaded down my cheeks. I was still fighting for my own emotional survival, for my own sanity, and I couldn't go through this again. These children were not my responsibility.

But when I looked at the little girls, again it was me that I saw. It was my brothers and sisters staring me in the face.

I knew that I was facing a major turning point of my life. If I touched one of these children I would be making a commitment from which I could not turn away. If I touched them, I could never go back.

'Give me. Give me,' the little girl said again.

I straightened my back and forced my face to be stern. 'No,' I said. I backed away. My dream had waited almost twenty years and it could wait some more.

The girl stood up, took a step in my direction and again reached towards me. This time with both arms. This time she was not begging. This time her palms were down and her fingers fluttered open. All she wanted was the touch of another human being. All she wanted was the comfort of holding my hand. I froze. Her hands and her expression were those of the girl in my dream.

A vagrant breeze suddenly sprang up, and suddenly it seemed as if the smoke-filled air was swirling about my head. Across the square, high up on one of the buildings, was a billboard advertising some product, I don't remember what. But the word 'Vietnam' was on the billboard, and the blinding afternoon sun suddenly made the word look as if it were bathed in a great white light.

I sobbed. I reached for the girl but I could not see through my tears. She found my hand. And then I was sitting in the dirt holding the children in my lap. I pulled them to me and I rocked back and forth and I cried for a long time and I promised them that I would take care of them.

Their bleak days as *bui doi* were over. I promised them that.

My decision was made. Here, my dream, my destiny, would be fulfilled. Here the pain and the sorrow and the anger of my childhood in Ireland would be resolved. I would work with the street children of Ho Chi Minh City. I would work with the ill and the unwanted, with the lonely and the misbegotten, with the throw-away children of this war-torn country. I would work with the children who were living as I had lived so long ago in Dublin.

This poor and crippled country would be the place of my salvation, the place where I would regain hope and rebuild my life. Here I would stay. Here I would find happiness. I knew that I would never leave.

Vietnam would be the bridge across my sorrows.

Ireland

1

I am a child of the Liberties as they once were, a God-struck, beer-soaked slum in south-west Dublin. When I think of my childhood I think of pain and betrayal, and when I talk of those years in Ireland my voice changes. It is not something I can control. My voice becomes high and tight and there is a hint of fear. I say 'mudder' for 'mother' and I revert to the grammar and the cadences of the Liberties, the part of Dublin where I grew up. I don't understand it.

I was born on 23 December 1944 at the Coombe Hospital about two miles from Grafton Street, the eldest daughter in a family of eight children. Two boys died, one of a fever and the other of milk from my mother's abscessed breasts. As I later heard the story, my daddy stumbled often on the way to the hospital because, as usual, he was drunk.

At the hospital one of the nurses said, 'Mr Byrne, we don't think you should come in. It's not good for your wife.' Daddy waved his arms and said, 'Get out of me way.'

My mammy looked up as daddy lurched into the room. Her eyes were black with fatigue and her head rolled from side to side. 'Tom, will you go home,' she moaned. 'In the name of God, go home.'

When daddy was drunk, his mouth became twisted. I grew to hate this sign. That day at the hospital, daddy smiled his twisted drunken smile, mumbled something about how sad he was, and left.

He drowned his sorrow as he always did, with Guinness. To go into a pub and talk about a dead son and a sick wife was a great way to generate sympathy and free drinks.

For daddy, that sad day passed quickly. But for years afterwards my mother cried when she thought of how her poisoned breasts had killed one of her children and how my father was drunk when he came to the hospital. One of my enduring memories of her is how she would sit at the window looking over that grey and terrible neighbourhood where we lived, as tears rolled down her cheeks. It was a silent crying.

While my mother was in the hospital, one of the children in the neighbourhood said, 'We heard your mammy was bringing home a baby in a bag again.' Children in the Liberties always said babies came in a bag; their parents didn't want them to know the truth about sex and how babies are born. Neighbourhood children were surprised when she came home without a baby. 'I thought you had a baby in a bag,' one said.

My mother, Annie Gross, was different from most women in the Liberties. She was very gentle and everyone called her 'The Lady'. Some called her 'The Jewess' because she had long black hair that was tied in a bun and she had dark skin and an aristocratic face. Philomena, one of my younger sisters, was always fascinated by the fact that our mother might be Jewish.

My mam was a gentle woman with a soft voice, but she could speak with authority. She was also a devout Catholic. For years she was a cook at St Kevin's Hospital which everyone in the Liberties called the Union. Many homeless people congregated around the hospital. It was said, 'If you go to the Union you come out in a box.'

When my mother worked at the Union she would leave the house before 6 a.m. and not return until about four that afternoon. She was always exhausted.

'She was born with rheumatic fever which damaged her heart,' my daddy said. Mammy was sick for much of her life. She was always in and out of hospitals. And from my earliest years I was terrified that she would go to the hospital and never come home.

My mother prayed a lot. She belonged to the Legion of Mary and spent much of her time visiting the sick and the poor. If someone in the Liberties died, it usually was my mam who washed them and laid them out.

At home she was always mending and darning, washing and scrubbing. When the collars on my daddy's shirts frayed, she turned them inside out, sewed them, and made them look like new. Her work was impeccable. And as she sewed she used to sing 'Danny Boy' and 'The Wild Colonial Boy'. Even today I can close my eyes and see her in her favourite woolly, a moss green cardigan with pink stripes on the sleeves, sitting at the window and sewing away on our clothes.

My mother wore no make-up and neither smoked nor drank. She hated liquor. 'Strong drink is the downfall of many and the ruination of families,' she said. There was an air of sadness about her. She desperately wanted her children to have a decent life. But she knew that my father's drinking made such a goal almost impossible. 'I want you to be educated so you can have a future,' she told us many times. She sent us to the convent schools and had to buy us uniforms. She was always in debt.

One of my earliest memories is how she walked with me all over Dublin. She would put on the moss green cardigan and we would walk hand in hand through Phoenix Park, one of the largest city parks in Europe.

Near the main gates it has neatly clipped hedges and numerous flower beds; further in, there are tree-lined roads, several lakes, herds of deer, and open space. We always went in the main gate on Parkgate Street. To the left of the entrance is the Wellington Monument, which stands sixty metres high. As a child, I could not say 'monument', and called it 'the mollyers'. I played often in the lush green grass surrounding the monument.

From time to time I was taken to the picture house. My favourite pictures were those starring Doris Day, the American film star. I remember her singing 'Que Sera Sera' and 'By the Light of the Silvery Moon'. Doris Day was always smiling. In one of her pictures she wore an apron and was taking cakes out of the oven and I imagined what it would be like to be in her family. If I could have stowed away on an aeroplane, I would have gone to America to meet her. I loved her. I love her still.

As mammy and I walked around Dublin, I sometimes could see Dublin Castle in the distance. It was on a hill, and on one side, over the gate, was a statue of Justice balancing her scales. On these walks, she sometimes told me about her life.

She was from Carrick-on-Shannon, a market town on the upper reaches of the River Shannon. She said her father, Michael Gross, was of German stock. But I never knew him. And her mother had died giving birth to her. Mam came to Dublin to study domestic science at college. She met my father, Thomas Byrne, at a bus stop and they were married within a year. They never talked to us about their courtship; I only remember her saying my dad looked like Errol Flynn, what with his being so tall and handsome. He had blond hair and beautiful blue eyes. He was a gorgeous man.

My father Thomas Byrne was born and grew up in the Liberties. He used to laugh and say, 'I graduated from the toss school,' which was the Dublin way of saying he gambled on the street for coins. As a young man, my daddy was a bare-fisted boxer.

'I'm a great boxer,' he used to boast. 'I fought Brannigan of Belfast.' As if we knew – or cared – who Brannigan might be. 'And I'm a great swimmer; I've saved many lives. The ocean has no fear for me. I was asked to play for Manchester United. Ah, your father was a great all-around sportsman: a brilliant soccer player, a swimmer, a boxer and a champion of the toss school.'

My daddy continued to box even after the doctors told him to stop. His knuckles and his nose had been broken and smashed many times. He had cauliflower ears and he was partially deaf.

I remember, too, that daddy used to talk occasionally of how he had once worked with Americans at a navy base in Scotland. He said he had wanted to move to America but that mother had refused.

'It would have all been different if your mother had come with me to America,' he said.

One of the few good memories I have of my father is how he would take me to the beach where we built sandcastles and he laughed and sang and talked to me about how important it would be when I was seven years old and had my first Holy Communion. 'Then you'll know right from wrong and you'll be responsible for what happens in your life, Ina,' he told me. He often said to me 'Ina, God has great plans for your life.'

About the only good thing I can say of my father today is that he never swore and that he was respectful of old people. Most of my memories of my father are sad memories. I still become angry when I think of him. I remember when I was very young, it was in the winter, he was carried home from a pub fight with blood gushing from his face. There was a silence in the air, the same sort of silence one feels before a great snow storm. At home, everything was in place. We had a fire in the fireplace and we were all feeling good. My father had taken the pledge and had been off the drink for perhaps three months.

But that night he was carried home, blood gushing from his nose, his eyes bleeding, his face bruised. Teeth were broken. Oh, he had been badly beaten.

My mother pulled out clean pillowcases and wrapped them around his face. 'Oh Jesus, Mary and Holy Saint Joseph,' she said. 'What have they done to you, Tom?'

He mumbled something and she said, 'I've told you, Tom, if you don't stop this drinking one day it will kill you.'

Daddy didn't answer. I thought then that the drink was wearing off and he was feeling the pain of his injuries. But we realized much later that he had sustained brain damage in the fight. It was that night the noise in his head began. He said it sounded like rashers of bacon frying. Many times he held his head in his hands and moaned, 'I can't stand the noise. Let me die.'

Almost every memory of my father involves the drink. If I close my eyes today and think of him, I see a man who was drunk, drunk, drunk. Blind paralytic drunk.

He would go to the priest, take the pledge to stop drinking, and then stop in a pub on the way home. He prayed for the Pope every day. He would stumble down the street drunk out of his skull, crossing himself and praying. He would come home and stand in the middle of the flats, surrounded by laughing neighbourhood kids.

They called him 'the clown' because he danced for them and sometimes he fell over. He would sing a song that began, 'You can roll a silver dollar . . .' and another one, an American song, 'Get along little doggie, get along . . .'

The children in the neighbourhood roared with laughter when he came home drunk. 'Come on, do some more,' they would say, and he would reach into his pocket and throw them all his change. Inside the flat we would be hungry and my mam would be crying and worrying. I was the one who always went out to get daddy. As the oldest daughter that was my responsibility. I spent much of my young life saying, 'Daddy, come home.' He would say, 'Go away, spoil sport.'

'Let him alone,' the children would sing out when they saw I was having no influence on him. 'He's a great dancer.' And often they would laugh and say, 'He's an awful eejit', the Irish way of saying idiot. And then I wound up fighting with them. 'Leave my daddy alone,' I shouted. 'Don't laugh at him.'

There were six children in my family. I had two older brothers, Andy and Michael, and then there was Johnny, three years younger than me, Kathy, five years younger, and Philomena, or 'Paw Waw' as I called her, who was eight years my junior. We lived at 326 Marrowbone Lane Flats in the Liberties. From the outside, the flats were grey and dingy. Clothes always hung on lines in the playing square. The rubbish chute was in the front of the flats and when it was opened rats scurried out. For most of my young life we lived on the fourth floor, the top floor. To get there it was necessary to climb up narrow, dark, concrete steps. Our flat was very small: it had one bedroom, a living room and a scullery that was not big enough to swing a cat in. The living room served as a bedroom for the children. And the one bedroom served as dining room and sitting room. My mother and father slept on a mattress on the floor and six of us children slept in one bed. The bed had a horsehair mattress that sagged in the middle. We had only one blanket. The room had a fireplace, in the back of which there was a small oven. My mam did most of the cooking in the fireplace as we could not afford gas for the stove. Most of our furniture had been sold or broken up and burned in the fireplace. About the only good thing I can say about the flat is that it was clean. My mother always said that just because we were poor did not have to mean we were dirty. She kept the flat immaculate.

In the scullery, our name for the small kitchen, was a little table painted green and cream. It stood beside a small tub sink that was cracked and broken. There was a wooden board with grooves in it for scrubbing clothes. The kitchen had a concrete floor. Many times I walked into the kitchen and found my mother crying. She was always crying. She usually blamed it on onions.

I remember my mam putting me and my two elder brothers, Andy and Michael, to bed and then she would go next door to talk with a neighbour. I was always terribly frightened when she left, even though I knew she was in the next flat.

I was afraid of the banshee. The banshee is the death witch and has long hair. I thought she was going to come through the windows and take me away. In Ireland, we have great respect for the banshee. Any noise in the night is the banshee, and when the banshee moans it means someone will die soon. The banshee sometimes drops her comb when she is grooming her hair and this comb is poisonous. Few people in Ireland will pick up a comb on the street because it is a premonition of death. I used to pray, 'Please God, don't let the banshee come here.'

We always knew when the banshee had visited: a white card with black edging was attached to the gate in front of the flats. A black ribbon was draped around the card. And on it was the name of the person who had died.

The Liberties was dominated by Guinness's Brewery which occupied seventy fenced-in acres of west Dublin: one of the largest breweries in the world. Millions of pints a year are exported out of those blue and gold gates. The smokestacks belched a smoke smelling strongly of malted barley that mixed with the fog and clouds and made it seem as if the sky itself was pressing down on the Liberties. Many people in the Liberties worked at Guinness's. The smell of stout dominated the neighbourhood and church steeples dominated the skyline. All around were dozens of pubs, betting offices – and poverty. This part of Dublin proves that the Irish have as great an affection for the drink as they have for God. I've never seen another place where the spiritual and the secular, the sacred and the profane, are in such abundance and in such open warfare as they are in the Liberties.

My dad worked at Guinness's for a while. He unloaded barges on the Liffey filled with supplies going to and from the brewery. Guinness workers were given two free pints every day and two more if the work was particularly heavy. Once my dad had a pint he was on his way. On Fridays one of my older brothers and I would try to catch him where he worked; if we stopped him when he came out the gate and talked with him before he went into a pub, we might get money to pay for rent, gas, food, or electricity. But often he left work early so we could not catch him, or he left by a different gate. The workers would see us and know why we were there. Men who love their pints are not uncommon in Dublin.

The poor in Ireland have always had a miserable existence, and nowhere was their misery more pronounced than in Dublin. Once I heard that when the Duke of Wellington was reminded that he was a Dubliner, he responded, 'Being born in a stable doesn't make one a horse.'

The institutional memory of many Dublin people is one of failure, deprivation, ceaseless toil, and monumental hardship. And nowhere in Dublin is that more true than in the Liberties.

My neighbourhood was one of the poorest in all of Ireland. Unemployment was as high as alcoholism. Like many poor people, we were also very strong. We had to be in order to survive.

People in the Liberties were known as grafters, as people who would do whatever they had to do to make a few pence. To say someone was 'a great grafter' was a compliment of the highest order. After working all day, many people sold fruit or fish on the street. The women, after work, gathered and washed clothes in communal washhouses. Everyone had to struggle to survive and to provide for his or her family.

There were always fights, both in the streets and in the pubs. But there was also a deep sense of community spirit. Our poverty and our toughness bound us together. Many people who grow up in the Liberties remain there. They marry and they perpetuate the poverty and the violence and the drinking as well as the closeness and the community spirit. I don't know what it was about the Liberties that influenced me the most. To this day I abhor many things about the place. But the most important years of my life were spent there. My strength came from the Liberties. They are the foundation of my life. Even though today I am half-way round the world from Ireland, I will always be a child of the Liberties.

2

My escape from the pain of my childhood was always in singing and dancing. It took me away from the Liberties and from a life where my mother was tired and sick and where my father was drunk and abusive.

I loved dancing and singing from as far back as I can remember. My mother thought singing would be my future. It was very serious to her. And even though we were very poor, mammy put money aside for my singing and dancing lessons. There were times when my family had no food because the money went for my lessons. One of my older brothers was very angry about that; he still remembers it and he still feels strongly about it. Once my mother sold the coat off her back to pay for my lessons at the Sweeney School of Dance. It was a navy blue coat with a belt, the only special coat she ever had. She sold it for three pounds and afterwards wore an ugly black one.

I was dedicated to my singing and dancing. I gave it my all. Rain, hail, snow and cold did not matter, I went to my classes. I never missed. I was not simply another child being pushed by her mother to go on the stage, I was a solo artist. And I was good.

My earliest singing was in the church. In fact, as a child, the only time I truly enjoyed being in a church was when I was singing in the choir. I was singing solos at High Mass when I was eight years old, in a high clear soprano. I was very intense when I sang in church. I believed that God was in me. I sang fervently, I sang for all the saints in heaven, I sang with love. I folded my hands, tilted my head to the side, rolled my eyes heavenward and sang, 'Sweet Heart of Jesus, we implore.' And then I was supposed to sing, 'Oh make us love you, more and more' but I instead sang, 'Oh please love me, more and more.' I wanted so much to be loved.

People in the church told me afterwards that I sang like a little angel. But I was no angel. Before going to Mass, I sometimes picked up damaged fruit and hid it in my knickers. When I stood up to sing I looked around the congregation and picked out a woman in a big hat. Then, when I sat down, I pulled the fruit out of my knickers, flicked it over the railing at the big hat, then ducked down on the kneeler, giggling.

Because of my singing in the choir at Mass, I was picked to be a rose petal girl for the Feast of Corpus Christi when I was only six years old. The Feast of Corpus Christi was a very big celebration in Ireland. I had a little basket filled with rose petals and during the procession my job was to take out a rose petal, kiss it, then toss it on the street.

As a child, I had a great relationship with God. I breathed Catholicism. I believed that nuns and priests were agents of God, that they were saints. I believed everything they said and I told them how much I loved them. But that was before I was abandoned to the ways of the world.

Not long after I began singing in the choir, I also began singing in the variety halls of Dublin. The variety halls were family places where all sorts of musical and dance acts took place. Anyone with talent could perform. Before each performance my mammy spent hours curling my long sandy hair. She was so proud of me. I sang ballads and other songs such as 'When Irish Eyes Are Smiling'.

I also sang in the pubs. I would run in, sing a song or two, collect maybe half a crown, and run out. I still remember hearing a man say, 'God love her. She's a great singer.'

My father, when he was sober, was very proud of my ability as an entertainer. I remember once when he had taken the pledge and our family seemed normal, my daddy and I were walking on the beach and he said to me, 'You are going to be a great dancer and singer. You will go to America and sing in Hollywood and the Americans will love you. Your name will be in lights and you'll be famous. It's in your blood, you know. You've been doing it since you were a child.'

I sensed in my father a goodness. I sensed the child in him. He was a monster when he was drinking, but, yes, there was good in my father and I loved him.

In our dismal flat on Marrowbone Lane I practised for my performances. We had an electrical cord hanging from the ceiling. But the electricity usually was cut off because we could not pay the bill. I removed the light bulb and tied a cup to the end of the wire. That was my microphone. The wallpaper in the flat once had been white but it had turned a dirty cream on which were tiny red roses. We had stripped off most of the wallpaper and burned it in the fireplace to keep warm. But a few roses remained. I pretended that I was in a theatre and that each rose was a person's face. I began by walking into the room, bowing to the roses, and introducing 'Christina Byrne, the greatest singer in all of Ireland who will soon be going to America to sing in Hollywood.' Then I would bow and leave the room. A moment later I would dance out into the room, smile at the thunderous applause from the audience, seize the cup in my hand and begin singing something like, 'Gee but it's great, after being out late, walking my baby back home.'

After each song I smiled and bowed to the rolling waves of applause. I actually heard applause coming from the roses. And when I left the stage the applause continued for so long that there had to be an encore. I would dance out, smile, thank the thousands of people in the audience, and sing again: 'I'll be down to get you a taxi, honey. You better be ready about a half-past eight.' Or I might tap dance. And proper tap dancing it was; I had big double taps on my shoes. I did a lot of Al Jolson numbers.

When I was about eight years old, my friend Lilly and I began putting on concerts for other children in the flats. To pull children in the Liberties to a concert requires an inducement. I used sweets. I sold rags or I chopped sticks and sold them as kindling, and with the money I bought sweets.

I went down to Donoghues' sweet shop. We called it Dirty Donoghues' because the sweets were squeezed and broken and melted and because rats ran loose in the store. 'Mrs Dunny,' I would say, 'can I have tuppence worth of your dirty – sorry – can I have tuppence worth of your worthless sweets?'

'They are not worthless, child,' she grumbled. 'They are only soiled.'

We wrapped the sweets in small pieces of paper then stuck them into another piece of paper in the shape of a cone. Each child attending the concert was charged a penny. Before each concert we lined the concert-goers up on the steps inside the building. A full house was twelve or fourteen people.

For some routines, I moistened red paper and rubbed it on my nose and lips, and I burned a match and rubbed the blackened tip around my eyes. If I was doing Al Jolson, my make-up was different. I would stick my hand up the chimney, pull down a handful of soot, and rub it over my face. And I would crush headache tablets and moisten them and rub the paste around my mouth and eyes to whiten them.

When we began the concert, I played all the different parts. Sometimes Lilly danced with me but usually she walked around with a flashlight, shining the light in the faces of those who talked and trying to silence them. I would run out and say, 'Now, ladies and gentlemen, we have Christina Byrne, the famous Irish singer who is doing her version of Al Jolson. Give her a big round of applause.' I made them shout and applaud and show lots of response.

Then I clutched my heart, dropped to my knees, and in what even today I think of as a remarkable Al Jolson voice, I sang 'Mammy'.

As I left the landing I might hear a voice from somewhere on the steps saying, 'Where are the fucking sweets?'

Lilly would shine the flashlight on the lad and say, 'Shoosh.'

Then I would dance out, go down on my knees, throw my arms wide, and sing 'California, here I come. Right back where I started from'. And I would do it in a strong American accent.

The kids clapped and whistled, but there was usually someone who said, 'Throw her out the fucking back door. She's no good.'

Between numbers, Lilly and I made the kids clap louder and scream, 'More, more, more.' We told them if they wanted the sweets they would have to show the proper response.

'Come on. Give me a big clap. A big one. I'm as good

as Doris Day and Lilly here is as good as Grace Kelly. You got the best. Now applaud.'

But by then they were demanding sweets. 'Our hands are raw from all the clapping. Give us the sweets.'

'Give us a "hip, hip, hoorah" for the very talented Ina Burns, Ireland's next great singer,' I insisted.

'Ina, will you pass out the sweets?'

So I would pass out the sweets. And every time there was a kid who would say, 'These fucking sweets are no good. She got them off the floor at Dirty Donoghues'.'

There was a lot of laughter during those concerts. We ignored the cardboard in the window that kept out rain and snow and the bitter winds. We forgot our poverty. I created normality during the concerts.

After the concerts Lilly and I would go down to the ice cream shop on School Street and buy two ice pops and two packets of crisps; cheese and onion they were. We spent a long time eating the ice pops. We licked slowly and took very small bites while we chatted away like two old women. The ice pops were almost as good as jelly. As a child I loved jelly more than any other food, perhaps because we had it so infrequently. Jelly was my comfort food.

Lilly and I sat on the steps and chatted, and when it was time for us to eat the crisps we rubbed our hands together in anticipation and pretended we were very grand, 'the quality' we used to say. We made a ceremony out of our after-concert outings.

When I began singing in the variety halls, my mother and I put together several wonderful costumes. I had a scarlet pleated satin skirt, with white shiny taffeta coming down the back in sort of a bustle. There was gold braid around the skirt. I don't know where she got the money, but mammy always bought a bottle of tan for my legs. I had to have tanned legs. I also had a sailor's outfit with a white pleated skirt and a navy top. And there was a Dutch costume. But my favourite was the one I wore in my solo act, my top hat and tails. It was made of mauve satin with a yellow satin collar. The top hat was yellow and mauve and I had yellow gloves and white buckskin boots with big double taps on them. I often did an imitation of Sophie Tucker while wearing my top hat and tails: 'One of these days, you're gonna miss me, honey. One of these days, you're gonna feel so lonely.'

My mother was very proud of me when I sang and danced. Seeing me perform was the highlight of her life. She used to say, 'One day you'll be on the stage. But you'll give it all away.' I did not know what she meant. If mammy had lived, she would have put me in drama school.

I rarely went to school when I was young. One reason was my frequent illnesses. Another reason was that I did not fit in. While most kids in Marrowbone Lane went to a national school, I went to a convent school and wore a navy blue skirt with a white blouse and a blue tie. Unlike the other students, I didn't pay to attend the convent school. Because of my mother's devotion to the church and all of her good works, I went there at no cost. The other children knew this. They also knew my daddy was a drunk and they often made comments about his drinking and then I would start a fight.

'Your father is an awful aul' fella,' they would say, using a Dublin expression that is particularly disrespectful.

'Don't be talking about me father that way,' I said.

'Oh, he's a terrible drunkard,' another would say. 'He's always coming home fluthered.'

'I'd be ashamed to walk up the street with him, I would,' still another would say.

'They are really poor, they are. Her father's always fighting with her mother.'

By then my temper would get the best of me. 'I'll tear every hair out of your head. I'll kill you.'

But there always seemed to be far more of them than there was of me. By the time the conversation had escalated to this point there usually was a ring of taunting children around me.

'Your daddy is a drunkard. Your daddy is a drunkard,' they laughed. 'Ha ha ha ha. Your daddy is a drunkard.'

I would put my fingers in my ears and bend over, just waiting for the moment when one of them became too bold and got too close. If I could get my hands on one of them, I would hurt them.

All the other children were happy and able to do their homework. They had someone at home to help them. They had paper and pens. I didn't have any of that. We couldn't afford it. At home there was no place to study. I would go to school with no homework done and the teacher would stand me in front of the class and beat me with a ruler and tell the class I was a dunce. And then I would have to stand in the corner with my face to the wall. I was forced to sit at the very back of the class. The teachers had no time for anyone who was poor and shabby and a nobody. They had no motivation to teach anyone like me. I was not going to university. The day would never come when one of those teachers would see me and say, 'She was one of my students. I taught her.'

Other children had priests or nuns in the family, or the family owned a grocery shop or was in business, and the teachers had time for them. But if you were poor, you were lazy. I told the teachers that I loved English and loved poetry and they laughed at me. Once I wrote a poem about my mother and father. I debated for days about whether or not I should ask the teacher if I could read it before the class. I was very proud of that poem. It would have shown the teachers and the students I was not at all as they pictured me.

Eventually I gathered my courage and one day I got out of my seat and walked slowly down the aisle to the teacher. 'I wrote a poem about my family,' I said. 'Could I read it to the class?'

She looked down at my grey face and my tatty clothes and at my wretched little body and she said, 'You wrote a poem? You?'

'Yes. I want to read it to the class.'

'I've never known you to write anything. Go back to your seat and be quiet.'

'I wrote a poem.'

'Stop talking. Go back to your seat.'

I still remember that poem.

Mammy cries, daddy lies.
Screaming, shouting, tears, and fear in the night.
I'm afraid they'll take my mammy away.
No daddy's little girl, my mammy's little girl.
Fight fight, cry cry, lie lie, die die.
Stranger tell me, who am I?

At a very young age I began staying away from class. Rather than going to school, I walked the streets and lived in a make-believe world. Because I frequently stayed away, I came to the attention of Dickie Clarke, the School Attendance Officer in the Liberties. Everyone in the Liberties knew Dickie Clarke. He was the greatest kid-catcher in all of Dublin. 'Our man, Dickie', we called him. He was very skinny and he wore dark clothes draped about his tall body. We thought he was about six feet seven inches tall. He had white hair and we used to say he looked like a lamppost. Because he rode a bicycle, the right leg of his trousers was always clasped in an aluminium clip. Dickie Clarke caught children who were not attending school, took them before a judge and had them sent away to an industrial school. These were Church-run training schools where life was said to be like something from another century. We used to say that Dickie Clarke had sent more kids to industrial school than any of the other inspectors. 'Dickie Clarke will swear your life away,' we warned each other. And whenever we were 'mitching' – our name for playing truant – we always looked out for Dickie Clarke. The sight of Dickie Clarke zooming along on his bike – 'scorching' we called it – with his mac billowing out behind him and his shiny black shoes going round and round was a sight that brought terror to our hearts. No-one wanted to be the next child Dickie Clarke sent away. We made up a song about Dickie Clarke to cover our fear.

> Dickie Clarke is a very good man,
> He goes to church on Sunday.
> The only thing he cannot do
> Is catch the kids on Monday.

Dickie Clarke was like God, he was everywhere, and he learned my name early. As I darted up a narrow alley, or climbed steps, or disappeared into an old building, he would shout after me, 'I know you, Ina Byrne. And if you don't go to school, I'll have you put away until you're sixteen.' He chased me many times. When he came to the house I locked the door or hid under the bed. But occasionally he caught me and then my mother would find out. Dickie Clarke would tell her he was going to have to take me to court if I didn't stay in school. Mammy would cry. She would be so angry with me. Nonetheless, I more or less stopped going to school when I was about nine years old.

3

Something happened to me when I was eight years old that contributed to my decision to drop out of school. My mam, somehow and somewhere, found the money for me to take bagpipe lessons. I was not anxious to go, but mammy said this would add to my education and to my musical talents. She said if I wanted to pursue a career as a singer and dancer I should be able to play a musical instrument.

On the first day of class I walked into that long oblong room and looked around. A few tables stood in one corner. The room was also used for ballet lessons so one wall was mirrored and in front of the mirror was a barre. The other girls in the class, perhaps a dozen, were all at the other end of the room. They were well-dressed and wore watches and bracelets and had ribbons in their hair. They looked at me and knew in an instant I was not one of their group. There was no 'hello' from a single one of them. I was on my own.

Carmen was the leader of the group. Her father was a wealthy businessman and she was particularly well dressed with more jewellery than the other girls. Carmen overflowed with self-confidence. She always had a box of Cadbury's milk chocolates that she passed out to the other girls. Privately, I thought of her as 'Toffee Nose'. I really wanted one of those chocolates. Such a treat it would have been. But I would never ask her.

I was very proud. I was also jealous of Carmen and quite insecure in her presence.

From the first day of class the teacher talked of Easter, which was about seven or eight months away. On Easter Sunday the bagpipe class would march in Dublin's Easter Parade. We would wear special uniforms. Measurements were taken from the girls and a great mood of anticipation began to build up. My ma began saving money so she could pay the ten shillings for my uniform.

I always arrived for the bagpipe class at the very last minute so that I could begin the lesson immediately and avoid standing around by myself while Carmen held court and passed out chocolates and laughed and joked.

Then one morning, Carmen looked at me from the other end of the long room and held out the box of chocolates in my direction. 'Would you care for a chocolate?' she asked in ever-so-proper tones.

'Yes, please,' I said and began walking towards her.

As I drew closer she turned, smiled at her friends, and took a chocolate from the box. She took a bite and threw the chocolate on the floor. 'There,' she said, 'you can have that one.'

The other girls giggled madly.

Being from the Liberties, I did not react well to such an insult. I picked up the chocolate with one hand, and with the other hand I seized the hair at the back of her head. Before she realized what was happening, I smashed the chocolate in her face.

It was stuffed with orange cream.

Then I ran out. I was crying, running and crying. I would never go back in that class.

For six months afterwards my mam thought I was

taking bagpipe lessons. 'Ina is learning the bagpipes,' she told everyone she met. I would go into the church, ask God to forgive me, then use the money for the bagpipe lessons to buy sweets. The longer this went on, the worse it got. And my apprehension grew because Easter was approaching.

On Easter Sunday Mam gave me ten shillings as payment for my uniform. 'Don't lose this ten shillings,' she cautioned me. 'Put it in your pocket. And when you march in the parade, hold your head up high. You're as good as anyone there.'

I didn't want to take that money. Mammy had worked hard for part of it and had borrowed the remainder. But I took the money and waved her goodbye.

I wore a bright yellow frock that Easter morning. It had a frill over the shoulders. I had on a nylon see-through slip that had little bubbles in it. I wore yellow socks and had a yellow ribbon in my hair.

I walked over the bridge and towards O'Connell Street where I stopped in front of a very posh chocolate shop. My heart was heavy. I had the worries of the world on my shoulders. And I thought to myself, 'I have all this money. If I die, I will go to hell.' And I remember the window of the sweet shop was filled with oranges and bottles of red lemonade and boxes of chocolates, all draped with brightly coloured ribbons. Next to them was a straw hat, sort of window dressing. Looking at the boxes of chocolates made me think of Carmen. There were lots of children on the streets carrying Easter eggs and chocolates. So I went in and looked up at the woman in the shop.

'Yes, child. What is it?'

I pointed to the window. 'Could I have a box of them chocolates there?'

'Do you want a pound, half pound, quarter pound?' She spoke very fast.

'That one there,' I said.

'The half-pound size.'

'And could I have a bottle of the red lemonade, please?'

She reached for a bottle on the shelf, but I told her I wanted the one in the window, the one with the ribbons on it.

She looked at me for a moment and then took the bottle from the window.

'And could I have the straw hat in the window?' I asked.

As I left the sweet shop I felt so swanky. I felt everyone was looking at me in my straw hat and I began to smile from ear to ear. 'God, I look beautiful,' I said to myself. For this one day I would be like Alice in Wonderland.

So I went down to the station and caught a train out to Bray, a small town by the seaside. It was not unusual for children to get on the train and go somewhere. We Dubs learn early to cope with the world. It was chilly out by the sea, not nearly as warm as in the city, and not many people were there. They must have been in Dublin watching the parade.

I sat by the sea and I held the bottle of red lemonade up to the sun, watching the light warm the lemonade and soften the colour into a lovely whitish pink. I ate the chocolates slowly, relishing each one, and thinking, 'If only Carmen could see me now.' The gulls were flying over, crying their ugly harsh noise.

'Fuck off,' I shouted. 'Go on. Get away.' I realized it was not me they were after but my chocolates.

That day by the seaside was a luxury I had never enjoyed before, a long languid day that was all the more precious because in the back of my mind was the ever-present knowledge that a time of reckoning was approaching. At the end of the day I would pay dearly for the hours on the beach.

When I climbed back aboard the train there was chocolate all over my face and hands and all over my yellow frock. It was beginning to get dark and the gathering darkness was a harbinger of the trouble I was in. I was going to get killed. I thought about going to live in the mountains.

As I rode back into Dublin I leaned over and put my head on the window to rest. I saw my reflection in the glass and thought of the two Christinas: the real one and the reflection. There was the Christina who sang in church and who obeyed her mother, and there was the Christina who disobeyed her parents and stole money from her mother. There was the Christina who was filled with guilt over the pain her mother would feel when she discovered her daughter was not in the Easter Parade, and there was the Christina who had lied to her mother for months.

I looked at the Christina in the window and knew mother was worrying about where I was and what I had been doing all those days when she thought I was taking bagpipe lessons. I closed my eyes. 'Jesus, Mary and Joseph, I give you my heart and soul . . .' I began. And then I wondered aloud, 'Am I bad? Am I really a bad child?'

The conductor came through, looked at me and said, 'You're a bit small to be out here on your own, aren't you?'

'I live in Dublin,' I said, in explanation.

I got off the train and caught a bus to the flats. By then it was late in the evening. The bus driver looked at me in surprise and said, 'Where have you been, young one? This is an awful time of the night for you to be out.'

Eventually I got home. I stood at the bottom of the flats and could see the lights were glaring and the door to our flat was open.

I knew they were all out looking for me. I walked quietly up the steps, crept inside and hid under the bed.

Several hours later the family came in. It was Andrew, my younger brother, who found me.

'She's under the bed. You can stop looking,' he announced.

Mam pulled me out and shook me and shook me and shook me. 'Where have you been?' she demanded. Her eyes were heavy and filled with pain. 'What have you done?'

I was crying. I could not answer.

'What were you doing until this hour of the night? Where did you go, Ina?'

I cried all the harder.

'It's too late to cry,' me mam said wearily. 'Where is your uniform? What did you do with the money?'

'I bought chocolates,' I bawled.

'What possessed you, child? What possessed you?'

'I don't know.'

'We can hardly eat here, let alone afford to have you stuff yourself with chocolates. Isn't it enough that I have to cope with your father?'

I had no answer for her.

'You've never had bagpipe lessons,' she said. 'You've been lying to me for months. May God forgive you.'

I dropped my head on my chest and cried even louder.

'Hold your head up and look at me,' mam said. She was horrified at the chocolate on my pretty frock.

She made me tell her about the money, about the chocolates, about my trip to the seaside.

'I want you to pray,' she said. 'I want you to ask forgiveness from God. It will be a long time before I trust you again.'

She looked at the chocolate on my dress. 'And it will be a long time before you get any more sweets.'

She even stopped my singing and dancing lessons and I was not allowed out of the house, except to go to school, for about two months. She walked me to school each day and pushed me into the classroom. But as soon as the roll was called I ran away.

Dickie Clarke was told about this and I was always on the alert for his tall black-clad figure pedalling madly down the streets and alleys as he searched for me. Occasionally he would get close enough to say, 'Ina Byrne, I know you. If you don't go to school, I'll send you away.'

I made many friends on the streets of Dublin.

One friend, who was later to play a surprising role in my life, was a house painter. He was about fifteen years older than me and my cousin's boyfriend. As I walked around the Liberties, I often saw him painting shops or homes and when I waved he always spoke kindly to me.

As I roamed the streets, I often saw people who were sick. Children could be very cruel to these people. If someone was crippled, he might be called 'gammy leg' or 'bandy leg'. And a mentally ill person was referred to as 'dopey'. I never did that. And if I heard kids saying nasty or cruel things to these people, I reacted strongly.

'Don't be calling him gammy leg,' I said angrily. 'He can't help it.'

Don't get me wrong. As you know by now, I was no model of good behaviour. But I was never deliberately cruel.

Sometimes the other children and I went up to the Grand Canal used by the CIE (the Irish transport company) boats, when they were bringing grain to the brewery. We used to swing on the bars of the drawbridge as it was opening for the boats. It was very dangerous. Children often fell and were rushed off to hospital. Occasionally a child fell into the canal and drowned. It was not unusual to see children dragged out of the canal. Any time children of the Liberties were late in coming home, their mothers would say, 'Jesus, I hope she's not at the bottom of the canal.'

When someone in the Liberties died, they were taken to what we called 'the dead house', a mortuary behind the Union. When someone we knew drowned in the canal, we used to show our bravado by saying, 'Let's go visit our friend in the dead house.' We sneaked in, eyes peering anxiously through the dim light and noses wrinkling at the awful odour. We walked on tip-toe and peered at the dozen or so bodies that were always there. The corpses were covered with sheets. Someone would always say they had seen one of the sheets move and that the dead person underneath had sat up and stared at us. The boldest boys used to pull back the sheets.

We saw nothing unusual about this. Death was always around when I was a child. It was part of my upbringing. We talked of the dead often. It is the way of the Irish.

During these childhood days, even when I was on the streets and playing with other children, I often thought of my ma. She was very much on my mind. I would worry about her constantly. I felt responsible for both my mother and father. Many people drank heavily in Dublin. But what they didn't do was stand in the middle of our flats as my father did, singing and dancing and throwing money around, then come into the house and smash things about and beat their wives.

I had a way with my father. When one of my brothers tried to talk him into coming into the house, he would get violent. Or even more foolish. But when he was dancing in the streets or bashing things up in the flat, I could stop him. Sometimes.

'Daddy, don't be doing that,' I would say softly. 'All the kids are laughing.' Or I would say, 'Daddy, come on in. I have something to tell you.'

'And will you sing for me, Ina?' he would ask.

'Yes, come inside and I'll sing for you. I'll sing the songs of Ireland.' And I would sing and he would listen so intently, and then he would join in, and we would sing together, clapping our hands.

I tried to stop daddy from going to the pubs. But if you lived in the Liberties, the smell of Guinness was always present. We never could get away from it. It hung in the air and soaked into our clothes and into our furniture and even, it seemed, into the very bricks and mortar of Dublin. I think it also soaked into my daddy.

When daddy worked at Guinness's, I used to wait for him at the gate. If he was with his drinking buddies and wanted to seem to be a good father, he would give me fifteen shillings or maybe a pound to take home and give to mam for food. If he was alone and tried to get away without giving me money, I would get very angry.

'If you don't give me some money, I'll follow you into the pub and tell everyone there that you give no money to your family,' I would say to him.

'Don't be talking to me like that,' he said. But the threat sometimes was enough.

If daddy left Guinness's by another gate, I began making the rounds of pubs in the Liberties. When I found him, if he had not been there too long, sometimes I could talk him into coming home before he was drunk.

After I learned the names and locations of all the pubs he frequented, he began going to different areas of town so I could not find him.

On those nights when I could not find him, and there were many, mam might send one of the children to buy a single order of fish and chips. We called it a 'one and one' because that's what the Italians who lived in Dublin called it. When the food arrived, we would all sit on the bed. Mam blessed the food – we always said grace before our meals – then we sprinkled vinegar on the fish and ate slowly, relishing every bite, knowing that when the last morsel was gone, we would still be hungry.

Even today, the smell of vinegar reminds me of those nights when we sat on the bed eating fish and chips sprinkled with vinegar. Vinegar reminds me of mam. Vinegar has a happy secure smell for me.

But then we had to contend with daddy. When he came near the flats I could hear him singing and hear children laughing as he tried to dance and fell on the street.

He would stagger into the flat, break whatever furniture he happened to grab, then lurch across the room and fall into bed. The lights would go out and a moment later I would hear me mammy's embarrassed and angry whisper, 'Tom! Don't, Tom. Not with the children in the room.'

But he would insist and I would hear his groans.

My mother's health worsened. She had taken a bad fall in the snow while carrying a load of groceries and it seemed that afterwards she could never get rid of the pain. Her breathing was ragged and she gasped for air much of the time. She became thinner and she coughed a lot.

Those were the days when I was ashamed of my

father. And I hated it that I was ashamed of him. I was ashamed that my friends made jokes about him, that they laughed at him. When we went out, I walked behind him and pretended he was not my father. But at the same time I loved him so much. I prayed often for him. I was in church all the time, praying, 'Please change my father. My mam is tired and we have no money. We are poor. Please change my father. He might bang his head and die.' I begged and pleaded with God to change him.

I lost count of how many times I took him to church and asked the priest to give my father the pledge, and a little pin you got when you promise God you will stop drinking. But it never worked.

I once took him to see Father Alexius down on Merchant's Quay. Father Alexius was at Adam and Eve's Friary on the south side of the River Liffey. I liked him because he was a Franciscan and he wore a brown robe with a cord around his waist and he wore sandals. I thought he looked like Jesus. And because he looked like Jesus, he must have a special relationship with God, he could do more than others. So my father took the pledge again. He came out pointing to the pin on his lapel and he said, 'Ina, I will keep the pledge this time. Your mam is sick and we need money. I am going to be a good father and everything will be OK with our family.'

As we were walking home I was so proud of him. I walked beside him and held his hand and skipped with delight and looked up at him in adoration. Then we stopped in front of a pub and my heart sank.

'Don't worry, Ina,' he said. His beautiful blue eyes were sparkling and he had a gorgeous smile. 'I'm just going in to use the lavatory.'

I hung my head and wondered, 'Will he?' He smiled,

ran his hand over my hair and said, 'I'll be right back.' So daddy went into the pub, out the back door, and down the street to another pub where he got drunk and then came home and fought with my mother and smashed up the place again.

4

I will always remember that Saturday night. I was nine years old. My father had taken the pledge, and this time it was working; he had not had a drink in months and he was a changed man. He was giving money to mam for food. The electricity had been turned on. And, best of all, daddy was eating dinner at home. Having my dad at home for dinner was like Christmas. Mam's face lit up when he sat down on the one chair that had not been broken and burned in the fireplace.

With daddy at home we were a family. We were like any family you see on the screen in the cinema. We were normal. We had confidence to go out and play with friends, to knock on their doors and say, 'Are you coming out to play?' We played chase and we felt we could live for a thousand years.

Daddy took me for walks by the River Liffey. As I walked beside him, he told me wonderful stories. And we talked about fishing and swimming and sports. But we talked most about mam, and about my singing and dancing. 'Your mother is a good woman,' he said to me many times. 'She is a lady. She comes from a good family, she does.'

I felt so special. I felt like any other child walking along with her father. I felt safe. Now and again I would skip and show him a new dance step. 'Let me show you a treble,' I said, and I demonstrated the fancy step and he laughed his heart out and applauded.

'Have you got your mouth organ in your pocket?' I asked.

'Yes.'

'And would you play for me?'

'Aah, Ina, of course I'll play for you.' And he played the songs of Ireland.

That dreadful Saturday came at the end of a wonderful week. My mother was happier than I had ever seen her. On Friday she had been paid at the Union and stopped at the shop and bought bags of groceries. She bought six half-moon cream cakes, rashers, sausages, and lots of groceries. And most important of all, she bought a little electric cooker. It had two rings on top and a little oven. Mam was so proud of that little cooker. She had worked so hard to pay for it. That night we had a wonderful meal and mam was smiling and looking over each of us in such a proud fashion.

Saturday morning she began changing the flat around. She put lovely white sheets on the bed. She cleaned all the windows and polished the sideboard. Everything in the flat was spic and span. Everything was so homey. She was feeling good. And she kept talking about the special dinner we would have that night. On the new cooker she prepared whiting in flour accompanied by potatoes and peas. She even made jelly and custard for the next day. She put the jelly in the window and the sun shone through it and cast a warm glow there in the scullery.

We were so proud of daddy. And on this Saturday mam went out and had her hair cut, which was very unusual. She was wearing new shoes; it was the first time I had ever seen her in new shoes. She had on a white cardigan with a little blouse underneath and she wore a navy blue skirt. There was a sensation in our house that something was beginning to happen in our family. The children were beginning to grow up. I know mam felt things were getting better. There was a pride in her. And we children were feeling more self-confident.

About five o'clock, mam took my whited shoes and those of my sisters and put them in the window to dry so they would look nice when we went to Mass the next morning. She washed our vests and knickers and put them on a little wooden frame to dry. A fire was going in the fireplace. Everything I had always wanted was there in the flat. I was skipping up and down the balcony and feeling as good as anyone. Dinner was ready but daddy was not home. Mam sat down and started to darn my father's socks. She wore glasses when she was darning and the glasses would slip down her nose.

About 6 p.m. mam said that daddy was late and we should go ahead and eat dinner. The fish and mashed potatoes and peas, all prepared on the new cooker, was a meal I shall always remember.

'I'm going to build a lovely home,' she told us at dinner. 'We won't feel ashamed any more. Your daddy has given up drinking.' And she smiled at all of us and I thought my heart would break from happiness.

After dinner, mam put daddy's dinner into the little oven and sat down at the window. She put on her little glasses and began darning socks again. I put the other children to bed and then sat down to talk with her. The flat was warm from the fire and smelled of fish and mashed potatoes and peas. Our flat was like a scene from a Doris Day film. Occasionally, mam looked up from her darning and her eyes searched up and down the street.

By about 8 o'clock she was getting anxious and she

said to me, 'Ina, would you go out and see where your father is?'

'Is he working late?' I asked.

'No. It's Saturday and he only worked a half day.'

So I went out, walking slowly, trembling in fear at what I might find. I wouldn't look inside my daddy's favourite pub or any pub where I knew he drank. I sat at a place we called 'the Fountain', a little square on James's Street where the giant dray horses that used to pull great carts up to Guinness's Brewery used to stop and rest and have a drink of water. It was here around the square that old men sat and talked about the past. I waited among all the old men and kept saying to myself, 'I hope daddy comes past and he is walking straight.'

About 9 o'clock Mrs O'Neill, a neighbour from the flats, walked past and said, 'If you're looking for your father, he's over there.' She turned and pointed to the pub. 'And, Jesus, is he locked.'

I couldn't go into the pub. I did not want to see my father drunk. It would have destroyed the world in which I had been living and brought back to me all the horror of my life. So I walked around for a while and then I went home and told mam I couldn't find daddy. I sat down and watched her darn socks. She occasionally looked out the window and she had the most painful expression on her face. Then for a long time she bent over her darning and I could not see her eyes. When she raised her head, tears were streaming down her face. She looked at me for a long moment and said, 'Ina, I think your daddy has broken his pledge. I think he will come home drunk again.'

I stood up and walked across the room and put my arms around her. 'Why does he do it, mam? Why?'

She didn't answer. She made no sound as tears streamed down her face.

'I don't think he will change, mam,' I said.

She wiped her eyes and looked at her watch. The pubs had closed and she knew daddy would soon be home. She did not want me to see what would happen. 'Go to bed,' she said.

'No, I'll wait.'

'No, you go to bed.'

I looked across the room. Johnny, my younger brother, was standing there. He was nervous. He knew what was going on.

I went to bed, but I could not sleep. I could never sleep when daddy was out drinking. We were all too fearful of what would happen when he came home. Many nights, more nights than I can count, I sat in bed with my hands over my ears, my legs pulled up into a ball, rocking back and forth and waiting for the shouting and the violence to stop.

That night we heard daddy before we saw him. 'Get along, little doggie, get aloooong.'

We saw him staggering around the sidewalk as he tried to tap-dance and we heard his groan when he fell.

To hear my father's drunken voice, to hear him cursing as he fell was the end of the world for me. All of my hope drained away that night. It would have been better had daddy never stopped drinking. I was afraid I would have to go out on the street and pick him up. I was afraid he would vomit all over himself and me and the flat.

But daddy managed to pull himself up the stairs that night. I came to the door when he staggered in. Mother made the sign of the cross then put her face in her hands and cried.

'Where's my dinner?' shouted daddy.

Mother didn't say anything. She stood up and took his dinner out of the little oven and put it on the table. He was belching and lurching about and kicking the furniture. He sat down and looked at the plate.

'What's this?' he growled.

'Your dinner has dried up, Tom,' mother said. 'It has been in the oven waiting for you since six o'clock.'

Daddy snarled, picked up the plate and threw it against the wall. He tried to smash the table and the one chair.

My little sisters and I were in the door watching. We heard mam say, 'Tom, please don't do this to us. Don't do this to us.'

'Get along, little doggie, get aloooong.'

He looked across the room and saw me. 'I fought in Belfast,' he said. 'Your father could have been a world champion. Did you know that? Aye, your father was a great athlete, he was. A champion swimmer and a great soccer player.'

Mam tried to come into the bedroom with us but daddy caught her and threw her across the room. She hit her back on the iron frame of the bed and her glasses flew across the room. I heard her gasp and saw the look of pain that cramped her face.

She stood up, gasping for breath and her face was red. Normally she was very pale. 'Tom, I'm leaving you this time. I don't care what the priest says. I'm leaving you. I'm taking the children and I'm leaving before you kill me. Before you destroy your family. As sure as God is in heaven, you're killing me. The devil has hold of you, Tom. The roaring drink has you. I can't take it any more.' She was trembling in rage and pain and impotence. Whatever good had been in her life during the past few months, whatever hope she had known, my father had taken away with fifteen pints of Guinness.

Daddy screamed and banged the furniture. My little sisters were crying, 'Daddy, don't hurt us. Don't hurt mammy.'

'Daddy, will you lie down?' I asked. But this time I could not control him. He threw me against the wall and returned to hitting mammy. I thought she was going to die. Her breathing was very bad.

'You're killing my mam,' I screamed. 'God will never forgive you.' He stopped and lurched across the room towards me. 'Please don't hurt mammy,' I said. I was very frightened. I wanted to hit my father, I wanted to smash him so hard he would never wake up. Daddy looked at me and for a moment I thought he was going to hit me again. Then suddenly his blue eyes danced and he sat down and pulled me on his lap. He smiled and his blue eyes danced.

'Oh Danny Boy . . .' he began in his wonderful Irish tenor. 'Ina, did you know your father fought in Belfast? He could have been a world champion boxer. Aye, your father was a champion athlete.' He went on and on. Mam thought his attention was diverted and that he had forgotten her. She tried to drag herself into the bedroom. But he saw her and pulled her back and he made her listen. He made all of us listen. For hours he talked about what a great man he would be one day.

5

I mark my Confirmation day as the beginning of my guilt. On the Saturday before my Confirmation on Thursday, mammy went to hospital. I knew that morning when I awakened that something was terribly wrong. It was March and the flat was freezing; it was so cold that Philomena and I were sleeping with mam. I think I woke up because of the noise mam was making. She was on her back gasping and wheezing. She was very thin, like a stick, and her face was hollow and yellow. She struggled to get out of bed and then she held on to the heavy oak sideboard and stood there sagging and weaving. She turned and stared into the mirror for a long time while I watched from the bed. With a trembling finger she pulled down the eyelid of each eye, sighed, and in a flat voice said, 'I'm dying.'

She turned her hands over and looked at her palms with an expression of disbelief. 'I'm dying,' she repeated in a hoarse whisper.

Still braced against the sideboard, she turned her head and said to me, 'Ina, go next door and get Mrs Kelly. Ask her to come over.'

Mrs Kelly rushed over, took one look at mam and in a voice of great concern said, 'Annie, what's wrong?'

Mam's voice was very weak. 'I don't know. Tom's gone off again and hasn't come back. There is no fire. We have no food. There is no electric.'

Mrs Kelly told me to go to the dispensary. 'You tell

Doctor Finnegan to come up straightaway,' she said. 'Your mother is very sick. Tell him she is very sick.'

Before I left, I heard mother say to Mrs Kelly, 'The children have had nothing to eat since yesterday. There is a bit of porridge in a box in the cupboard. Would you put something in their stomachs for them?' Mrs Kelly looked in the empty cupboards and shook her head.

I ran about ten blocks to the dispensary. Several people were waiting. I ran to the person in charge and said, 'Me ma is very sick. Mrs Kelly said Doctor Finnegan must come straightaway.'

'Sit down and take your turn,' he said to me.

'I can't. Mrs Kelly said he must come straightaway.'

But it was almost two hours before a doctor came. Mrs Kelly ushered him into the bedroom so quickly that the door was left ajar. A few moments later I heard the doctor say to Mrs Kelly, 'You'd better go find Mr Byrne. This woman is dying.'

My heart was beating so fast. Mrs Kelly came out of the room and in a very kindly way told me to find my father and bring him home as quickly as possible.

I ran and I ran and I ran to all the pubs on James's Street, to the Cozy Bar, the Canal Bar, Maher's, O'Reilly's. My legs were freezing and I wondered if something was wrong with me. My legs shouldn't hurt this much just from the cold. I went everywhere.

'Do you know where my daddy is?' I asked. But I could not find him. And I thought it was my fault that I could not find my father when mammy was so sick. And the guilt and the sense of failure made me cry. By then it was lunchtime and everyone in the pubs was singing. I went everywhere, even down on the Quays, but I couldn't find him.

When I returned to the house, I sat next to mam on the bed. Philomena was standing in the corner and crying. The grate in the fireplace was empty and the ashes were dead. The scullery was dead; no cooking, no pleasant smells. Everything was dead.

The ambulance came and the attendants gently placed my mother on a stretcher and covered her with a red blanket. As they were about to leave, my mother held up her hand for them to wait a moment. Her eyes roamed around the room and then looked for a long time at Philomena and me and then around the room again.

'I don't think I'm coming back,' she said.

Outside the flat the whole neighbourhood had seen the ambulance and had gathered. When I went down I heard them talking. 'My mammy said that Mr Byrne killed her.' I heard another say, 'My mam said he has been killing her for forty years; he's a drunkard.'

'My mammy is not going to die,' I screamed at them. 'Don't you say that. And don't talk about my daddy that way.' Then I ran after the ambulance, chasing it as it made its way slowly through the entrance to the flats and along the walls surrounding Guinness's Brewery.

My father came home later that day. He was too drunk for us to tell him about mammy so we let him sleep in the chair for a few hours. We sat on the floor and stared at him as he snored and coughed and dribbled spittle down his chin. He stank of beer.

About six o'clock that afternoon we told him about mammy and I walked to the hospital with him. It was a soft day, rainy and misty. When we arrived at the hospital, visiting hours had passed.

'I'm Thomas Byrne and I'm here to see my wife, Annie Byrne,' daddy said to the receptionist.

'Visiting time is over. And you can't take the child in there.'

Then the receptionist looked at my father in a strange way. 'What did you say your wife's name was?'

'Byrne. Annie Byrne. She is here. She took sick.'

'Can you come in for a minute, Mr Byrne?'

The receptionist motioned for me to stay outside. He whispered something to my father and gave him a piece of paper. I heard him say something about a 'dying pass'.

When my father came out he was shocked. I could see it on his face. I thought there were tears in his eyes. He was scared and he was walking fast and he would not look at me.

'Why did he give you that piece of paper?' I said. I was holding on to his coat trying to keep up with him. He did not answer me.

'I heard him say something about a dying pass,' I said. 'What does that mean?'

'You are imagining things, child.' He wiped his eyes.

'Then why are you crying?'

'It's the March wind biting into me. Don't you be talking like that.'

'My mammy is not going to die, is she?'

'Stop talking like that. Don't you be talking about your mother like that. And don't you be crying. If she sees you upset, she *will* die.'

When we went into the ward, the nurse told daddy where mammy was. Her bed was near the window and she was looking outside at the grey and rainy day.

I wanted to be strong. So I smiled and held her hand and said, 'Hello, mammy.'

She asked me about her favourite cardigan, the moss green one with the pink stripes. She wanted me to bring it to her. But mostly she wanted to talk about what I would wear to my Confirmation. She had bought me a beautiful pink dress that had a rosette on the belt and two ribbons hanging down. There was a little hidden pocket. The dress was covered in small white bumpy dots that had a bit of glisten to them. A big frill was around the bottom and it had a round collar with a bit of pink lace. It had big puffed sleeves and at the bottom of the sleeves was more lace. Underneath was a petticoat of pink taffeta. The dress was fastened at the back with little pairs of buttons. It was the most beautiful thing I had ever owned.

Mammy was as proud of my Confirmation dress as I was. But she was very concerned about the hat I would wear. She wanted me to wear a half-moon hat but there was not one to be found. So I decided to wear a beret. Mammy was very upset about that and she talked on and on about my wearing the proper hat.

For some reason, I don't know why, I said to her, 'Mammy, I'm not going to sing any more.'

Her head lolled in my direction. 'You'll continue singing. You'll find a way. It's in your blood.'

She smiled and asked me to sing for her. 'Sing me one of your Sophie Tucker songs,' she said weakly.

'Some of these days you're gonna miss me, baby . . .' I sang.

'It's very good,' she said. She raised a finger. 'When you sing, sing with your heart. Always sing with your heart.'

Daddy was very contrite that day. He had on his I'm-going-to-stop-drinking-and-take-the-pledge face. Mammy looked at him and shook her head. She had seen it so many times. She had always tried to believe, to have hope. But now she was dying and she could at last be honest with my father.

'Tom, you'll never change,' she said. There was sadness in her voice, sadness and anger. 'And now it's too late, Tom. I'm going to die and what will happen to my children? What will happen, Tom?'

'Stop talking like that,' he blustered. 'You're a young woman.'

'Tom, what will happen to my children?'

My daddy could not answer her. And I've never felt, before or since, the fear I felt at that moment.

Mammy turned to me. 'I want you to go out and find that half-moon hat. Don't wear a beret to your Confirmation.'

Daddy was silent as we left the hospital. 'What's wrong with mammy?' I asked.

'When she fell in the snow, she shifted her heart.'

I didn't know what he meant.

A block away from the hospital where my mam lay dying, daddy stopped in front of a pub. I was far too young to go into the pub where they were drinking stout and singing. Daddy left me outside. It was bitterly cold. I crouched down by the side of the door, wrapped my arms about my legs and huddled into myself to keep warm. After a long while daddy came out and gave me a few pence. 'Go get a single,' he said. Before I could answer, he was back inside the pub.

I stood up, legs stiff with the cold, and walked down the street to get an order of chips.

Then I went home. I was terrified that mammy was going to die but I had to pretend I was not afraid. Mam was worried about my Confirmation and wanted to make sure all my clothes were right, that my hair was right, and that I was learning my catechism.

The next day I put on all my Confirmation clothes and wore them to the hospital so she could see what I would look like. As I was leaving I heard one of the nuns say, 'The poor woman is holding on until the child has her Confirmation.'

The night before my Confirmation, I bathed in our tin bath and washed my hair. I got up early the next morning and dressed in my new outfit. I felt so special. I thought I was the most special child in the whole world; everyone would look at me because my dress was more beautiful than anyone else's. I was dancing around like a little fairy and every time I saw a glass of any sort, I stopped and looked at my reflection. I sang happy songs all morning and made gestures as if I were bowing in court. Mrs Bourke, a neighbour who was looking after us while mammy was in hospital, said to me, 'Stop that nonsense. You'll be late. Stop singing this time of morning. You should be saying prayers for your poor mother.'

There must have been several dozen children being confirmed that day; I don't remember the exact number. I just remember that St James's Church was crowded. During the ceremony, a child takes another name, the name of the saint he or she loves most. I took the name Annie, my mother's name. The Bishop asked each of the children questions from the catechism, but for some reason he didn't ask me anything. He looked at me for a moment, patted me on the head, and passed on to the next child. I thought it strange that he asked me nothing, that he did not want to test my knowledge of Catholicism before I was confirmed.

The crowd at the church did not include my father. He was off drinking. After the Confirmation I immediately ran off to the hospital to tell my mother all about it.

She was gasping for breath but her eyes lit up when she saw me. She waved her hand for me to turn round in a circle so she could see everything. She told me how to adjust the little angora beret – she still did not like it and she was very upset that I had not found a half-moon hat – and she looked me up and down examining every detail of the dress. Tears inched down her face.

I told her that I was going to work and make money and buy her a sofa and everything she wanted, and that daddy was not going to drink any more, and that everything would be OK. I told her that in a few more years, when I was thirteen, I would not have to go to school any more, that I would work. And I told her I would stop singing and dancing lessons so we could save money.

She weakly waved her hand at me and there was a look of distress in her eyes. 'You go to school,' she said. 'And you continue with your singing.' Her voice was so soft and faint.

My father and one of my brothers walked in the door at that moment and I turned to the window so mammy could not see the tears on my cheeks. Then I ran from the room and out of the hospital and down to the Meath Street Grotto. There was a stone in the grotto that came from Lourdes, and when I was very young my mother used to take me there and press the stone against my neck in an effort to heal the infected lymph nodes in my neck.

'O God and Baby Jesus and the Holy Ghost,' I prayed. 'If you let my mammy live I'll be a Carmelite nun for the rest of my life. I'll join the toughest order in the world and stay inside a convent. Just let me mammy live. Don't let her die.'

For the next day our flat was filled with family members, most of them members of my father's family, and I heard several of them say, 'Annie is going to die.' They seemed very calm about it.

When I went to see my mother on the Saturday after my Confirmation, I wore the Confirmation dress because she liked it so much. I walked down the hospital corridors looking at the peeling dingy paint on the walls and smelling that awful smell of disinfectant. I hated the smell then and I hate it now. To a ten-year-old that corridor seemed as if it would never end. On either side were trolleys filled with dirty sheets and dented oxygen tanks. Big pipes ran along the walls. It was all very dark and drab.

When I walked into mam's ward, the nuns scurried in my direction, their beads rattling, and one of them seized my arm, pulled hard, and said, 'Child, you can't go over there. Your mother is very very sick. We're waiting on your father.'

As the nuns pushed me from the room I heard the mumbling of Latin and wondered if the priest was there. My stomach was rumbling and my heart was beating fast and I was sweating.

I ran down the corridor and out the front door and around to the side. The ledges for the large windows were about a foot off the ground. I stepped up on a ledge and looked into my mother's room. I tapped on the window trying to get her attention but she could not hear me.

'Mammy, mammy, it's me. Look at me, mammy.' Tears were choking me. 'Oh mammy, don't die.'

A screen was around mam's bed so people at the door could not see her. A candle burned on a little table beside the bed, and there was a crucifix next to it. Mam was lying very flat. She pushed the bedclothes away as I watched. Her mouth was open and I sensed that she was gasping. Her eyes were as dull and flat as a doll's and seemed to have retreated into dark pits.

The sheer horror that came over me was so great that I fell off the window ledge, wet my pants and began vomiting. When I tried to stand up my legs were shaking so much I could not use them. I sat there and sobbed for what seemed like hours. When I did manage to stand up my Confirmation dress was soiled with dirt and wet with urine.

I walked back around to the front of the hospital and sneaked back into mammy's room. No-one was there when I entered. I noticed a chipped enamel bowl on the table by her bed. It was partially filled with blood. Mam was taking deep breaths. She would seem OK for a moment then begin gasping. Her eyes were sunk deep in her head. She was sweating like mad. Blood dribbled from the corners of her mouth. Occasionally she coughed and more blood came up. She had the rosary beads in her hand and she was very uneasy; her fingers moved constantly over the beads.

I leaned over her. 'Mammy, don't die,' I said. 'Please don't die. God, please don't let my mammy die. Mam, I'm sorry. I'm sorry I cried. I'm sorry I was naughty. I'm sorry I couldn't stop daddy from drinking.'

For a second my mother's eyes rolled open. Then they glazed over and she vomited a great gout of blood that sprayed over the covers and over my Confirmation frock.

At that moment the nuns in the hall must have sensed something and they rushed in. Several leaned over my mother while one seized my arm and pulled me screaming from the room.

'Your mother is going to God,' the nun said. 'And when you scream you bring her back. You have to pray for her soul to go to heaven.' But I was thinking about hell, about mother burning. What did the nun mean that I had to pray for mother's soul? My mother was a good woman. Of course she would go to heaven.

I was put in a room and told they were going to wash the blood from me. When one of the nuns said something to me about God's will, I grew very angry and kicked her and ran out of the room and down the hall and out of the hospital. I continued running across the road and down an alley where I leaned against the wall, rocking and sobbing. My face was to the wall and my back to the hospital, but I remember looking over my shoulder and seeing the iron gates of the hospital and the name Saint Kevin's.

Suddenly, I was seized with uncontrollable diarrhoea and cramps. I rocked back and forth, covered with blood and faeces and smelling of urine and wondered if I had killed my mother. I thought of my many sins. I had lied to my mother about bagpipe lessons, spent the money for my parade dress on chocolates, and not marched in the Easter Parade. I had done so much I was ashamed of.

Sometime later, I saw some of my relatives and my father come out of the gate. Daddy was carrying a parcel, and from the parcel dangled the sleeve of a cardigan, a moss green cardigan with pink stripes.

6

I don't know how long I ran through the streets. All I remember is that hours later I ended up west of the city and miles out in the countryside. I was near a river. Below me I could hear the sound of the water. I sat in the high grass and rocked back and forth. I thought that if I went to sleep, when I awakened everything would be OK, that none of this would be real and my mammy would be well and my daddy wouldn't drink any more. I slept for a long time.

I was awakened by the rain. It was dark and I was shivering with cold. I stood up and began walking. When I passed under a street light I saw that the rain had washed away much of my mammy's blood from my Confirmation dress. The few streaks left were a faded pink.

It was a long time before I arrived at the flats. A card was pinned on the front gates, a white card with black edging and draped with black ribbon. The ribbon, soaked though it was, twisted and snapped in the cold wind. The rain had smudged the writing on the card, but I knew what it said. I couldn't bring myself to read it.

A boy my age was coming out of the gates as I went in. He pointed at the card and said to me, 'Your mammy is dead, she is. That's your mammy.'

'My mammy is not dead,' I shouted. 'You mind your own business.'

I was cold and hungry and frightened and I kept forcing myself to believe that it hadn't really happened. God had not taken mammy away. I walked slowly up the concrete stairs into our tiny flat. It was filled with loads of people, mostly daddy's relatives, and all of them were talking and drinking black Irish stout and eating sandwiches made from boiled pigs' cheeks. And they were all talking about my mam. They were telling stories about dead people and about my mam. They were all drunk and didn't even notice me coming in.

All of those people and none of them cared about my mother when she was alive or when she was sick. I knew she didn't like any of them. They had contributed to her death. And now they were drinking in her flat. She would have hated that. Daddy was drunk too. I suppose he thought he had a legitimate excuse.

That night is very hazy to me. I remember that I went to bed in my Confirmation frock that smelled of urine and was stained with my mother's blood. I thought of Doris Day and how I wanted to sing in Hollywood and make mammy really proud of me. And as I went to sleep, I prayed aloud: 'God, when I awaken in the morning, will you let my mammy be alive and will you let it be like it used to be?'

But it was the same the next morning, I heard daddy's family talking about the doctors at the Union having to perform an autopsy on my mother. I remember that I wore black stockings for several days before the funeral. The stockings had holes in them. When one of my relatives saw the holes she said to me, 'Those holes mean your mother is turning in her grave.' Was mother really unhappy with me, so unhappy she could not find rest even in death?

One of the first things my father's family did was to take my beige three-way coat that my mother bought for my Confirmation and put it in a pawn shop. They wanted my pink dress but I would not give it to them. I wore that dress day and night. They took my other clothes and pawned them, and they took my brother's Confirmation suit and pawned it, all so they could have money to buy strong drink for the wake.

It was the day before the funeral, when my mother was in a coffin in the death house (the hospital mortuary), that the family went to see her. We had to see her before they put the lid on the coffin and took her to the church.

It was raining, as usual. I remember licking the rain from my lips.

Someone in the family, one of my uncles I think, was going around taking up a collection to help with the funeral costs. The Burial Society insurance had lapsed and not been reinstated.

One of my father's female relatives took Philomena and me into the death house. She had never liked my mother. My mother was different from her and from everyone else on daddy's side of the family. When my mother was alive, we rarely saw these relatives.

Bodies covered with sheets were on slabs all around us. The smell, oh, the smell. Mam was at the far end. The lid of her coffin was on the floor.

Slowly and fearfully I approached the coffin. Mam had false teeth and the top plate had fallen out of her mouth and was dangling over her lower jaw. Her face was twisted in a grimace. This was not the way I wanted to remember my mammy. I turned away.

Then I felt the big and all-too-anxious hands of that woman on my head. She twisted me towards the coffin. 'You have to look,' she demanded. 'You have to say goodbye to your mother. That's the proper thing to do. Go on, say goodbye to your mother.'

I resisted. She tightened her grip and forced my

head down into the coffin towards my mother's face. Philomena backed away. She was terrified. She screamed and screamed.

'None of that nonsense now,' I was told. 'Go on, kiss your mother goodbye. Go on.'

'I don't want to,' I shouted. 'I don't want to kiss her goodbye. That is not my mammy. My mammy is not dead.'

'Ah, stop talking like that,' the woman said. She lost all patience and pushed my head down until I was touching my mother's face. Her face was icy. My warm wonderful mam was icy. And there was a horrible smell coming from my sweet mam.

In my head I could feel blood, clouds and clouds of blood. It was as if I was being taken through pain and gore and clouds of blood. I couldn't breathe.

When I was at last released I fell to the floor and vomited. What happened afterwards is dim and vague. I only remember that very faintly I heard Philomena's screams as she in turn was pushed into the coffin and held against mother's cold face.

A few days later my nightmares began. Hovering over me in the night were people, actually it was faces, disembodied, distorted, ugly, strange faces. And I was being pushed into the ground, into a grave. And I kept saying, 'I'm alive! I'm alive!' But they kept pushing me into the ground.

Then there were the nightmares where I was being chased over the roofs and along the streets by people who wanted to hurt me, to kill me. But the most frightening of all were the dreams of being in a slaughterhouse. The knives were coming down towards me to cut me into little pieces. Over and over I would scream, 'I'm human. I'm human.' But the knives kept coming until I awakened.

I don't remember my mother's funeral. I only remember it was 1955 and I was ten years old. My mam was buried in a pauper's grave. I did not visit the grave for more than thirty years. I did not know where it was. Then several years ago I took my daughter Helen to the cemetery. She got a map from the manager and we walked through the cemetery until we found the plot. There is no marker, no name there. But, as Helen pointed out, there is a tree.

One day when I have a few pounds I'm going to put a gravestone there for my mother. She should have a monument. And on that stone I will write a poem in which I'll tell her of all she did for me. And I will tell her about my work with the street children of Vietnam.

One day I will do that for my mother.

7

A few days after the funeral one of the neighbourhood women asked me to come to her flat. I did not hesitate. Mammy had known her well, liked her, and spoke very highly of her because she had raised several children by herself after her husband had left her. The woman was a bit gruff, but my mother always said that her bark was worse than her bite.

The woman sat me down and brought me a big piece of apple tart. I had barely begun eating it when she said, 'Ina, you're a lovely child and you're a good girl.'

I looked at her expectantly. 'This is a very big piece of apple tart,' I said.

'I want to have some straight words with you, child. Now you have no mother. And this is a very dangerous world for young girls. I think it is time for you to live with me. I want to adopt you.'

'What's adopt?'

'You'll come here and live with me and be like my own daughter.'

'And what about my little sisters and my little brother?' I did not like the way this conversation was going. I began eating faster.

She shook her head. 'I want only you,' she said.

'Like hell you do,' I said. I was scared. That was the first time anyone had hinted that my family might be split up.

'We are going to stay together,' I said angrily. I

quickly finished the apple tart. 'I am their mammy now.' I leaped up. At the door I turned. 'My mammy is coming back,' I shouted defiantly, and I ran from her house. As I raced across the street to the flats, I wondered again if this was all a dream.

Back in the flat, I jumped on to the bed and hugged the pillow that my mother had slept on. 'You can't leave us. You must come back,' I whispered. 'Oh, God. Don't keep her in heaven. You don't need her. We need her here. Please send her back.'

I looked out of the window, searching for my mother. I stared for a long time, seeing her in my mind, her dark hair, the lumpy black coat, her slow shuffling walk, the frequent pauses to catch her breath.

If, in my childhood fear and denial, I wondered if I was living in a bad dream, I knew that what was happening to my father was all too real. His drinking became worse. Many were the nights I searched for him in the pubs of Dublin. And many the times I was patted on the head and told, 'Ah, your father's a good man, a generous man. He always stands his round.'

That was money that could have bought us food and clothes, money that would have restored the electricity and bought coal for the fire.

Daddy would come home drunk and he would sit there in that cold empty flat horrified that he was going to die, horrified that he would go to hell. He had such a fear of the devil. The flickering light of a single candle etched the angular lines of his face and made him appear like a monstrous piece of sculpture.

'Can you see the devil at the window, Ina?' he asked. 'He's there he is. He has lovely grey hair, a face like wax, and he's wearing a tuxedo suit. The devil is trying to take me over.' The light in his beautiful blue eyes would dim and be replaced by an awful fear and he would mumble about how terrified he was of dying. If he was not fleeing from the devil, he was wrestling with guilt and fear.

'Annie, Annie,' he wailed in the night. 'Why did you leave me? Come back. I know you are around, I can hear you breathing. Annie, come back to me. Annie, help me with these noises in my head. What am I going to do with the children?' Then he would scream, 'Ina, get up. Your mother is in the other room. She's crying. She wants to talk to you.'

'Daddy, you make me frightened.'

'Talk to your mother. She is breathing over you. She wants you in the other room. She is crying. Can't you hear her?'

'I don't hear her, daddy.'

'She is turning in her grave, she is. She is very unhappy. Look at the way she is moving all the furniture around.'

'Daddy, there is no furniture.'

'Ahhhh, you'd better talk to her.'

So I would have to talk to my dead mother.

'Mammy, I don't know if you are here. Daddy says you're here. If you are, please come back to us. We need you. We miss you. I'm worried we will all be put into orphanages if you don't come back.'

Often this was not enough for daddy. 'Ina, make your mother a cup of tea. She's moving the furniture around. She's not happy.'

'She's not here, daddy. She's not here.'

Daddy would often come in, sit down, and stare off into the distance for a long time. Then he would say, 'I'll have a smoke and me pipe, Annie.' He would talk to mother as if she were in the room. 'Annie, I think there's a chance at a good job down at the docks. If I get it, we can buy a little house and get out of the flats.' Pause. 'By the way, Annie, I saw Boxer Kelly today. He's not looking good. Drinking too hard, he is.' And when he had smoked his pipe he would say, 'It's getting on. Shall we go to bed, Annie?'

You might think it strange that my daddy thought he saw my dead mother and that he talked to her. But it is not uncommon in Ireland for people to talk to the dead or to talk about the dead as if they were still alive. Every Irish family knows that. Someone will die and invariably a friend will ask, 'And exactly what time did he die?' Someone will think for a moment and say, 'Nine forty.' After a moment's pause, someone will say, 'Well, it was ten fifteen when I ran into him on the road. I was walking down the road when I saw him. He had his head down and was walking right along, he was. I spoke to him but he never answered. I thought there was something strange about that.' And the man is perfectly serious when he tells this story. He will be highly offended if you suggest that he is imagining things.

Perhaps because he had never been a good husband or a good provider, daddy always made a great occasion of the rare times when he did bring home food. He would bring some pig's feet or pig's cheek and say, 'I'm going to boil a nice bit of dinner today.' He thought of himself as the great provider. He would cut the fat off the meat and eat it and say, 'There, that will lubricate me lungs.' He would point to the gobs of fat on the plate and say to us, 'Get that fat down you. It's good for you.' And then he would go off to a manual labour job and we wouldn't see him until late at night.

Now that I considered myself the mother of the family and responsible for my two younger sisters and younger brother, I no longer made any pretence of going to school. Dickie Clarke would see me on the streets and he would shout, 'Ina Byrne, I'm going to send you away.' He chased me many times on his black bike with his long mac flapping out behind him like the devil's cape. He was something out of a horror movie, he was.

Looking after Philomena and Kathy and Johnny was a full-time job. 'You're the mother now, Ina,' my father said. So I pretended to *be* my mother. In one sense, that meant she was there, she had not gone. By pretending to be my mam, it was easier to cope with the emptiness, the isolation, the deprivation of love, and to cope with my father, who had become more twisted than ever.

In the year after my mother died, daddy sold the few things left in the flat worth selling; he even sold my mother's earrings, the only thing we had left of hers. He used the money for beer. He would have sold my Confirmation frock but I wore it every day for a year. I washed it and wore it wet. It was all I had. There was nothing left in the flat to show we had been a family, not even photographs. They were all gone. There was nothing of our childhood. The electricity had long been cut off and we began peeling the linoleum off the floor and burning it in the fireplace.

I went around Dublin collecting scrapings from people's plates; pig food, we called it, because some people collected their scrapings and sold it to farmers for tuppence or sixpence. I knocked on their doors and said, 'Have you got any slop for the pigs?' I collected the slop in a big bucket and took it home. If any of the neighbourhood kids saw us, I told them I was taking the bucket to a farmer and I left it by the door until no-one was in sight. Then I quickly brought it inside, put a piece of newspaper on the table and emptied the bucket onto the newspaper. I can still see little Philomena and Kathy and Johnny sitting around the table, their black eyes wide and with serious expressions on their gaunt little faces as I picked through the slop and shared it out.

Most days I got up at 4 a.m. and went to the Smithfield Market while vendors were preparing their stalls for the day. It throbbed with energy. The sound of horses' hooves rang on the cobblestones and drivers would shout, 'Get outta me fucking way. I'm late.' The eyes of the horses rolled anxiously and the smell of their fresh sweat hung in the air. The chatter and the banter of Dublin voices rising high on those cold mornings I shall always remember. 'Ah, get your potatoes here. Lovely potatoes.' A saleswoman might see a handsome man and say, 'Ah, you handsome thing. Come here and I'll give you a hug.' Or if she saw a sour-faced old man she might say, 'These potatoes will do you a world of good. They'll put colour in your weatherbeaten cheeks. Come on. I've got the best potatoes on the street.'

Whatever fruit or vegetables I found on the street, I hid in my clothes and took home to the young ones. I also went to the open market on Moore Street. You could smell the fish when you turned off Parnell Street. I walked along slowly looking for cabbage leaves, rotten oranges, or onions that had fallen under a cart. I would dip quickly, and then slip the scavenged vegetable up my sleeve. Whatever fell to the ground was fair game, but I didn't want anyone to see me doing this, the shame was too great.

In the year after my mam died, we had scabies, scurvy, and fleas. Scabs covered our heads and down our neck. Our heads constantly bled from the scratching. I cut the hair of the young ones very short and then poured paraffin over their heads to kill the lice. They screamed with pain.

One day after I cut their hair and all the pus-filled scabs where they had scratched open wounds were visible, Kathy stood staring into the mirror for a long time. Then she took an old pair of nylon stockings, cut them into long strips, and stuck them on top of her head so the pieces of nylon hung down to her shoulders. She walked to the mirror, sighed, flicked the nylon strips and said, 'I don't know what I'm going to do with my hair. It's getting far too long.'

One Saturday, the day when I combed fleas out of our hair, I noticed Philomena's jumper was seething with millions of fleas. She had been wearing that jumper for six months, day and night, and it had grown very tight on her. I had to cut it off with a knife. Her body was covered with flea bites. I was very scared. I poured more paraffin over her.

'Mammy, you're hurting me,' she said.

Afterwards I went outside and cried. I hated my father so much. 'I hate you. I hate you,' I screamed. And I asked God to let us die so we could be with mammy. I got down on my knees and I said, 'Please, God. Let us die.'

I didn't know how to look after children. I was only ten years old. Johnny was seven, Kathy five, and Philomena only two. Michael came in from time to time, but not often. However, my other brother Andy did help us. He brought biscuits. He would drop a biscuit into a cup of tea and we would share it. Some days that was all we had to eat. Other days I would buy a potato each and we would save the skins. The next day I would peel back another piece of linoleum and build a small fire in the fireplace and cook the skins and pretend they were crisps. Some days we never ate at all.

Sometimes the burden of worrying about my father and caring for my younger brother and sisters was too much for me. I would go up to Guinness's brewery where there was a pretty house with a big blue door and a big brass knocker. I sat on the steps and pretended this was my home and that I had a room inside with books and dolls on white shelves and lots of dresses. 'Would you care for a cup of tea?' I would ask invisible guests at parties. I imagined I had a dolls' house and a bed with a big yellow cover. Everything in my room was yellow, I don't know why. Even today, yellow is my favourite colour, bright, bold, sunshine yellow.

Many mornings, very early, I went out with a woman who sold fish. I had no coat and I remember those mornings were terribly cold. I sold mackerel, whiting and herring. They were placed on a board on top of a pram and I pushed it through the streets shouting, 'Whiting, lovely whiting. Get your whiting. Penny each the whiting; tuppence each the herring. They are lovely with floury potatoes. Come and get your whiting. Come and get your herring.' I was ashamed to be going through the neighbourhood this way. But it earned me money to feed the young ones.

Singing was my island of sanity. It was an enormous struggle for me to continue singing after my mother died, but I did. I kept my buckskin boots and my tuxedo clean; they were all I had in the world. I kept them rolled up in a bag and hidden in a vent in the wall in order to keep my dad from finding them and taking them to a pawnshop.

I still did my concerts on the stairs and I still sang to the red roses on the walls, although most of the wallpaper was gone now and my audience was very small.

Occasionally I sneaked into the cinema when there was a Doris Day film. And when I came out of the cinema and walked slowly back to the flat, I listened to the cadences of Dublin. A group of men on the corner might see a young girl walking by, and one of them would say, 'Ah there, Mary. God didn't give you a brain, but He gave you a lovely pair of legs.' And she would look over her shoulder and flounce her hips and say, 'Don't be talking like that, you dirty thing. You should be in confession, you should.'

But Doris Day and the vibrant chatter of Dublin would eventually give way to the reality of my young life. I was so afraid we would be evicted from our flat. And for a while I tried to meet my father at the pubs in the afternoon and talk him into coming home. There was one pub where a local priest drank. He began coming out with an orange juice and gin hidden in his robes and would ask me to drink it. He was always talking about his fine furniture and grand rooms. He wanted me to see them. When anyone entered or left the pub, he would suddenly grow very stern and begin lecturing me in a loud voice about hanging around on the streets and how I should attend church. But as soon as the people were out of earshot, he tried again to get me to drink the gin. I was ten years old and a priest was trying to get me drunk and take me home with him.

Occasionally, perhaps once a month, my father brought home a rasher of bacon. And he was really the big man as he broke up another piece of furniture for the fire and cooked the bacon in the fireplace. He wanted us to fall over him in our thanks.

'Ah, your daddy is a good man,' he would say. 'He is a good provider, he is.'

I wanted to kill him.

As we moved into the cold and rainy autumn after my mother's death, I began to fear Christmas. My birthday is 23 December, but we had always been too poor to celebrate birthdays. Once or twice mam gave me a glass of lemonade as a birthday present. Christmas was enough of a financial and emotional strain without adding my birthday. I knew that this year, as I turned eleven years old, there would be no glass of lemonade and nothing for the young ones.

'Mammy,' Philomena said, 'what is Father Christmas going to bring us this year?'

'Paw Waw, what would you like him to bring?' I asked. She always liked it when I used her special nickname.

She smiled and looked up and said, 'I want a doll with eyes that move and it says "ma ma". Will Father Christmas bring that to me?'

I thought for a long time. 'Father Christmas has to bring gifts to so many children this year, he can only give you one small present. If he can give you a doll, he will.'

My eleventh birthday came and went with never a nod or a smile from my daddy. And on Christmas Eve I prayed that he would come home carrying a bag of groceries. Maybe he would even bring presents. I had visions of him coming home with food and presents, and maybe even sober.

I knew God could work miracles and I thought that on Christmas He might work a miracle on my father. But there were no presents. Father Christmas did not visit our house the year my mother died. And that night I gathered the children around me and they asked me to tell them the story of Bethlehem. I wanted them to sleep so I could go out and find my father before he got drunk. I hoped he had saved a few shillings for food. We had one old blanket on the bed and some newspapers and a little coat belonging to Philomena. Snow and wind blew around the piece of cardboard in the broken window and chilled the room.

We had a small stub of a candle but I wanted to save it. Outside was a streetlight that lit a bit of the bedroom. So I put my arms around my brother and sisters and told them the Christmas story. I told them how the baby Jesus in the stable had nothing: 'But that doesn't mean if you are poor you are not special. Jesus was the most special person in the whole world and he was poor.'

After a while, they went to sleep and I went out looking for my father. About midnight I came home and sat on the pavement in front of the flat and wondered about mam and how things used to be. I could remember a Christmas when the smell of cabbage and boiling ham filled the flat.

Daddy came in sometime after midnight. He was drunk of course. He made me light the candle and put it on the table. The flat looked particularly empty and eerie that night. In the flickering light, I saw that most of the wallpaper was gone. The linoleum was gone. The table and one chair were all that was left. Daddy sat there early that Christmas morning, burping and stinking.

Suddenly I lost control. 'I hate you,' I screamed at my father. 'I hate what you did to my mother and I hate what you are doing to us. You don't love us. You don't care. You are just a dirty stinking drunkard and I hope you die and go to hell and burn for ever. I hate you.'

8

The noises in my father's head grew louder and more frequent. The doctor said he had a mastoid infection and that an operation was necessary. When daddy was told he would be in the hospital for weeks, he talked to some relatives and asked if they would take in Johnny, Philomena, Kathy and me.

Daddy had four children underfoot. At eleven, I was the oldest. My two elder brothers were gone. Andy was living with family friends. Michael used the birth certificate of the brother who had died to prove he was sixteen and joined the Irish army.

Daddy encouraged us to move in with our relatives. 'If you don't like it there, you can always come back home,' he said to us. We had no choice.

But we believed that as soon as daddy was released from the hospital he would find a way for us to be reunited as a family. Staying with these people was a temporary thing.

Our new home was in the James's Street flats, a twenty-minute walk from our old flat. James's Street was where the snobs among the poor of Dublin lived.

Daddy put all our belongings into a brown paper bag and walked with us to the house. 'You'll only be here until I get out of the hospital,' he reassured us. 'It's only for a little while.'

But we were apprehensive. The flat on Marrowbone Lane had been our home all our lives. Johnny and my two younger sisters huddled around me as we walked. I was the mam and I would protect them.

When we arrived, my father gave the woman who was to look after us a little money and the Social Welfare children's allowance book. My elderly granny was there and she smiled at us and talked a lot. She had osteoporosis and a large goiter and was stooped and gnarled.

The first thing the woman did after daddy left was march us into the bathroom and give us all a good scrubbing. I was afraid of her. She was stern and forbidding and almost a complete stranger to us.

In the beginning, however, she appeared quite kind. She took us to Mass and occasionally to the pictures. She bought us sweets and macaroon bars. Sometimes she would look at us and cry, and I knew she was thinking of our dead mother and the fate of children whose father was destitute and an alcoholic.

The living conditions at our new home were cramped and the place was infested with fleas. When we returned to the convent school we had so many flea bites that the children thought we had measles; when we played in the schoolyard the other children pointed at us. Soon, none of them would play with us. 'Flea heads,' they called us.

Then one night something dreadful happened. We were being looked after by granny, who was sharing our room. It was after midnight when she leaned over and softly called to my brother.

'Johnny, Johnny.'

'What is it, granny?'

'Put on a kettle of water, and get me a basin.'

'It's the middle of the night, granny. Are you all right?'

'Do it fast.'

Johnny awakened me. 'There's something strange

about granny,' he whispered. 'It's half twelve and she wants a kettle and a basin.'

'Granny, are you all right?' I asked her.

'I'm going to die and I must wash me self,' she said.

Johnny brought granny a kettle of water and a basin, and then she sent all of us into the other room. We heard her getting up and I knew that she was sitting in a chair and sponging herself. We drifted off to sleep. An hour or so later we were awakened by rasping and gurgling noises. When we reached her she was slumped over in the chair.

'Johnny, you'd better go and get the priest,' I said. 'I think granny is dead.'

Later, granny was moved into the bed where Kathy and my aunt slept. As her body cooled, we could see the fleas jumping from her. She stayed in that room for two days. People kept coming in to see her body. They were moaning and weeping and wailing. They talked to my dead granny. Many of them leaned over and kissed her. Candles were burning all around the room. Crucifixes were everywhere. The curtains were drawn. People stood around drinking and talking of death and ghosts. The presence of so many people raised the temperature inside the room. The smell of granny's body grew and grew until it permeated the entire house.

After granny's funeral, things became worse for us children. My relatives said we were the reason granny died. The man would come home drunk, waving his arms, and shouting, 'Get them fucking kids out of here. I don't want them here.'

He, like my father, was an alcoholic. I remember he used to put a poker in the fire and then threaten Johnny with it. Several times he burned my brother. While we were there, Johnny's leg was broken. I think the man was responsible, but I am not sure. I remember that when my little brother returned from the hospital he was a different person, quiet and frightened.

Our female relative was permanently consumed by anger. After a while, she began pulling my hair and hitting me with the broom handle. She would grab my hair and throw me against the wall, then catch me and fling me against the wall again. Many times she locked me inside the wardrobe. 'Your mother's in there,' she would shout gleefully. 'Being in there with your dead mother will teach you a lesson.' She appeared to me then as nothing short of monstrous. 'The devil is eating the living daylights out of you.'

Our diet consisted primarily of 'lap', the fat cut from lamb and boiled with potatoes and an onion. We ate that every day except Sunday and Friday. Some days we ate nothing but bread and butter.

Kathy and Philomena couldn't eat lap because it made their stomachs heave. But if they left anything they would be beaten, so I ate it instead. And then I would become sick and vomit. The woman would sometimes make me eat the vomit as punishment. She would force my face into the vomit and say, 'You eat it. You'll eat the fucking vomit or I'll fucking kill you.'

Sometimes I went to the poor house to buy a bowl of stew. Everyone called these meals 'penny dinners'. The penny dinners were for the homeless, for the people called 'the men of the street'. The stew had a peculiar and distinct odour. You could smell it a mile away. When I bought a penny dinner, I hid it under my coat as I came out. I didn't want anyone to know I was getting food from the poor house. But invariably I would hear a triumphant shout from one of the children on the street, 'There's Byrne with her stew. Let's get her.' I ran like mad and spilled the stew all over me. After this had happened a number of times the sour smell on my coat became so bad that I had to get rid of it. The smell of those penny dinners would not come out.

Our health deteriorated rapidly. Kathy developed rickets and her legs began to turn inwards. Her foot is deformed today. She also had kidney problems but was too frightened to tell anyone about the pain. Sometimes she would lose control of her bladder. That brutal woman would hold Kathy's hand and beat her and all the time Kathy would be saying, 'I love you. I love you.'

Throughout the period we stayed with our relatives in James's Street I continued to perform secretly in variety halls. On one occasion a talent competition was held and, along with a double-jointed acrobat and a rock-and-roll singer, I became a finalist. The winner was to be decided at a special performance in a carnival on Cork Street. I was billed last. It was while I was giving a Sophie Tucker song everything I had, singing from the heart just as my mam had told me to do, dancing all over the stage, that I noticed, towering over everyone in the crowd, a very tall man with white hair and black clothes.

'Oh, my God,' I said. 'It's Dickie Clarke.'

He stood there staring at me, unsmiling, looking as if he had just emerged from a haunted house. As my number ended, I danced across the stage and made my exit. I did not stay around to learn who the winner of the talent competition was and I was not there when the judges called my name. I was not there to receive the silver tea-set that went to the winner. I was running from Dickie Clarke.

One day I was playing in the yard when I sensed that my knickers were wet. I went into the toilet and found blood in them. I was terribly frightened. No-one had ever told me about a girl's menstrual cycle.

'My daylights have come out,' I told my relative in a voice quivering with fear. I thought of daylights as something on the inside of my body and I reckoned the devil had eaten them out.

'What are you fucking talking about?' she snapped at me. 'What do you mean your daylights have come out?'

'Well, it might be me inners. There's blood in my knickers from me innners.'

I was dragged into the kitchen, where she turned on the tap and stuck my head under the water. 'Dirty little bitch,' she said. 'The devil is raving inside of you. You are never to talk of this again.'

I stood there in the middle of the kitchen, cold water down my face and body, and so racked with fear that I turned to the sink and retched. 'Make sure your blood doesn't get on anything,' I was told. A moment later she reappeared, 'And you stay away from boys.'

Later that afternoon I went to see Doreen, a friend of my age, and I told her what happened.

'It's not the devil,' she said. 'Girls get that. It means you can have a baby. But you can't tell anyone when it's happening.'

She gave me an old vest that had belonged to her father. We hid it in the shed behind her house and she told me I could use it every month. We cut the vest in half. Whenever I had my period, I would roll up half the vest into a cylinder and place it inside my knickers.

While I had been warned about boys, I was never warned about the man we lived with. I did not like the way he looked at me when we were alone. And his smile frightened me. One night when I was twelve, he came home with the stench of Guinness about him.

He was a big man; to a child he was enormous.

I closed my eyes when I heard his footsteps coming across the linoleum towards my bed. He leaned over me for a few seconds, then went across the room to his bed. I heard him removing his clothes. Then he was sitting on the edge of my bed. He held my breasts and kissed me. I could smell the stout on his breath. And his oily hair was in my face. He tried to force himself upon me. I whimpered and the noise awakened Philomena. She began crying. The heavy man stopped for a moment, fearful that Philomena's crying would wake the household. For what seemed a long time he held me as he waited. I wondered why he was doing this. What had I done that caused him to come to my bed?

Then Philomena went back to sleep and he put his hand under the covers and fondled me. He forced my hand to hold his penis. Then he held my hair and tried to push his penis into my mouth.

'I'm going to tell my daddy,' I whispered. I was frightened of Philomena waking again.

'If you tell anyone, you'll be sent away,' he said angrily. 'Nobody would believe you. They would say you're a devil.'

He continued fondling me. 'You be good to me and I'll be good to you,' he said.

The man came to my bed many times afterwards. When he returned from drinking, the sound of the door handle turning would fill me with fear. I would lie there trembling in the dark. His heavy footsteps would resound in the hall, and the door handle would turn. The squeak of the door knob became the signal that began night after night of terror.

For as long as we lived there I was sexually abused by him. Many times he pulled me into his bed and tried to have sex with me. But he was too big. For days afterwards my vagina burned. Or he would force his penis into my mouth or masturbate while fondling me.

I wanted to tell someone but I was afraid. What if the authorities split us up and sent us away to different homes? We had no rights. We were at their mercy.

I was so terribly afraid for Philomena that I began taking her to school with me. She was too young for the convent but I did not want to leave her at home and in danger of abuse. Because of Philomena I found the courage to talk to my female relative. I told her I wanted to move into the room she shared with Kathy. I thought if I was moved into her room, she might also move Philomena. When I asked her, the woman snapped around and stared at me. I think she knew what was happening. Her eyes were filled with denial.

'Don't you be talking like that,' she shouted. 'You ungrateful little bitch. You'll end up in a home, you will.'

One night the man came home from the fish shop. Grease was all over his mouth and chin. He was belching.

'Sit down there,' he ordered, forcing me to sit in a chair facing him. He stuck the poker into the fire and left it there.

'Have you got your knickers on?' he demanded.

'Yes,' I said.

He pulled the poker from the fire. It was red hot. 'How'd you like this between your legs?' he said with a smile.

I have wondered many times if my female relative knew any of this. I think she refused to let herself think of the possibility. This sort of thing was hardly heard of and never talked about in Ireland. I came to think of myself as a devil. I was not a victim; I was a dirty filthy bitch with evil ideas in my head.

The beginning of the end came in a most unlikely

fashion. Philomena became very sick with an ear infection that may have come from being repeatedly boxed round the head, and Kathy was ill with a kidney infection. I took them both to Dr Stevens' Hospital where the doctors and nurses were horrified at the fleas and lice on us. They stripped us and put us in a small room. I was asked about our family and replied that we lived with our mammy and daddy. I thought if the doctor knew our home situation, he might separate us. We were terrified of this more than anything. The doctor also asked if I went to school. I had stopped attending months earlier, but I told him that I went to a convent school. I think he sensed I was not telling the truth. He gave me a letter to take to the chemist for vitamins and medicine to treat the lice, but I was afraid to take the medicine back to where we lived for fear of punishment.

'Let's go home,' I said to Philomena and Kathy. We thought of our old flat on Marrowbone Lane as home. So we went there to apply the medicine but the flat was boarded up. My father had been operated on and released from hospital but, unable to pay the rent, he had been evicted. I eventually discovered that he lived in a hostel for drunks and the down-and-out, an end-of-the-road sort of place.

We had no choice but to return to our relatives' house and use the medicine there. Later, I hid the bottles but inevitably they were found. 'You are a crafty sneaky little bitch,' I was told. 'You will die roaring, you devil.'

One day a few weeks later a man from the Society for the Prevention of Cruelty to Children showed up at the James's Street house. I remember he was wearing a big peaked cap. I shivered and put my arm around Philomena. The man explained that the doctor who had treated us for lice had reported us and that we had to go to court. Our father had to take us back or he could go to prison for neglect.

A few days later we went to a hearing at Dublin Castle. It was to change our lives for ever.

9

We went to Dublin Castle with our father on a bus. The sights of the city, the streets we knew so well, we ignored. Instead we stared at our hands and sneaked glances at our father. He stared straight ahead and said nothing.

Dublin Castle sits on a ridge south of the River Liffey. We entered through the Cork Gate on Palace Street, an enormous gate over which there are heavy grey stone arches folded like the wings of a bat. Over the arches is a statue of Justice, blindfolded with scales in one hand and a sword in the other. I noticed as we went into the Upper Castle that her back was towards us. She seemed to disappear in the rain that was falling.

We were taken to a waiting room on the ground floor of Block 5, a room located under the court-rooms for children. Dickie Clarke was there. It was the first time I had ever seen him smiling, and I knew then that this was serious. His eyes followed me and I could almost hear him saying to himself, 'Ina Byrne, I told you I'd catch you one day.'

'Oh, God,' I said under my breath. 'Dickie Clarke is going to swear me life away.'

Other children were there. They, too, were waiting for Dickie Clarke to swear their lives away. Several social workers were in the room. It was large and square with rows of seats; it felt cold and sterile. All of the people there were poor. Their shoes were worn, their clothes shabby, and some of the boys had their hair greased back with margarine. The mothers were angry and anxious and the children were tough and scared.

Philomena and Johnny and Kathy and me were crying without end. We were a ragged-looking lot: dirty, insect-ridden. We looked neglected. We knew that our ultimate fear, the fear that had gripped each of us since our mother died, was about to be realized – we were going to be separated. I wandered around the room desperately looking for a way that we might escape. But the police were there and kept us away from the doors and windows.

My daddy looked like a dog that had been kicked in the arse.

'Daddy, you won't let them put us away, will you?' I asked him.

'Ah, you won't go away.'

'Please, God,' I said to myself. 'Keep us together. Don't let them separate us.'

'It is all for the best,' daddy said two or three times. I think I sensed he was glad the responsibility for his children was being taken away from him.

I stood close to him and said, 'Please, daddy, don't let them take us away. Fight for us. I'll look after you and I'll not shout at you about your drinking. Just fight for us. And don't let them take us away.'

'It's for the best. It's all for the best.'

When daddy was pressed about something, he would put on his I'll-never-go-in-the-pub-again look. He was wearing that look. I tried to hold his hand but he pulled away. I realized then that my father had never said to me, to any of us, 'I love you'. And now we were being taken away and he would never have to worry about us again. We were told to proceed upstairs. And a few moments later we lined up in front of a judge.

I don't remember much of the proceedings. But I do remember that people we didn't know testified to how neglected we were; they talked about our malnutrition, the lice and fleas, and about how poor we were. And someone testified that it would be for our own good if we were sent away.

There was no testimony about how Philomena and I had been sexually abused. We kept that secret locked in our young hearts. We thought that if the judge had known the truth he would put us away for the rest of our lives.

Then the judge asked Dickie Clarke for his recommendations. Dickie Clarke stood up, pointed at Johnny and said, 'The boy would get what he needs in Artane.'

I gasped. Artane was an industrial school for boys, located in Dublin. I was afraid for Johnny. But I would have been even more afraid if I'd known that Johnny would soon be transferred to Letterfrack, another industrial school, but one located in the remote wilds of western Ireland. Letterfrack had the reputation of being the most inhuman place a young boy could go. And once a boy entered there, he stayed until he was sixteen. Everyone had heard of Letterfrack. It was matched in reputation only by St Joseph's Industrial School in Clifden, a school for girls.

But I had no more time to worry about Johnny. Dickie Clarke turned, looked at me for a long moment, and announced to the judge, 'This one is wild. On a number of occasions she led me on chases. She lives on the streets. She never goes to school. And on one occasion she was singing in a carnival when she should have been in school. She is a bad influence and I think she should not be with the others.'

Dickie Clarke was enjoying this, I could tell from the light in his eyes. All those times I had hidden from him or outrun him, and now he had won, just as he always said he would.

In our hearts we hoped that the judge would order us back with our father. After all, a bad parent, even if he is an alcoholic, is better than distant relatives.

We were given no chance to speak. The only time we were spoken to directly was when the judge looked down at me and said, 'The testimony indicates that you are out of control and that you must be put away for your own protection.'

The judge then leaned towards a social worker and began whispering. They were discussing our future, our lives. But to them it was just another hearing and they wanted to get it over with quickly and move on. When they appeared to have made a decision they motioned for the police to take us back downstairs. The stairs seemed endless.

We were children whose only crime was that our mother had died, our father was an alcoholic, and our relatives beat us and abused us, but we were being treated like criminals.

Even my daddy appeared heartless. We pleaded with him not to let us be taken away but all he could say was, 'It's for the best. Do what you're told. Your mother is watching over you.' I looked into his eyes and thought, 'You don't care what we feel; you don't even know that we love you.' And I knew this was the end of the line for us as a family, that we could never be together again. I made one more effort.

'Please, daddy, don't let them take us away.'

'Stop that,' he said.

We were ushered into the back of a Black Maria. I saw my daddy turn and walk away.

We travelled for about half an hour. Then we stopped, the rear door opened, and Johnny was seized by the arm.

'Ina, don't let them take me away. Please, Ina. Don't let them take me away. Ina, please.' His feet were dirty, his trousers were dirty, his big eyes were filled with tears that streaked his face. 'Ina, I haven't done anything wrong.'

'I love you, Johnny,' I said to him. 'We'll find a way to get you back.'

'Do you promise me, Ina? Promise you won't let them keep me.'

'I promise you, Johnny. I'll come and get you.'

There were two policemen guarding us, ready to grab us if we tried to get out the door. 'Can't you let us run away?' I pleaded with one of them.

'I'm doing my job, child,' he said.

I turned back to Johnny. 'Whatever happens, one day we will find each other again,' I said. I was the mother and my family depended on me.

Tears coursed down their cheeks.

'Every night, when we go to bed, we will think of each other. Every night. Promise.'

We crossed our fingers, reached out, and there in the back of the Black Maria we linked our fingers to seal the promise.

And then Johnny was pulled away, on the beginning of his trip to Artane. Philomena and Kathy and I stood up, trying to see him out of the rear window. We could see only his head.

After perhaps another half-hour's drive, it was my turn. I had hoped all the girls would be kept together, but it was not to be. The van stopped, the back doors opened and we were facing a brick building. The police motioned for me to climb out. I took Kathy and Philomena's hands, but one of the policemen barred their way.

'You stay,' he said to them.

Philomena's eyes widened in fear. She reached for me and whimpered, 'Mammy, mammy, mammy.'

We clasped each other.

'Paw Waw, I love you,' I said to her. 'Kathy, don't worry, I'll find you.'

The police forced us apart and dragged me towards the brick building. It was one of those old-fashioned square buildings so typical of Dublin.

As I marched inside, I looked over my shoulder towards the Black Maria. I could see Philomena's hands pressed against the dirty rear windows and the shadowy outline of her face. Kathy was standing behind her and appeared even more shadowy. The van drove away. And that was the last I saw of my sisters for many years.

I gave up on big people that day. Something happened to me that was forever to make me afraid of grown-ups.

I was taken through the enormous doors of the orphanage and met by a nun. She talked with the policeman a moment, then took my hand and walked me down a long corridor. The floors were so brightly polished they were like mirrors. And there were statues of Mary and Jesus everywhere.

I stumbled as I walked down the long corridor.

'You'll be all right, child. Now stop your crying. You'll get used to us like everybody else does.'

'Can you bring my sisters here to be with me?' I sobbed.

'No, you're too wild to be with them.'

'I'm their mam. They need me.'

'Don't talk nonsense, child. You're not their mother.' She looked me up and down. 'You need a good wash. We'll put you in a bath and scrub you and you'll be all right.'

My first stop was a red-tiled bathroom where the nuns took my clothes and scrubbed me with thick brushes.

I was given a navy skirt and jumper and told to wait in the laundry while they sorted out where they would put me.

The laundry had a door with light underneath and I figured it opened into a hall or corridor that in turn led to the outside and freedom. I tried the door but it was locked. Then I told one of the nuns I needed to go to the toilet. When I came out I ran for another door and tried to open it. It was also locked. The nun smiled. 'We thought you'd try that,' she said. And then her smile disappeared. 'There's no escaping here, child. We keep the doors locked. You are with us to stay.'

I looked up at her and said nothing. They could not take me away from my sisters.

All that afternoon the nuns kept me in the laundry, and every moment I was thinking, 'I will escape. I will escape. I will put my family back together.' I knew what my brother and sisters had suffered during their short lives. I knew the fear they must be going through. I knew they were crying. I knew they depended on me to put our family back together. I was the mammy.

That evening the nuns gave me a long flannel nightgown. It had been washed so many times it was an off-white colour. But it was thick and warm and comforting. And then they took me to the dormitory on the second floor and locked me in. I did not talk to the other girls there and they did not talk to me. The only human sound was when they said their evening prayers. The dormitory was filled with rows and rows of beds. It seemed enormous. And in those beds were the orphans of Ireland; the orphans – and me, a girl whose family could not care for her.

In the middle of the night, I crept from my bed, struggled some clothes over my nightgown, and lifted a window ever so slowly. I looked out. A bed of pebbles surrounded the building. It seemed such a long way to the ground.

'O God and Baby Jesus,' I prayed. 'I'm going to jump out of this window and escape. I don't want to die. I want to put my family back together. But if I do die, don't put me in hell.'

I made the sign of the cross and said an act of contrition: 'My God, I am heartily sorry for having offended thee. And I detest my sins above every other evil. Because they displease Thee, my God, who, for thy infinite goodness art so deserving of all my love. And I firmly resolve nevermore to offend Thee and to amend my life. Amen.' I jumped.

I remember hitting the ground very hard and then I passed out. When I awakened my nose and cheek were bleeding. I put my left arm down and tried to push myself up but the pain was so great that I almost passed out again. I shook my head and tried to stand. My leg collapsed with a searing pain. I rolled over and began crawling, pulling myself along the cold ground with my right arm. Finally, by using my good right arm, I pulled myself upright. I was hopping and skipping and dragging my right foot.

The only place I could think of to go was the tenement houses where a young man I knew, the house painter who was a friend of my cousin, had a flat. I hobbled along, stopping frequently because of the pain. Several times I spotted police cars and hid behind bushes or dustbins. It seemed that every policeman in Dublin was looking for me.

It took hours to reach my destination. When my friend opened the door he looked at me and said, 'Jesus Christ Almighty. I heard you were locked up. What happened?' He carried me upstairs, put me on the bed, and fixed me a cup of tea.

'I ran away. I think I've broken my arm and my leg.'

'We'll sort something out for you,' he said. I felt safe. He was going to let me stay until I was healed and I could move on.

'You'll have to go to the hospital,' he said.

'I can't. The police will catch me.'

When he said nothing, I reached out and took his arm. 'Promise you won't tell anyone about this. Promise me.'

'What are you going to do?'

'I don't know. Can I stay here with you until I'm doing better?'

He nodded. 'I think we can sort something out,' he repeated. But then and there he changed. Just as I was beginning to feel safe, his expression shifted and he crawled into bed and grabbed me. He tried to kiss my mouth.

There I was, eleven years old, vulnerable, dirty, in more pain than I've ever known, and a man I thought I could trust was trying to kiss me. I was astonished and then filled with disgust.

I shoved him away. He persisted. I shoved him away again. 'You're a bloody nuisance,' he said finally. He stood up. 'You've got to get out of here. The police will come after you and I'll be in trouble.'

I began crying; crying for my mother, crying for my broken family, crying from fear. 'Get out,' said my friend. 'You're a mad one, you are.'

I hobbled away.

10

The pain in my leg and arm was so great that I went to the Adelaide Hospital. As I was being X-rayed, the technicians whispered to each other and stared at me. I thought they knew I was on the run. As soon as they left the room I balanced myself on my one good leg and hobbled down the hall and out of the hospital.

The only place I knew to go was back to the flats on Marrowbone Lane. I crawled and hobbled two miles; it was mid-afternoon when I arrived. I went to Mrs Sweeney who had lived nearby. When she answered the door all I had time to say was, 'Mrs Sweeney, will you help me?' before I passed out.

Afterwards, I vaguely remember an ambulance ride to a hospital where casts were put on my leg and arm and where the doctors asked many questions. They knew I had run away. One of the doctors was disgusted.

'She deserves it,' I heard him say.

'Oh, she's a child,' Mrs Sweeney said.

My daddy visited me. He never mentioned the hearing at Dublin Castle that had broken up our family, and he never mentioned my brother or sisters. I felt as if everyone was waiting for me to get well so they could have me taken back to the orphanage.

One afternoon when I was almost healed, I whispered to my father, 'Today I heard the doctor say to the nursing sister I was ready to go. He said to tell the police to come and collect me. Daddy, they will send me back to the orphanage. Can you get me out of here?'

Daddy looked at the floor. 'What do you want me to do?'

'Bring me a frock and a pair of shoes and a cardigan and let me walk out with you.'

'What time?'

'Eight o'clock when the shift is changing.'

Daddy did as I asked. And that evening, when it was time for all the visitors to leave, I put on the new frock and daddy walked down the corridor with me as if we were visitors. I still had a cast on my arm. Rather than go to the front gate where the guard might stop us, daddy took me around to the back gate where I climbed over.

'I'll get us a place in a few days,' he said. And then we went our separate ways.

I slept that night in the basin behind the Grand Canal. It was not far from the convent school I had attended and near an iron foot-bridge. I felt like a criminal when I woke up the next morning and realized I was on the run. I was eleven years old and a fully fledged street child. The police would be looking for a child wearing a cast, so the first order of business was to remove the heavy plaster on my arm. I walked down towards James's Street and when I saw a man trimming hedges, I sat down and waited. He took a break to have a cup of tea and I grabbed his clippers to cut the cast off my arm.

Two teenagers were passing by and they stopped to watch. 'Young one,' one of them said. 'Why don't you go to the hospital to get that taken off?'

'I'm on the run from the police. Will you help me?'

To them this was very exciting. They helped me cut away the cast and stared at my white and skinny arm.

Now I thought the police could not recognize me.

I went back to the relative I had lived with and asked if I could live there again. 'I can't have you here,' she said. 'The police are looking for you.'

My father had many relatives in Dublin. One by one, I went to them all and asked to be taken in. They all refused. I went back to the first one and asked again, and again she refused.

So I lived on the streets of Dublin. During the winter, I slept in public toilets and coal sheds; in the summer and on balmy days, I slept under the bushes in Phoenix Park where I had spent so many happy hours with my mam.

You can easily find the place where I stayed if you come in by the main gate and turn left towards the 'mollyers'. Beyond the monument is a spike-topped metal fence, and beyond the fence a copse of trees and bushes that extends down to the stone wall along Conyngham Road. Under the thick overgrown branches along the wall, I had a little burrow. Cardboard was stuffed in there for me to sleep on, and paper and rags to sleep under. But it was so cold there; even in summer it was cold. I had a piece of plastic to cover me when it rained, but I was wet and sick all the time. Living in the park destroyed my health. But what I loathed most of all about living under the bushes were the worms. I dug a little depression to sleep in and have some dirt to cover myself with, and every time I dug, the long sticky worms emerged from the soil. I was terrified they would crawl on me at night. I never lost this fear.

Sometimes in the afternoons there would be children in the park. We would play around the mollyers, running up and down the slabs of stone at the base and then gathering grass, putting a forefinger under our noses, and goose-stepping across the park singing a song known to all the children of Dublin:

Hitler has only got one ball,
Rommel has two but they're very small.
Himmler has something similar,
And Goering has no balls at all.

As the afternoon drew on, one of the children would say, 'I have to go back for tea. Me mam will kill me if I don't get home.'

They would begin to disperse and then one of them would turn to me. 'And will you be going home as well?'

'Yes, but I'm going to take a short-cut.' I dallied along the park road, and when all the children were out of sight, I went down the hill behind the mollyers, crawled over the green metal fence, and crawled into my cave under the bushes, my 'magic cave', I called it.

Daddy knew I lived in the park. 'I'm going to try and get us a place,' he said every time we met.

From where I slept in the park I could hear the trains in the switching yard across Conyngham Road. All night they hooted and banged and jerked and pulled. I never became annoyed at the noise, it meant I was not alone. Sometimes it was too cold to sleep in the park. Behind a home in Rialto, a neighbourhood of Dublin, was a toilet where I sometimes slept. And there was a tenement building where I slept if I got in before the doors were locked in the late evening. I moved around a lot, and many times I was chased by the police. The closest I came to being caught was the night I slept in a train. The police found me but I told them my name was Christina Kavanagh and that I was there because my mammy and daddy were fighting and I wanted to get away from home. They released me.

Finding food was a constant chore. I was like an animal that spends its entire life seeking food. I ate leaves off the trees. Sometimes leaves were my breakfast and my lunch. I ate flowers. I gave the leaves names. Some leaves I called 'bacon' and some 'cheese' and some 'bread'. I sucked honeysuckle in the summer and called it 'milk'. I drank water out of taps. And I sat in the parks of Dublin and watched people eat their lunches and toss scraps to the ducks. They opened brown paper bags and pulled out sandwiches. I could smell the meat and onions and cheese and my salivary glands would start to work. The people were all so casual as they ate. They were so casual about their food that sometimes they tossed pieces of their sandwiches to the ducks. Every scrap they threw away tore at my stomach. After a leisurely lunch, they would wrap the remains of their sandwiches, place them back in the bags, and toss the bags into the rubbish bins. As soon as I was alone, I pulled the bags out of the bins and wolfed down the partially eaten sandwiches.

Some nights when it was too cold to sleep, I walked to keep warm. I walked through more nights than I remember. Cars often stopped and men tried to pick me up. I learned to ignore them. Sometimes late at night I would go down to the Quays, to restaurants where prostitutes hung out, and they often gave me food. Sometimes they even took me home and hid me so their mams would not find me. There was one girl, tall and skinny with bright red lipstick and a long grey coat and white high-heeled shoes who was very kind to me and often bought me a plate of chips and eggs or a cup of tea. I think she sensed that my health was not good. She also gave me a toothbrush. Once I went into a restaurant for a cup of tea, pulled the toothbrush out of my blouse, dipped it in the tea and began brushing my teeth. When I was through, I spat into the saucer. This was terribly upsetting to the people at the next table.

'Jesus, did you see that?' one of them said. 'Spitting in a saucer. What's the point of drinking tea if she's going to spit into a saucer?'

They told the waiter and he tossed me out.

During the days I walked around the city looking in the shops. I walked and walked. Every time I crossed one of the bridges over the River Liffey, I looked to the west to pick out the tall spire of the mollyers. I convinced myself that I was the luckiest girl in Dublin. That was my home, my castle. My home was visible from much of Dublin. Down below was my den, and when I returned I would be warm and cosy.

It was a very exhausting time. I was always on the outside looking in: looking in the shops and hotels and cafés and restaurants. Sometimes I was so tired I could hardly walk, but I was occupied constantly with the thought, 'What's going to happen to me?'

I used to walk near the Gresham Hotel and Jury's Hotel and the Shelbourne, because they were places where Americans stayed. Whenever I heard an American accent in the street, I followed it, hoping I might be taken to America. Maybe there I would get to meet Doris Day. She would take me to a house with lights and a big cooker. She would dress me nicely and love me and let me sing and dance. With her I would be safe. In my imagination her eyes were always warm and happy, her smile bright.

In the summer it seemed that everyone in Dublin turned red from the sun. Sunburns were worn proudly. But I did not burn, I tanned. So I took red crêpe paper, moistened it, and rubbed it on my face to make me appear sunburned. Even my skin was against me.

To vary the monotony, I sometimes slept during the day and walked around much of the night. I watched the lights inside the homes being switched off as those inside retired for the night, and I wondered if I would ever again be part of normal life.

My health grew worse. I was very thin and had ulcers on my legs. Glands in my neck became swollen. I had ear infections and was often sick. Occasionally, if I thought I could avoid capture, I went to the Adelaide Hospital for basic treatment.

All the time when I was twelve and thirteen and living on the streets of Dublin, I thought of my mother. And I thought too of my brother and sisters in children's homes, of our broken family. Often I cried aloud for my mammy and as I walked the streets I would look at women's faces. A woman's black hair or her walk would make me momentarily think God had answered my prayers and sent my mother back to me. This was not something that happened every month or so, it happened almost daily.

Once in a while I saw my father. And once in a while he would give me enough money to buy some chips and a glass of milk. He was still living in Keogh Barracks, the end of the earth, a place for the dregs of society, for those who were poor beyond poor. Occasionally I visited him. I had to have a light on constantly when I was there. I don't know if it was because the electricity was always off when we lived in Marrowbone Lane or because of what had happened with my relative in that dark room. I had no light in the park or in the coal shed. But when I visited my daddy at Keogh Barracks, I didn't allow him to turn the light off.

His room was a haven for me. Even though my daddy was an alcoholic, he was still my daddy. He was a link to my hope of reuniting the family.

When I tell people about my life after my mother died and about staying with my father in that tiny room, they sometimes ask whether or not he sexually abused me. He never did. My father was very modest around the children, almost shy. He always covered himself. One reason I never gave up on my father was that he never sexually attacked me. I felt safe with him.

One morning when I was staying with him my dad said he was going to work early and I knew something was about to happen. He looked at me for a long time and I saw tears in his eyes. He just stood there and stared down at me and his beautiful blue eyes were softer than I had ever seen them. It frightened me. Was something bad about to happen to him?

'Daddy, will you be coming back?'

He nodded. 'Yeah.'

'Will you promise me? You will be coming back today?'

Again he nodded. 'Keep out of the way so the guards don't catch you,' he cautioned me. 'They are looking for you.'

A short time later the door was kicked open and four Gardai, big uniformed policemen, rushed into the room. I was terrified and huddled in the corner with my legs drawn up and my arms wrapped around myself.

'Ina Byrne?' one of them asked. 'Are you Ina Byrne?'

My mouth was dry and my stomach in knots. They were going to take me away. Every dealing I ever had with the police was bad.

'Come with us, young one.'

'I'm not going anywhere with you. I'd rather die.'

'Watch this one,' one of the policemen said. 'She's mad. She jumped out of a first-floor window before.'

'There are bars on the windows where she's going.'

'Yeah, but this one will get between the bars. Watch her.'

I kicked and screamed when the police seized me. 'Get away. Get your hands off me.'

But they quickly cornered me. I screamed for my father and one of the policemen laughed. 'You may want your daddy. But he doesn't want you. He told us you were here.'

My arms were twisted behind my back and I was pushed into a car and driven to Kevin Street Garda Station. I sat there for hours. The policeman had been right, there were bars on all the windows. When I was caught trying to escape between the bars of the toilet window I was told, 'You're going to a place you won't get out. Far away it is. No more jumping out of windows for you, me lass.'

'Where am I going?'

'Connemara.'

I didn't even know where Connemara was.

I was put aboard a train with two women. During the journey I tried desperately to figure out where we were going. I knew that I would escape and I was mapping out in my mind the route back to Dublin. We went to Galway on the west coast of Ireland, a trip that took several hours. And when we arrived, a police car met us. The two women marched me out. I asked repeatedly where we were going but they would not answer. I was taken to another police station and then put into another car with the same two women who had held on to me all the way from Dublin. They squeezed me into the back seat, in between the two of them, and a man drove the car further west into Connemara, that wild, desolate, wind-swept and storm-lashed part of western Ireland. This part of the country is bleak, with a lot of marsh and turf and bog and hills and outcrops of cold granite.

Cromwell used to tell the Irish, 'To hell or Connacht.' Many chose hell. He banished many Irish to this harsh, remote countryside. I could see the black mountains of Connemara, the Twelve Pins. And I could see the deep lakes. Sitting between those two big women I looked out at the high intimidating mountains and I was very frightened.

'Where are you taking me?' I asked several times. They would not answer. About the only time they talked was when I asked one of them how far it was to Dublin.

'Don't get any ideas,' she said.

The road from Galway to North Connemara was single-lane. In many places it went through deep cuts in the rock and it seemed the mountains were closing in on me. Stone walls were everywhere. I had never seen so much stone in my life. As we came closer to our destination, I sensed the increasing cold.

After an hour or so we arrived at our destination. I saw a sign at the entrance to the village of Clifden and I gasped. Clifden was the location of St Joseph's Industrial School, at that time reckoned the worse place in all of Ireland for a girl. This was where Ireland hid its illegitimate daughters and its orphans, as well as young girls who were sent there by the courts. I felt like a criminal.

Dickie Clarke had done it. Our man Dickie had sold my life away.

11

Almost everyone who drove through the front gate of St Joseph's Industrial School wanted to photograph the grounds. The lawn was green and lush and the gardens well-tended. Tall imposing statues of St Joseph and Our Lady reminded all visitors that this was a place of contemplation. The convent in front of the school was serenely appealing, a stately building painted a soft yellow and trimmed with muted grey. The glistening mahogany door let visitors know they were entering a sanctuary of dignity and well-being.

I never walked through those lovely grounds and I never entered through that shining mahogany door. The police drove past the front of the school and turned up a side road to enter through a gate on to a track that led behind the convent.

The school seemed to have grown out of the bleak hills of Connemara. The half-dozen buildings of cold grey stone looked as if they had been there a thousand years. I stepped from the car into a wind so cold it brought tears to my eyes. The school was on the crest of a hill and the wet and unrelenting wind swept over the mountains from the Atlantic, chilling me to the bone. My entire time there it never seemed to stop blowing.

Catholics like to start everything with a bath, so as soon as I walked in the door I was taken to the washroom, stripped, and forced to bathe in scalding water. The water was from the bogs of Connemara and it was brown and gritty.

After I was thoroughly scrubbed, the nuns gave me a faded red institutional pinafore dress that was to be my everyday uniform. On the back was a number – 69. The number made me feel like a prisoner. I was also given a pair of black cumbersome lace-up brogues. And then there was a set of clothes for Sunday: black stockings, navy skirt, blouse and a sweater of royal blue. There was a navy mac for the rain that never seemed to end, and, finally, two night-dresses, shifts made of a heavy material that came down to my ankles. There was nothing at all feminine about these nightgowns, the nuns did not want us to feel like young women.

'Is there a toothbrush?' I asked.

One of the big red-faced nuns looked at the other. 'What did you say?' the nun asked me. 'Would you repeat that, child?'

'I asked if there is a toothbrush. I need a toothbrush.'

'Ah, did you hear that?' one nun said. 'She's come down from Dublin and she wants a toothbrush. Well, you won't get one of those here,' she snapped at me. 'You'll get a bit of soda once a week.'

She was right. Every Saturday morning a bit of soda was put out on a communal sink. And that was it as far as brushing my teeth went. I felt as if I had not got off to a very good start at the industrial school. And it was to get worse.

I had entered a relentless, merciless, work-filled world. In later years, someone described St Joseph's as a Dickensian workhouse. And they were right.

The nuns belonged to the Sisters of Mercy, an order with the most unsuitable name as it was a harsh disciplinarian order. The nuns tended to be large with red faces and they spoke Gaelic. They could not pronounce my name and called me something that sounded like 'Christiana'. They all seemed personally offended that I was a city girl. I was proud of being from Dublin. And even though I was only thirteen, I thought that the Connemara accent would be ridiculed all over Ireland. In Dublin, people who speak like that are known as 'culchies', a derogatory name for a country person. Now I was on the other end of that prejudice. 'Hello dere, you little Dublin jackeen,' one nun said to me. Being surrounded by Gaelic-speaking nuns who made fun of me caused me to be fearful that I would soon sound just like them. And then what would happen when I escaped and returned to Dublin sounding like a culchie?

'Jesus, Mary and Joseph, I give you my heart and my soul,' I prayed that first night. 'Jesus, Mary and Joseph, assist me in my last agony. Jesus, Mary and Joseph, may I breathe forth my soul in peace with you. Amen.' I paused, took a deep breath, and added, 'And please, dear God, please don't let me lose my Dublin accent.'

It was here at the industrial school that I first began to have doubts, not only about my religion, but about those whom we normally think of as 'good people', in this case, the nuns. I was a frightened and vulnerable child, in a place where even the language was different. The nuns not only showed me no love, they singled me out for ridicule and punishment.

My fellow inmates quickly realized this and, of course, tried to join in. But the first time one of them called me a 'jackeen', I turned to her and said, 'Yeah, and I'll pull the hair out of your head if you don't watch your bloody tongue.'

And that ended that.

I'm sure that any child entering a place such as St Joseph's would have adjustment problems. I was no different. I asked one of the nuns if I could have pen and paper to write to people in Dublin and ask about my brother and sisters. 'You haven't got any family,' the nun said. 'They are all dead.'

This was the standard response from the nuns if we enquired about our families, or, as I was to find out years later, even when relatives came to the door. My little brother Johnny was now at Letterfrack. He may have been the only boy ever to escape from there. He had found out from relatives in Dublin that I was at St Joseph's, and one day he turned up at the convent asking for me. The nuns told him I was dead. Not long afterwards, Johnny was caught and returned to Letterfrack.

I don't think I've ever known of a place where cruelty was as institutionalized as it was at St Joseph's. Part of the reason was our location. We were in such a remote place that the nuns could do whatever they liked. There was no-one to check up on them.

The second day I was there I saw a little girl running around the wind-lashed hill top with a wet sheet over her arm. Little ones who wet the bed had to carry the urine-soaked sheet round and round the grounds until it was dry.

A week or so after I arrived, the nuns brought us together in the assembly hall to ask about our future plans. In reality, it was a way to take our theological temperatures, to see if we were absorbing the spiritual lessons forced upon us daily. The highest sign of this acceptance was the publicly stated desire to be a nun.

'Who's going to enter the convent?' one of the nuns asked.

'I am, Sister,' said one of the girls. Of course she had no more intention of entering a convent than I did. But it pleased the nuns to hear this. And it made the speaker a special person in the eyes of the nuns and meant she would not be treated as harshly as the others.

'And what order would you be wanting to enter?' the nun asked.

'The Sisters of Mercy,' said the girl with a beatific smile.

'Ah, you're a lovely child,' said the nun. 'Stand over there nearer the window.' And as the girl walked to the window the nun nodded in approval, turned to the rest of us and said, 'Look at the light shining on her hair. She's such a lovely child.'

Several other girls said they wanted to be nuns and there were some who said they intended to become nurses, a profession the nuns also liked. Our guardians were in a good mood: so many children who wanted to become just like them. Then one of the nuns looked over the room and her hard eyes settled on me. 'Dublin girl, what do you want to do?'

'I want to be an actress,' I said. 'I want to go to Hollywood and be a dancer. I want to sing.'

I had gone far beyond the limits. Even Dublin girls were not thought to be so debauched and worldly as to want to go into acting. My questioner was horrified. 'Oh, and have you heard that?' She pointed a bony and imperious finger at me and said, 'Christiana, come to the front of the room and say that again. I don't think they heard you.'

I knew she was going to hit me. I came out of the seat giggling, and turned to a girl in the next seat. 'I should have said I wanted to be a prostitute in London.' I was a street-wise Dubliner, and putting me among these girls, many of whom could not remember ever stepping foot off the grounds, was like putting an alien among them. They did not know what to make of me.

I walked to the front of the room and stood there

with my hands behind my back. I looked at the nun, smiled, and waited. The only question in my mind was whether she would simply give me a hiding or if she would expound on my evils first.

'And would you tell the class what you said?' she demanded again. 'I don't think they heard you.' The nun was almost choking.

Perhaps she thought I would experience some sort of conversion during the walk to the front of the class, a quick redemption that would cause me to see the error of my ways and lead me to announce that I wanted to be, if not a nun, then at least a nurse.

'I want to be a dancer and a singer in Hollywood,' I repeated. 'And I want my name in lights.'

In the end there was no delay. The nun took me outside the classroom and whacked me hard with a cane. She beat me several times and then told me to return to my seat. 'We all know where you're going to end up,' she said in a voice audible to the entire school. 'You're going to end up like your father, in the gutter.' And then she delivered what to her was the supreme denunciation. 'Even worse,' she shouted, 'you might wind up in that pagan country, England.' She tightened her lips, shook her head, and muttered, 'Ah, the devil is burning in you, child.'

If the devil was indeed burning in me, I must have been the only one there to suffer from such a possession. For the girls in that place of horror were the sweetest and saddest I have ever known. Almost one hundred girls lived at St Joseph's, and most of them were either illegitimate or orphans.

In Ireland at that time, it was better to commit murder than to have an illegitimate child. Some of the children had been at the industrial school since shortly after birth. They did not know their mothers or fathers or where they had come from. Many was the time I saw someone steal a telephone book from one of the offices, and pore intensely over the lists of names in an attempt to discover someone who might conceivably be a relative.

The nuns told me I was in the school because I was wild. They beat us often; they used sticks and they really whacked us. 'This will make you a good girl,' they said as they beat us. They also shaved our heads.

Many of the younger girls cried at night. Because I was a bit older, some of the young ones would come to me. 'I wonder if I have a mother somewhere,' one said to me. 'I wonder if my daddy knows I'm here,' said another. When I cried at night I had to do so silently, as my mam had done. I could not let the little ones know.

Occasionally we sang together. The song we sang most often was called 'Nobody's Child'. We would all cluster together, and sing the slow haunting words:

> I'm nobody's child, nobody's child,
> Just like a flower, I'm growing wild.
> Nobody loves me, nobody cares.
> Nobody wants me, I'm nobody's child.
> I'm nobody's child, nobody's child.
> No mama's kisses, no daddy's smiles.
> Nobody wants me, nobody cares.
> Nobody needs me, I'm nobody's child.

When it was bedtime, each of us first had to put on our long night shifts. We undressed under the shift. Each dormitory was ruled by an older girl, who might have been in her early twenties, and she may well have been at St Joseph's all her life. It was her responsibility to make sure we stuck to the rules when the nuns were not there to enforce them. By law, we could leave when we were sixteen. But these girls had no place to go. They did not know how to catch a bus or how to buy groceries or how to find a cup of tea or how to go to a cinema or how to live in a flat. They knew nothing. So they stayed on at the school and they became embittered and angry, and they took great pleasure in beating and intimidating the younger ones. They were known as enforcers.

One of the enforcers always carried a stick and walked up and down the dormitory aisles looking for the slightest reason to hit someone. If a shift came up and she saw any part of our bodies, no matter how small, she would swing the stick and say, 'Cover yourself up.' The industrial school engendered in me what remains almost a fanaticism about not exposing any part of my body. Even today, I have great difficulty wearing a bathing suit in public.

On going to bed, we had to sleep with our arms outside the covers, preferably crossed, it was said in case we died during the night. We could not have our hands under the covers and we could not cultivate close friends among the other girls; the nuns were afraid we would become lesbians. If two girls exhibited any signs of becoming friends, one was quickly transferred to another dormitory.

We all attended school on the premises. And I did not do well.

Not only was everything taught in Gaelic, but I had missed so much school that it was very difficult for me. 'You're stupid,' one of the nuns said to me. 'You can't even read and write properly.' More times than I can remember, the nuns told me I was 'a thick Dublin tramp'.

I could understand their frustration with my difficulties at lessons. But I did not understand why they called me a tramp. Simply because I was from Dublin did not make me a tramp. Although, God knows, I'd had the opportunity when I lived on the street. If I had been a weak person, I would have become a prostitute. That's for sure.

Working in the laundry was deemed the lowest and most menial of all the jobs at St Joseph's. And I was constantly threatened with being assigned to that job. 'You'll end up in the laundry because you're too stupid to be educated,' said one of the nuns. 'You'll never pass your Primary.' The Primary Certificate was sat at about the age of fourteen and, if passed, allowed the student to enter secondary school.

I could do nothing about the nuns' derision towards me because I was from Dublin. But I could do something about my lessons. And I picked the Primary Certificate as the ground where I would make my stand.

The Primary test hinged upon a knowledge of Gaelic. I knew the Gaelic test would come from a book of essays called *Peann agus Duch,* or *Pen and Ink*.

I was determined to do two things: first, I would prove to the nuns that I was not as stupid as they said. Second, I would do this by not only passing my Primary but by receiving a distinction in the all-important and most difficult Gaelic part of the exam.

A workman had left a flashlight by the door of the school and I used that light to study under the covers every night after the dormitory was dark. Until the bulb burned out, I studied every night. I memorized every line of every essay and every mark of punctuation.

The Gaelic part of the exam was to write an essay entitled 'An Fáinleoge', which means, 'The Swallow'. I wrote it without a mistake. I still know that essay today and I can recite it flawlessly.

I received my distinction. This little girl who had rarely been to school got a distinction in her Primary.

What a glorious day that was. 'Ah ha,' I thought to myself when I saw the look of astonishment on the nun's face. 'You won't be calling me stupid any more.' So the nuns had to send me to the secondary school, adjacent to the industrial school. This was where the town children in Clifden attended.

One day I was doing Latin exercises. We were conjugating verbs when I came to the verb 'to love', and tears began falling on my book. The nun teaching the class had a stick in her hand and she pointed it at the book and said, 'And what are you doing to your book? The ink is running. You're a dirty untidy girl. Lift your head up.'

'I'm thinking about my mam,' I said.

'Thinking about your mother at your age? She is dead and buried.'

'I'm so lonely for my mam,' I said.

The nun hit me on the shoulder with her stick. 'Stop that nonsense and get on with your work.'

I was never able to mourn for my mam. Our relatives had never let us mourn. And when I was on the streets I was so taken up with my own survival that I was unable to mourn her. Although I thought of her often I never properly mourned her. Now that my food and clothing were taken care of and I had a warm and secure place to stay, my thoughts turned ever more frequently to my mother. But the nuns would not let me mourn her. After that day I never let the nuns see me cry.

The girls at St Joseph's studied every afternoon and evening. A particularly large nun sat at the head of the class to make sure our attention was devoted to our books. Late one afternoon when I was studying, the nun left the room for her 6 o'clock prayers and no-one came to replace her. So I climbed on top of her desk and began singing. I was laughing and dancing and really putting on a performance.

'Cupid, Cupid, you're a real neat guy,' I sang. And when it was over one of the girls shouted, 'Go on, Christina. Give us another one.' And I did. The nuns would not turn me into a vegetable. I would not be stamped and moulded and compressed into the form they wanted. So I began singing a Buddy Holly song. I was shaking my hips and swinging my arms singing, 'All my love and all my kissing/Baby you don't know what you been missing' and I thought I was really good. Then I noticed the faces in the class were no longer looking at me, but rather towards the door. I looked over my shoulder and there was the big nun. And she was carrying a cane.

'Maybe this will help you dance,' she said, waving the cane. She took me outside the classroom and belted me across the legs. Time after time she hit me. And when it was over she said, 'You won't dance for a long time.'

Soon afterwards the nuns took me out of school. Even though I was one of the few girls to be admitted to secondary school, the nuns stopped my education and put me in the laundry two days each week and in the dairy every morning. I had to get up at about 3.30 a.m. to go into town and light the furnace at the secondary school.

We were always working or praying. And I never seemed to have enough to eat. I used to rob eggs from under chickens and eat them raw. The nuns fed us bread and tea in the morning, potatoes and lamb at noon, a bowl of porridge with no sugar or milk in the afternoon, and bread and tea in the evening. Raw eggs were a special treat.

Sometimes the nuns would take us around the outskirts of the school, where we might encounter townspeople. We were told there were Protestants in town and that if we were out walking and came upon a Protestant to turn our heads away. 'Don't be looking at the Protestants,' the nun said. Don't ask me how we children could look at someone and know if they were Protestant, but we could. We Irish Catholics can spot a Protestant a mile away.

Sometimes I would run across the meadows and sit in the long grass. Only in the meadows could I relax and be me. I was growing up. My breasts were becoming large. And the nuns made us so ashamed of our bodies that most of the time I walked around stooped over with my arms crossed. But in the meadows I was not concerned with what the nuns might say. I could sprawl out in the long grass and dream of escaping and returning to Dublin and reuniting my family.

One night a friend and I sneaked out of the dormitory and ran full speed down the long dark road towards Galway. All we could see were clouds and lakes. We had heard the lakes of Connemara were filled with fish so big they could eat a human. We ran and ran with no idea as to where we were heading. Finally we stopped and realized there was nowhere to run, we would never reach Dublin. So then we had to turn round and run back as fast as we had run away. Now we were terrified that if we did not get back soon the nuns would discover our absence and beat us. We were exhausted when at last we stumbled back into our beds. We had not been there five minutes when one of the enforcers came round with her stick knocking on the beds to awaken us. Running away was something I never tried again.

I don't know what would have happened to my life had the nuns not decided to send me back to Dublin. When I was sixteen, they told me it was time to go. I think the nuns knew I would never become one of them or a nurse or even an enforcer. They knew they could never change me. They gave me a birthday present of a bar of soap, a five-pound note, a big suitcase, a long grey institutional coat, thick black brogues and a navy jumper, and they put me on the train to Dublin. I was so happy. All I could think of was that I was going back to be with my family.

The nuns notified my father that I was on the train and he met me at the Westland Row Station. I had not seen him during the two and a half years I had stayed at St Joseph's. The greatest surprise was that he was sober.

'Are you still drinking, daddy?'

'I packed that game in, Ina. It's a fool's game.'

Those lovely blue eyes of his sparkled as he told me how he was going to get a house. 'We will all be together again,' he said.

'We? You mean the two of us?'

He laughed. 'No, Ina. I mean all of us. Johnny, Philomena, Kathy, you and me.'

I could not speak for a moment. Tears sprang into my eyes. 'But they're all dead. The nuns told me they were all dead.'

'Dead? Get away. Kathy and Philomena are at an orphanage in Booterstown. And Johnny is now at Letterfrack.'

Joy that my brother and sisters were alive overshadowed my fear for Johnny. I had been at St Joseph's and knew what these institutions were like. And I knew that Letterfrack was worse. But he was alive. He was alive.

'We'll see them one of these days,' daddy said. 'But now we have to take care of you. I went to your relatives up in Fatima Mansions and they said you could stay there.' He said this would be only until he had arranged where we were to live and gathered his children together.

'Can't I live with you?'

'No, Ina. It's with your relatives you'll be living for a while.'

As we walked along the street, I looked up at him and said, 'Daddy, I have five pounds. Could we have some fish and chips?' It would have been such a luxury for me to eat fish and chips with him, just like in the old days.

He smiled and I thought my heart would break with happiness. I was out of St Joseph's, my brother and sisters were alive, my father was not drinking, and we were all about to be united.

'I know a good place,' he said. 'We can go on the bus. Have you any change?'

'No. Only the fiver.'

He looked at the door of a nearby pub then waved for me to give him the money. 'I'll go in here and get some change. We'll catch the bus, get some fish and chips, and then go to the place you'll be staying.'

The past suddenly rushed back and for a moment I was worried about giving him the money to go into a pub. 'You promise you'll come out? You won't go away?'

His blue eyes softened in pain. Then he nodded in agreement. 'I'll come right out,' he said.

'Can't you just go in a shop and get change?' I asked.

'Ina, you know what the shops are like. They won't give you change unless you buy something.'

So I gave him the fiver. 'I'll be out in a minute,' he said, and disappeared into the pub.

I stood outside in the freezing cold. I waited and waited. And suddenly it was just like the Christmas after my mother died. I was standing shivering outside a pub, waiting for my daddy. After a long time, I went inside to look for him. But he had gone out the back door and I didn't see him for weeks.

I was now broke. I went to a church and told the priest what my daddy had done. He told me of a hostel on the south side of the town. I walked across town in my industrial-school brogues, heavy coat, and carrying the suitcase, and I stood in front of the hostel. I took one look at the building and walked away. It reminded me too much of the last two and a half years. I couldn't go through that again.

Realizing I had nowhere else to go, I went to my relatives' house on James's Street and waited and watched from around the corner to see if the man would emerge. A woman selling oranges nearby told me he was in England. So I knocked and went inside.

I was horrified by what I saw when I looked around. The industrial school, whatever else it was, had at least been clean. When I saw the filth and the fleas and smelled the odour of that place I knew I could not stay. And then I received an even ruder shock. As I turned to leave, the man walked in. He stood between me and the door. I turned to jelly. I was shaking with fear as he stood there smiling and leering at me.

'When did you get out, Ina?' he asked.

I could not answer. He came closer. 'You're not a little one any longer.' Reaching out, he put his hand on my breast, smiled, and pulled me towards him.

I jerked away and ran. I left my suitcase. I had only the clothes I stood in. I had no money, no family, nothing. That night I returned to Phoenix Park. My first day in Dublin in two and a half years, and once again I was a street child.

12

I was more frightened of the streets when I was sixteen than when I was twelve. Perhaps it was the abrupt shift from the orderly and structured life at the industrial school. My first and most pressing need was to find a home. I could not stay in the park, so I went back to the coal shed in Rialto. I used newspapers to protect my clothes. Again, I was terrified that the people who lived in the house would see me and put me out. To lessen those chances, I alternated nights there with nights in my old burrow in the park.

My next need was to find a job. And I had to do that while I was still clean and had a neat appearance. I knew all too well what would happen to my appearance after a few weeks on the streets. I found a job assembling telephones. It was my first real job and I quickly noticed how different I was from the other girls. They dressed better, wore make-up and high heels, and had a light-hearted air about them. I had no money for clothes and I was anything but light-hearted. But I had to try. I rubbed red crêpe paper on my lips. And I went to the market and bought high heels. But I couldn't walk in them, so these I gave up on.

After a few weeks I began occasionally meeting my father. He gave me bread and butter for lunch.

'Daddy, it's cold in the park, freezing cold.'

'Ah. You're hardy, you are.'

The girls at work talked of their mothers and fathers

and their families. 'Me sister is getting married on Saturday. We're all going down,' one would say. Comments like this cut through me like a knife. They talked about their frocks, their first dance, all the normal things. I wasn't part of that life, but I couldn't let them know. The pain of being so different was inexpressible.

Even more painful was the knowledge that my two sisters were in an orphanage in Booterstown and I couldn't see them even though they were only four miles away. If I went there, the nuns would call the police on me. I wondered if the nuns had told Philomena and Kathy that I was dead. One day I would have enough money to visit them and to take them gifts. And when they were sixteen and able to leave, we would have a home together. We would be a family again.

One day a woman at work asked me where I lived. I made up an address. The woman must have been suspicious because she checked and found the address was no good. She told everyone at work. I was so ashamed that I left. I know this doesn't make sense considering how much I needed the money. But I was filled with shame about living in a coal shed, about the pretence, about wondering if the girls I worked with knew I had no home.

So I found a job on Francis Street at a silk-screen printery. The woman who ran the shop was very kind to me and I worked there for almost a year. I told her that I lived in Rialto. My father met me every Friday after I was paid and I gave him a third of my pay. I then went to the Iveagh Market to buy second-hand clothes. The shoes I liked always seemed to be too big and I had to stuff the toes with paper.

I wanted desperately to be normal, to be like everyone else. I used to stand in front of the dance halls and watch the girls. I tried to copy them. I tried to walk the way they walked: a bouncing, flouncy sort of walk. But every time I tried to go into one of the dance halls, the manager turned me away. 'Go on, you're a child,' he would say. 'And look at the state of you.'

Almost never was I able to take a proper bath. Behind a tenement house on Earl Street was an outside tap where I washed my hair. One of the most difficult things I ever had to do was stick my head under that tap. I did this either very early in the morning or late at night in order to avoid the embarrassment of people seeing me. I carried a bar of soap and washed my knickers under the tap and then put them in my pocket.

At work I told stories about my mother and pretended she was alive. Sometimes on Friday night the girls in the printery would buy ice pops and then we would all walk home with one of the girls, after which we all went our separate ways. One Friday night they wanted to walk home with me.

'Oh no,' I said, shaking my head. 'I can find my way home by myself.'

But they had been home with every other girl and now it was my turn.

'I'm not going straight home,' I said. 'I have to do a few messages.'

They insisted. The moment I had feared for so long had come. My heart was beating madly. I imagined the shame that would be mine. Eventually, we came to the house in Rialto and I said, 'This is my home.'

The girls clustered around, looked appreciatively at the house. 'What a lovely home,' one of them said.

'Oh, God,' I prayed. 'Please don't let the owners come out. And please make everyone go now.'

The girls were waiting for me to go inside and I was waiting for them to leave.

'Go on in, Chris,' one said.

'No, you go on. I want to see you off. Off with you.'

So they walked slowly up the street, looking over their shoulders as I waved at them, keeping one eye on the front door. The minute they rounded the corner I dashed down the street in the opposite direction.

Occasionally one or two of the girls at the printery would take me home with them. But their mothers always made it clear I could not stay the night. Usually they were nice about it. 'That young one better go home,' they would say.

I was soon to leave the printery. I knew the girls there were beginning to wonder about me, and in looking back I believe they must have known I had no home.

I was beginning to have serious problems with my legs. I had always had poor circulation, and the year of living in the park when I was twelve, and selling shamrocks in the freezing weather, had probably aggravated the condition. Now that I was back in the park and was again subjected to the cold and damp, the circulation problems became even worse. I developed chilblains which became ulcerated and then septic. The condition got so bad that my employer could ignore it no longer.

'You must go to a hospital and have that treated,' she said. 'You shouldn't come back to work until you are cured.'

At about the same time a girl came to work at the silk-screen printery who knew my family background. I think she even knew I had been at an industrial school. I could not face the other girls. Now they would know I had lied to them. So I left and never returned. I asked my father to take me to the Adelaide Hospital where they bandaged both my legs from ankle to hip and gave me two walking sticks. Every day for two weeks I hobbled to the hospital for injections. I had to visit regularly for months afterwards.

'I can't live like this any longer,' I told my daddy one day when we met on the street. 'It's too hard. Won't you try and find a place for us? Then we can bring Philomena and Kathy home and we can all live together again.'

'There's nothing I can do for you now,' he said. 'You'll have to fend for yourself.'

'Daddy, I've always fended for myself. But I need your help now.'

'I have to go,' he said. And he was off to the pub.

And I knew then that my father didn't care about me. He had a soft and gentle side, and there were times when I thought that he hated what he was. But he was a lonely and broken man. If he wasn't going to care about me, then I wasn't going to care about him. Or anyone else.

I went back to my hole under the bushes in Phoenix Park. Many nights I quite literally ate paper or cardboard to quell the hunger pangs.

By this time I was physically grown. My body was well developed and despite my living conditions I had lovely fair hair. I knew from the way men looked at me that it was not safe for me to walk the streets at night. I had the body of a woman and the face of a child. And in many ways I was still a child. I behaved like a child. I would go up to people on the street and ask, 'Do you want me to sing for you?'

At night I returned to my burrow in the park. But often it was so cold that I would have frozen if I had stayed there. So on the coldest nights I walked the streets of Dublin to stay alive.

We have a song in Ireland called 'A Mother's Love is a Blessing'. It is about an Irish girl who leaves Dublin for America by sea. Her mother walks with her down to the quay. There mother and daughter throw their arms about each other before they are parted for ever. Many nights when the cold rain was lashing the streets, I would go into a public toilet and sit there and sing this song, sobbing my eyes out.

Sometimes I would go to John's Lane Church in the middle of the afternoon when there might not be anyone inside. The church was filled with lighted candles. I would kneel and pray through the stations of the cross, my feet freezing and my legs aching, and then I would sit down and continue praying. Then I would collect melted wax from the bases of the candles, soften them over a flame, pretend I had found a big piece of bread, and chew it slowly.

Once, a priest caught me eating candlewax and threw me out. I've never forgotten that. He wore warm clothes, lived in a nice house, and worked in a church where there was gold everywhere. And there I was with nothing but candlewax to eat and he saw fit to throw me out.

On nights when the banshee was howling and I was afraid to go to sleep for fear of nightmares, I would walk the streets instead. One night was to prove worse than all my nightmares. I headed down to the Quays and then I walked west along the Liffey River. It was about 1 a.m. when I passed the Four Courts, the imposing building where the most important trials in Ireland take place. Here, a car ran alongside and stopped beside me. I was asked if I wanted a ride. I ignored the question and kept on walking. Then two men jumped out of the car and stood in front of me.

'How old are you?' one of them asked, looking me up and down.

'My father is a policeman. And he's a boxer. I'm going home now.' I tried to step around the men but they moved to block my path.

'And where is home?' one of them asked with a broad smile.

'Marrowbone Lane,' I stuttered.

'What are you doing out here at one o'clock in the morning?' The men looked at each other. 'How old are you?' one of them repeated.

'Sixteen.'

'Get her in here now,' shouted someone from inside the car. The men grabbed me, shoved me into the back seat of the car, and held me down on the back seat. There were four of them in all.

'Mammy, help me,' I screamed as we drove away. 'Mammy, please, please help me.'

'She's calling her mammy,' said one in mock sympathy. He reached down and touched me.

'Please don't hurt me,' I begged. 'Please don't hurt me.'

'We're not going to hurt you, love.'

I tried to get up but the man seized my hair and pushed my face down into the seat.

'Keep your fucking head down,' he shouted.

The car stopped at some flats in the Westland Row area and I was forcibly walked to the end of a balcony, pushed into a room and shoved down on a bed.

I looked up. There were four men looking down at me. I screamed. And that is when they began beating me. They tore off my clothes, pulled at my breasts and beat me until I was only half-conscious. And then, one by one, they raped me. I remember only bits and pieces of conversation.

'Let me get in there and get at her loaf.'

'I want to eat her loaf. It's a fresh one.'

'Let's ride her all night long.'

Laughter. 'Who's next?'

I don't know how long this went on but it seemed an eternity. Once I came to and bit and scratched one of the men. He hit me in the face and knocked me out.

At last I remember one of the men saying they had to get me out of the flat before someone came home. Then they were walking me down the balcony. I could not stand. They dumped me out of the car somewhere near College Green, tossed me out as if I were a bit of rubbish.

After a while I regained consciousness, straightened my clothes, and stood up. I was shaking and shivering and terribly confused. I was also in a great deal of pain. I began walking. Although at one stage I passed a police station I did not go in for help. In fact I panicked and ran. I was afraid the police would send me away. I was a street child. I had no rights. I walked slowly through the breaking dawn until I came back to the park. I wanted to scream but my mouth was swollen and torn and my face was contorted and locked in a rictus of horror. My thighs ached. My lower spine ached. I was bleeding badly from my vagina and knew that the men had done me serious harm. It was very difficult to climb over the fence. Half-way across my clothes caught on the tips of one of the spikes and I couldn't move. I had to use all my remaining strength to pull myself free and tumble into the weeds below. Trembling uncontrollably I crawled into my burrow and scratched around, covering myself with earth.

'Mammy, why did you leave me?' I moaned.

I began hitting my body, beating myself in anger and self-loathing. This went on for a long time.

'Mammy, please let me go to sleep,' I cried. And eventually I slept.

The thing I remember most vividly about the aftermath of that experience was the horrible realization that

1. With two of my sunshine children, Vietnam, 1993.

2. My grandfather, Michael Gross, on his farm outside Carrick-on-Shannon with my mother (right), *c*. 1930.

3. My father in Dublin with two of his sisters, *c*. 1930.

4. Mam (top, third from left) with nurses at St Kevin's Hospital where she worked.

5. In the Marrowbone Lane flat, 1950. (From left) Me (aged six), Kathy, Johnny, Andy (plump due to a recent stay in hospital).

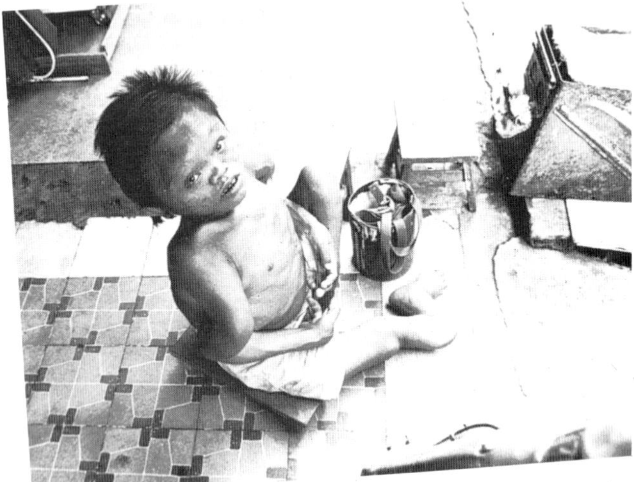

6. Ho Chi Minh City as it struck me on first arrival: a street child resting on a fruit barrow and (below) a young man horrifically malformed.

7. On the steps of the Centre with a group of nurses, 1992.

8. Resting after dinner in the kindergarten. Most of these children will be collected by their parents at the end of the day.

9. On a day trip to Vung Tau. For many of the children it was their first view of the sea.

10. Discussing the work of the Foundation with Nguyen Huu Tho, President of the Patriotic Front National Committee.

11. Play can sometimes get quite riotous.

12. My father at eighty, still with his pint of Guinness.

13. At daddy's funeral in 1991 with (from left) Philomena, Michael, Johnny and Andy.

14. With Nicolas, Androula and Helen in 1992.

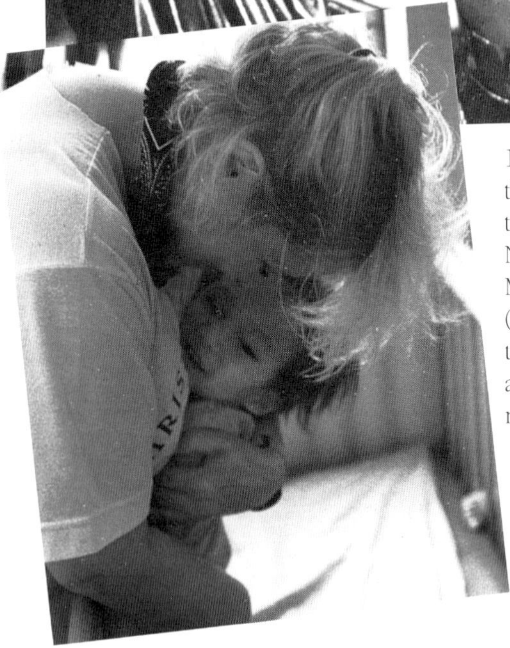

15. Singing for the children at the Quan Van Nghe in Ho Chi Minh City and (left) finding time for a hug at a quieter moment.

there was nobody for me to go to. I needed just one person who would not see me as dust, or barely more than an animal. The sense of being punished that I had felt ever since my mammy died, the sense of being cut off from the rest of the world, increased.

For days I stayed in my cave. I came out in the evenings and ate leaves or cardboard and I drank water from puddles. Late one afternoon I finally emerged in the daylight. My face was still bruised and swollen. And I knew from the pain in my stomach that I had suffered serious internal damage from the gang rape.

I went to the Adelaide Hospital and tried to tell the doctors what had happened. But I couldn't do it. I couldn't tell anyone of the horror of that night, not only the multiple rape but the lengthy physical beating.

I had to talk to someone. I had a desperate need for someone to listen. About eight o'clock one evening I went to see a priest. A housekeeper came to the door. I tried to tell her that something terrible had happened to me but she would not listen. And she would not disturb the priest.

'Go home and come back tomorrow,' she said. 'And say your prayers tonight.' She slammed the door.

Now the nights were too horrible for me to stay in the park. The banshee howled in my ears and the nightmares returned every night. I went back to the coal shed and a few days later began making the rounds of my father's relatives. I could no longer survive on the street.

One by one my father's relatives turned me down.

One actually shut the door in my face. 'You're your father's responsibility,' she said.

I was afraid of everything and everyone. In addition to the nightmares that had begun when my mother died, I now had nightmares about being raped. I was so filled with anxieties that I could never sit still for more than a few minutes.

Sometimes, if the priests did not catch me and toss me out, I slept during the day on the back pews of various churches. I slept, too, on park benches.

'You look very delicate,' my father said to me one day.

I could not meet his eyes. I could not stand still. I kept looking over my shoulder and looking all around me.

'Why are you so nervous?' he asked.

I turned and walked away.

Three or four months later I found a job at the Union, where my mother had worked. I was employed to clean the wards. It was the same sort of back-breaking and gruelling work my ma had done, and I found that my appetite was increasing. I began gaining weight. Late one afternoon the supervisor came to me and said, 'There's no need for you to come back tomorrow. We're paying you off.'

I had been sacked. I accepted this without question. I was a street child and thought I had no rights. It was simply more of the punishment that had been visited on me since my mother died.

Early one morning, it was about 3 a.m., I was lying in the coal shed when I was gripped with terrible stomach pains. I went to see one of my father's relatives. The woman opened the door, took one look at me, and said, 'Never knock on this door again.' She closed the door in my face. Much later their daughter told me she had been ordered never to talk with me.

I went back to Marrowbone Lane, the only home I had ever known, but none of the neighbours would take me in.

'If I was you, I'd go and buy a brass wedding ring,'

one of them said. What was the woman talking about?

Eventually a female relative took me to a distant branch of the family where everyone began whispering, talking behind their hands, and casting sidelong glances at me. Even today I grow angry when I see people talking behind their hands and looking at me. One of the relatives pointed to my stomach and said, 'How long have you been in that state?'

I looked down in confusion. 'What state?'

She said angrily, 'You do know you're having a baby? Who's the father?'

'Having a baby? The father? I don't know.'

They looked at each other in amazement. 'She doesn't understand,' I heard one of them say.

As odd as this might sound, I did not realize I was pregnant. I knew so little about my own body. Although I knew in theory how women got pregnant, and I knew how babies were born, it never occurred to me that this could be happening to me.

By then I was in constant pain. It felt as though my insides were coming out. I was more frightened than when I had my first period. The relatives took me to the hospital. I was very sick. And I was crying for my mother. 'Mammy, if you were here, this wouldn't be happening. They think I'm bad. They all think I'm bad.'

A social worker came into my room and asked me about the baby.

'Somebody hurt me,' I said. 'But I can't talk about it.' I began crying. The social worker did not understand. She was impatient.

'You're homeless, aren't you?' she said.

I was suddenly ashamed. I had never thought of myself in that light. But she was right, I was a homeless person.

'After you've had the baby you'll be sent to an unmarried mother's home,' she said.

In the spring, the most glorious time of the year in Ireland, I gave birth to a son. He was such a lovely baby. When I held him in my arms it was the greatest joy I had ever known. I was a mam. I had someone to care for. I named my son Thomas after my daddy.

Then it was time to go to the home for unmarried mothers. I had joined the ranks of the worst outcasts in Ireland. I hated the idea of going into another institution. But I had no choice.

I was there for about three months. Other girls who were there used to talk of the boyfriends who had fathered their children. When they asked me about my son's father, I could tell them nothing except that I thought he had black hair.

One day I was asked to sign some papers regarding Thomas. I was confused and fearful for what might happen to my life. I signed, not fully understanding what the papers contained.

The nuns who ran the home separated me from the others and put me to work in the kitchen. There I felt happy. I was allowed to sing the Doris Day songs I loved so much. The nun who administered the kitchen used to put her arm around me and say, 'You're only a child. You're a good girl.' Not only did she allow me to sing, she encouraged it. 'Sing another song while you're mixing the dough,' she would say to me. I began to feel hope for my future.

One morning I fed Thomas and went down to work in the kitchen. A few hours later when it was time to feed him again, I found him gone. I panicked. I ran downstairs to the kitchen. 'Sister, where is Thomas? He's not in the nursery. It's time for his feed.'

'Sit down, child,' she said kindly. 'Do you remember

a few weeks ago when you were given some papers to read, some papers you signed about Thomas's future?'

'Thomas is gone. Is he dead? Is that what you're telling me?'

'No, he's not dead. You know your situation, child. You know you're a homeless person. You can't give Thomas a home. We have found good Catholic people who will give Thomas a good home.'

I shook my head in disbelief.

'We've found you a job in the home of a doctor, a good Catholic home,' she said. 'You'll look after his children and work in the house. You'll be leaving at two o'clock.'

'I don't understand. You mean Thomas has gone away? They've taken him away? But they can't do that. He belongs to me.'

'Stop your crying. It's not going to change things. Just be glad he's got a good home and that nobody will hurt him.'

'But I love him. He knows me. He won't know them.'

'You're going to have to live with this. The best thing for you is to put him out of your mind.'

'He is not in my mind, he is in my heart. He grew inside *my* body.'

She stared at me, unmoved. 'You'll never know where he is. You'll never see him again.'

I knew she was speaking the truth. The Catholic Church was so horrified by illegitimate children that when they were taken from their mothers, it was impossible to find them.

'I hate you,' I screamed. 'I hate you.'

My job at the doctor's house lasted only a few weeks. All I did was work. Never once did the doctor or his wife say anything to indicate they knew of my great sorrow and that they understood or that they had sympathy for me. I used to go upstairs and lock my door and cry for hours. I couldn't bear to touch their children when my own child had been taken from me.

So I returned to the flats in the Liberties, to our old home on Marrowbone Lane, and looked up Mrs Sweeney. She told me that my brother Andy now lived in England, in Birmingham. She did not know where, she only knew it was a part of town where a lot of Irish lived. I decided to go there.

The cheapest way to get to England was on what we called the cattle boat, a B&I Line ship that left from the North Quay and crossed to Liverpool. I booked a passage.

I wanted to leave everything behind. I wanted to remember nothing of Dublin. So I never told my father I was leaving. I simply caught a bus and then walked along the North Wall until I came to the boat. I was cold and sad and felt then that I would never return to Ireland. My mother was in an unknown grave. My father was in a home for end-of-the-road alcoholics. My two younger sisters were in an orphanage. My family was scattered all over. As the boat pulled from the harbour on a wet and windy evening, I said goodbye to Dublin, the city where I had spent most of the first eighteen years of my life.

The Irish Sea was wild that night. Cold winds pushed the waves high. I stood on the upper deck near the bow and let the wind and the spray drench me. I spent most of the all-night voyage on deck, as far as possible from the Irish folk who crowded into the bars aboard the boat. The Irish might cram themselves into a cattle boat as the cheapest means of transportation, but they always have money for booze.

My anger kept me warm during that all-night journey. 'I'll never go back to Dublin again as long as I live,' I said to myself. 'I'll never be Irish again. I died here in Ireland and no-one ever knew it.'

When a person is almost destroyed on the inside, you can't see it. But that person must live with the loss, and get on with life. That was what I intended to do in England.

England

13

On the black anvil of the open deck, between lowering skies and stormy seas, I hammered out my new life. When I arrived in Birmingham I would be Tina Hamilton, daughter of a wealthy sweet factory owner, who drove a fancy red car and lived in a big house in Dublin. My mother would be a teacher and a kind and wonderful woman.

After I disembarked in Liverpool I waited hours for the train to Birmingham. It struck me as ironic that I was going from one dirty, grubby, poor city to another. When I arrived in Birmingham, it reminded me of the Liberties.

I asked a woman at New Street Station if she could tell me what part of town the Irish people lived in. 'Oh, that would be Aston,' she said. She told me which bus to catch.

When I got off the bus I was given directions to a local pub. The minute I walked in I knew I was in the right place. The voices of Ireland filled the place. I asked if anyone there knew Andy Byrne and was told immediately where he lived.

I knocked on the door. A moment later there was Andy staring at me in curiosity. He did not know who I was. We had not seen each other since he left home many years earlier.

'Hello, Andy.'

He continued staring. He still did not recognize me.

'I'm Ina. Your sister.'

Andy was married. He and his wife had a little girl whom they had named Christina. They fed me dinner, part of which was tomatoes that came out of a tin. I had never seen tomatoes in a tin.

'Why'd you come over?' Andy asked.

'I can't live in Ireland any more.'

'You all right?'

'Yeah.'

'You'd better get a job.'

That was about the extent of our conversation, apart from talking about his house and his job. His wife and I talked. But Andy and I did not talk about Ireland and about home and family. We had not seen each other for almost ten years, but we could not talk. My brothers and sisters and I never learned to talk with each other about the things that truly matter.

Andy and his wife let me sleep on the settee that night, and they said I could stay there while I looked for a job. The next morning I tried again to bring up the subject of family.

'Where's Michael?'

'Germany.'

'What's he doing?'

'I don't know.'

'Do you know where Johnny is?'

'In Germany with Michael.'

He told me that GEC, a local company, was hiring women to assemble electrical products, and that's where I found a job. I would pull a piece off the assembly line, screw in a part, put it back on the line, then pull off another piece and repeat the exercise.

After work, and at the weekends, I spent most of my time hiding in the cinema or in churches, just as I had done in Dublin. Then one day at work I went to the canteen for a cup of tea and met Joan, an Irish girl from Cork. She was a tall bubbly blonde who looked like Barbra Streisand.

A few days later she said to me, 'Tina, why don't you go out with me this weekend?' I was incredulous. Why would someone as extrovert and popular as Joan want to go out with me? I was nobody. And if she got to know about my life in Ireland, my real life, would she turn her back on me? But I liked Joan so I agreed to go with her.

'Come by my flat after work Friday,' she said.

Joan laughed when she saw me. I had on black lace-up shoes, a long navy skirt, an old-fashioned blouse buttoned to the neck, and a heavy coat.

'We're going to the Rendezvous Café, down on Broad Street. You can't go like that,' she said. 'I'll have to dress you up.'

She gave me a new blouse and skirt and high heels. I couldn't walk in the heels. I'd worn high heels but once, and then only for a few minutes. I lurched back and forth across the room and kept falling down. Then she gave me a pair of stockings to wear. I pulled them up and tied a knot in the top of each to hold them. I had no garter belt. Joan also gave me a bra, my first.

'Put this on,' she said.

I took a sheet from the bed, draped it over my head, and tried to put the bra on under the sheet. I got the straps horribly confused. When I emerged from under the sheet Joan was roaring with laughter.

'Haven't you ever worn a bra?'

'No.'

She reached out to show me how to put it on properly. I recoiled as I remembered the admonitions of the nuns at the industrial school.

'Don't touch me. Don't put your hands on me.'

'I was only trying to help.'

'I can do it me self.'

I finally got it right.

'Gorgeous,' Joan said. 'You're lucky. You don't need Vienna Rolls.'

'Vienna Rolls?'

'Most girls don't have nice titties. So they scoop the dough out of Vienna Rolls and put the top of the roll in their bra. Then everyone thinks they have pointy titties.'

I nodded as if I understood.

Joan put lipstick on me, bright red lipstick. Then she lit a match, let it burn down, and used the blackened tip to put a black beauty mark on my face.

'That looks dirty,' I said to her.

She laughed. 'It's all the fashion.'

She sprayed my hair, backcombed it, then pulled it up in a bouffant style. The sight of my reflection in the mirror was deeply comical. I was stumbling around in my high heels and laughing at the stranger in the mirror. Joan showed me how to walk in the shoes and how to swing my hips. But I had great difficulty and couldn't take more than tiny mincing steps.

'Don't walk like that,' Joan said. 'You look like an orphan.'

I stopped dead. Did she know about me? Did she know my mam was dead and that my father was an alcoholic? Did she know my family had been broken apart years ago? Did she know I had been abused by my relative and raped by those four men? Did she know I had lived on the street? I looked into her eyes for what seemed a long moment. Then I relaxed. She did not know. It was just an expression. But it was odd that she should say that.

The Rendezvous Café had a big neon sign outside it.

A juke box was on the right wall. And there was an espresso machine in the rear. The place was packed.

As we walked in, Joan waved at all her friends, including two lads sitting at the bar. Very handsome, they were. They both had black hair and dark skins. I did not take much notice of them beyond recognizing they were foreigners. I knew little about people of other nations. In Dublin I rarely saw anyone from abroad apart from a few Italians.

Once we had sat down I leaned over towards Joan. 'Are they foreign?' I whispered.

'Of course,' she laughed. 'Greek Cypriots. This restaurant is owned by Greeks.'

The two men came to our table and asked to sit with us. They ordered coffee and Joan introduced me as 'Tina from Ireland'. One of the lads turned to me. He introduced himself as Mario Pistolas. 'What would you like to eat?' he said. His accent was very strong. I remember being taken aback by that.

'I can't eat anything,' I said. My experiences with men were extremely limited. This was one of my first times in a normal social situation, the first time I had felt included in the human race. But I had no idea what to do.

Mario offered me a cigarette. And then he lit it for me. He was ever so nice. But I was terribly frightened.

'So you're from Ireland?' he asked. 'Are you from Cork like Joan?'

'No, I'm from Dublin.'

'And what did you do there?'

'Well, not much. You see, my father owns a sweet factory and my mother is a teacher. Lovely parents. I drove my father's red car sometimes. And I had my friends over to our new house. It's north of the Liffey. Do you know Dublin?'

'No.'

'Well, you see the north side of Dublin is the nicer side of town. That's where my father built our new home. Very large, it is. And lovely.'

He smiled but did not enquire as to why I had left Ireland. 'What would you like to eat?' he repeated.

I shook my head. 'I can't eat anything.'

'Of course you can eat something,' Mario said.

Joan nodded for me to accept.

After a long pause I said to him, 'Can I have a sausage sandwich? And perhaps a little packet of those sweets?'

When the sweets came, I put them in my mouth, stuck out my tongue and asked, 'What colour is my tongue?' I was making myself giddy in an attempt to hide my fear.

'You're like a child,' Mario said.

The waiter brought the sausage sandwich. Mario handed it to me. Buying me a sausage sandwich was the nicest thing anyone had ever done for me. I was overwhelmed.

At the end of the evening, Mario and his friend asked if we would like to ride home with them in a cab. My eyes widened.

'No,' I said before Joan had a chance to answer. She looked at me in surprise. 'I'd rather go back on the bus.'

'It's more dangerous to go on the bus. You still have to walk down a dark road,' Joan said.

She was right. But I had begun hyperventilating and my heart was pounding. I was sweating and my hands were twitching.

'I'm frightened,' I said.

Mario drew back in surprise. 'Why are you afraid? We won't hurt you.'

Joan was embarrassed. She leaned closer to me and whispered, 'They're not going to hurt you.'

'I don't like being in cars.'

'It's OK,' Joan insisted. She was becoming impatient. I was afraid she was regretting having invited me to go with her. 'They just want to go with us for a ride.'

'No,' I said, shaking my head.

'They won't hurt you. They always give me a lift home. They're good people.'

The two young men were looking at me in astonishment.

'It's OK,' Mario repeated. 'Nothing will happen to you.'

It took a while for them to convince me it would be all right to get into the cab. As we walked outside, I grabbed hold of Joan's arm.

'Could I sit by the window?' I asked.

Joan clambered into the back seat. I waited for Mario to get in so I could sit by the window, but he was standing there laughing because I was so nervous. And the driver kept saying for one of us to get in. So I got in and then Mario followed.

My throat was constricted. I was panic-stricken. The only other time I had been in a car with young men was on that awful night in Dublin, and the memories of pain and fear nearly overwhelmed me.

As the car pulled away, I seized Joan's arm. I thought I was going to pass out. 'I can't breathe,' I said. 'Something is wrong with me.'

She stared at me in bewilderment.

'They're not going to hurt us, are they?' I asked her.

Mario turned towards me and in a very kind voice said, 'We are civilized people. We will not hurt you.'

The next day he called Joan and told her he wanted to see me again.

'Really? He wants to see me? Why would he want to see me?'

'He thinks you are lovely and innocent.'

'I'm not. And I don't want to see him.'

'It's nothing serious. Come out again and have a laugh.'

The shadows of my past were very much with me when we met in a café on Coventry Road a few days later. He brought someone to meet Joan. She had lent me a cream plastic raincoat which, because she was so tall, was far too long for me. But it was very stylish and it made me feel glamorous and important. I was going to meet a man. He was kind and considerate and gentlemanly, the first I had ever known. He was also very handsome and dressed smartly. Several of his brothers owned fish and chip shops, and one day Mario planned to open one himself. I wondered what he saw in somebody like me.

Afterwards I began seeing Mario regularly. My brother would get upset with me because I was coming in later and later. Nor did he like it that I was using the name Tina Hamilton. He said he knew more about England than I did and did not approve of my dating a Greek man.

So I moved in with Joan. Mario and I became very close, spending more and more time together. Being with him was so exciting that I did not go to work for a week. Then he suggested we take a flat together. Other girls I knew lived with their boyfriends. I could not forget how kind Mario was to me. He had bought me a sausage sandwich the first time we met, and that was the sweetest thing anyone had ever done for me. He was the most handsome man I'd ever met. I wondered every day what he saw in someone like me. I wanted the family I never had; I wanted to be normal. So I moved in with Mario and gave up my job at the factory. A few months later I was pregnant.

I was eighteen, but I was still a child. I think that is part of the reason that Mario's relatives treated me as if I did not exist. They always spoke in Greek and never made any effort to include me in their conversation. Another reason they treated me so poorly was that they had a very old-fashioned view of women. To all of them, women were little more than receptacles.

Another thing about my relationship with Mario that disturbed me was sex. I never enjoyed sex with him. I never initiated it; it frightened me. It felt like a duty and I was always glad when it was over.

One day I went to the hospital for an ante-natal check-up. I returned early to the flat and found Mario sitting on our bed talking with a beautiful young girl.

He looked up, very surprised. But not as surprised as I was. 'What's going on?' I asked.

He stood up, pointed his finger at me, and shouted, 'It's none of your business.'

The girl continued to sit on my bed and smile up at me. I had seen her a number of times at the fish and chip shop where we worked. Suddenly I realized she was having an affair with Mario.

'Mario . . .' I began.

'Oh, shut up,' he said in disgust.

The two of them left the flat and Mario did not return until very late that night.

'I know you're having sex with that girl,' I said to him.

He did not answer. Then, very slowly and with great emphasis, he said, 'It's none of your business. I am Greek. I do what I want and you have no right to question me.'

'Why are you doing this?' I cried. I was afraid he would abandon me. What would I do?

Mario softened. 'Come on,' he said gently. 'I won't see her any more. She is only a *budana*.'

In order to save money and to spend more time at the fish and chip shop, Mario and I moved into a bedroom in his brother's house. The house was adjacent to the shop. I worked there all day and began to feel as if I was working for something of my own. I began to feel a sense of security. It was exciting. In return for our work in the shop, Mario and I received free lodging and a small salary. Mario was in charge of our money. Every Monday he deposited almost all our weekly salary into the bank. 'One day it will buy us our own fish and chip shop,' he would say. He was very confident.

In 1966 Helen was born. She was our first child and she was beautiful. Mario was so taken with her. And he was a wonderful father. He called her 'princess' and told her he wanted her to marry a Greek tycoon.

After Helen was born, Mario began pressurizing me to marry him, but I refused. Deep down I was afraid of him. Perhaps I thought that as my husband he could exploit my greatest fear, which was that Helen would be taken away from me by the welfare people.

Then I found that Mario had not been truthful about the woman I caught him with. The affair had never stopped. When he told me he was going out gambling, he was, in fact, going to see her.

I confronted him but he told me to 'shut up' and not mention it again. Psychologically, I was still a Dublin street child. I thought I had no rights. So I accepted the situation. I did not want to lose my job at the fish and chip shop. I did not want to be homeless. Where would I go? What would I do? I was an emotional prisoner.

Perhaps because of his guilt, or perhaps simply because he had such a low opinion of women, nothing I did pleased Mario. He was very critical, even of small things such as how I hung up his clothes. He wanted his clothes, particularly his suits, placed on hangers to his exact specification. He would look inside the wardrobe and complain bitterly that I had not hung anything properly.

One Sunday evening Mario dressed very tidily and said he was going out with his brother, a man who was very fond of gambling. As he walked out he pointed to the clothes he had tossed on the floor and said, 'Hang them up.' I did.

Mario also told me that he did not want me to smoke. It was all part of his fault-finding. One night after he had gone out with his brother, I lit a cigarette and turned on the television in the living-room. There was someone with me, a Greek friend of Mario's who was often around. We disliked one another intensely. She came in and turned the television off. I could not resist it: I decided to have a showdown with her. She would not treat me as if I was dirt. I turned the television back on. She shouted at me in Greek and turned it off. I turned it on. She went to the telephone, dialled a number, and spoke rapidly in Greek. Then she smirked at me and sat down as if she was waiting.

About half an hour later Mario flung the door open and came striding into the room like an enraged tiger. I remember his topcoat was draped over one shoulder and his face was pale with anger. Mario did not say a word. He walked up to me and punched me in the mouth as if I were a man. I was knocked to the floor, dazed, my lip spewing blood. I still have a scar on my lip where he hit me. He stood over me, shouting. 'I told you not to smoke. You do not smoke. You do as you are told.'

'I'll smoke if I want to,' I said.

He punched me again. Then he seized my hair and banged my head against the floor.

'Where are the cigarettes?' he said.

'I don't know.'

But he found them. He lit one after the other and then forced them between my lips until I had a dozen cigarettes filling my mouth.

'Now you smoke,' he shouted.

As he stood up and tried to regain his breath, he noticed one of his suits on the bed.

'You stupid Irish bitch. You never listen to me.'

He seized my hair and told me that a hanger for a suit was curved and that a suit jacket should be hung so that the curve pushed the front of the jacket forward. I didn't know what he was talking about. He hit me with a hanger as if to beat the information into me.

'You don't smoke. You don't wear lipstick. You do exactly as you are told. And you hang up my clothes properly.'

Mario spat on me. Then he put his foot on my hand and ground his heel into the bones as if he was stubbing out a cigarette. I almost passed out from the pain.

'That's a lesson for you,' he shouted. 'You will obey the Greek way of life or next time maybe I will kill you, huh?'

Without a backward glance he walked out. I lay on the floor crying in horror and disbelief. I had not found a new life in England; instead I had entered a horror even worse than that of Ireland.

My existence began a downward spiral. Mario now had no patience with me. Everything I did angered him. I know that some of this was justified. For instance, Mario once gave me five pounds to buy groceries and I spent it all on jelly. All different colours of jelly. As a child I had never had enough of anything. For the first time in my life I had the money to buy more than enough jelly. I wanted to put it in the cupboard and look at it and have the security and comfort of knowing it was there.

Of course Mario did not understand this. He came home, looked around, and said, 'Where are the groceries?'

'I bought jelly.'

'Do you mean you spent it all on jelly?'

I nodded.

'Are you crazy? Who's going to eat it? You crazy,' he shouted. 'You crazy.' But this time he did not hit me.

In the next few years I became pregnant again and again. Three times I miscarried. But we were also to have two more beautiful children. They are the most wonderful thing that happened during the thirteen years I lived with Mario. Another good thing to happen was when I saved up a little money, bought a few presents, and returned to Dublin to see Philomena and Kathy for the first time since our family had been broken asunder that day at Dublin Castle. Daddy told me where they were and I was given permission to visit. So I took the boat train to Holyhead, a boat across to Dun Laoghaire, and then a bus to the orphanage in Booterstown. It was Easter and I was carrying bonnets for my little sisters.

Girls at the orphanage were assigned various jobs, one of which was opening the door to visitors. I was trembling with excitement when I arrived. I knocked and the door was opened by a tall girl with long legs, a very thin girl she was, with big blue eyes.

'Hello, my name is Christina Byrne,' I said. 'I've come to see my sisters, Philomena and Kathy Byrne.'

The girl's eyes widened and I thought for a second she would cry. She took a step backwards. Her eyes never left me. 'I'm Philomena Byrne,' she whispered in an anguished voice. 'But you can't be Christina. She's dead. My sister is dead.'

'I'm not dead. And I *am* your sister.'

'No, you're not. The nuns told me my sister died a

long time ago. Who are you? Why are you saying you're my sister? Don't say that.' She was shaking her head from side to side. 'Please don't say you're my sister. Everybody knows she is dead.'

'I'm not dead, Paw Waw.'

She froze. Then her eyes filled with tears and her lips trembled. In that moment she knew I was her big sister. She threw the door wide. 'Mammy, mammy,' she cried.

We hugged and kissed and danced in a little circle and looked at each other and hugged again and cried. Then Philomena turned and shouted in a voice loud enough to be heard throughout the orphanage, 'They told me my sister was dead. But my sister is alive and she's here.'

Philomena took both my hands, and said, 'Mam, I love you.' Then she pulled me down the hall to see Kathy. Later the three of us went into Dublin. I bought them shoes and socks and ice-cream. We talked about what would happen when they were sixteen and old enough to leave the orphanage.

Later that day I took them back. Of course we were sad as we parted, but there was also a sense of joy. After all, we were alive. 'We will be together again,' I promised them. 'Remember what I told you that day at Dublin Castle. This family will be together again. It may take a while. I must save money and get us a place to live. You and daddy will come to England to live with me. This family will be together.'

14

There is much about my thirteen years with Mario that I do not remember, and there is much that I will never forget. There was a terrible blackness about those years; it was then that my hopes and dreams of a normal life were forever destroyed.

Like many immigrants, Mario worked very hard. In addition to the fish and chip shop attached to our house, his family owned a well-known grill bar called the Mexicana. Keeping the restaurants profitable was an eighteen-hour-a-day job, and I shall always be grateful for the work ethic that Mario demonstrated to our children.

On 15 December 1968 Mario and I had a second daughter, Androula, whose dark hair and quiet ways were to be a wonderful counterpoint to Helen's blonde hair and zest for life. It was the middle of the afternoon and I was cleaning the restaurant after the lunchtime rush when I went into labour with Androula. Mario was out so I went to the hospital alone in a cab. I remember the driver was so terrified that I would have the baby in his car that he went the wrong way down a one-way street in order to get me to the hospital fast.

As with Helen, I had almost no voice in what my child would be named. This was the province of Mario and his family. In fact, he was outraged that I should even suggest a name.

'You want my daughter to have an Irish name?' he

shouted in angry disbelief. 'I'll kill you before that happens.'

When Helen was born Mario had decreed that her name would be Helenita Savvas Pistolas. And at the Greek baptism service, that became her name. However, on her English birth certificate she is Helenita Christina Pistolas. I could not prevent Androula being baptized Androula Savvas Pistolas, and this broke my heart. But I could not push too hard. After all, Mario thought my name was Tina Hamilton.

The first night home with Androula one of Mario's girlfriends came to the house, walked into the bedroom where I was feeding my new baby, and said, 'Now that you've had the baby, I can tell you something. Mario loves me. He wants to live with me.'

I did not have the strength to argue with her or to fight her. I told her to leave my house. I knew that Mario was friendly with the woman. He would go to her house two or three nights a week. When I asked him why he was visiting her, he said, 'Her door lock is broken. I told her I would fix it.' If I asked any additional questions, or if I indicated I did not believe him, Mario would beat me. So I stopped asking.

But when a woman comes into my bedroom and tells me the father of my two children wants to live with her, then I think that deserves an inquiry. Mario said he was not leaving me for her. But he did continue to work on her lock. I've never known a person who had as much trouble with her door lock as did that woman. Mario had to repair it two or three times a week. You'd think she could have found a better repairman.

Androula was only a few weeks old when Mario said I must go back to work. I was amazed.

'I can't go to work,' I said in amazement. 'I am not yet well. And what about Androula?'

'Flossie can take care of her,' he said. Flossie was our neighbour across the street. She had five children and wanted more. She loved children as much as anyone I've ever known. Mario said he had already paid Flossie to take care of Androula. I hated this idea but Mario was adamant. So Androula began spending her days at Flossie's and I went back to work.

Helen was then two years old and came to the restaurant with me every day. One morning I had a premonition that I should not take Helen to work with me that day. The feeling was so strong that I turned to Mario and told him my fear. His response was predictable.

'You crazy Irish girl. What are you talking about? We have to open the restaurant. Come on.'

But I nonetheless asked Flossie to take care of both girls. Mario was angry at my disobedience and he appeared to drive very fast on the way to the restaurant. We were in his new car, a Ford Corsair of metallic blue that we could not afford but that he insisted on buying.

'Mario, please drive slower.'

'Shut up.'

'Mario—'

'I told you to shut up.'

He drove through an intersection and had a horrific crash with an enormous lorry.

'Oh my God,' was all I had time to say before the lorry hit the left side of the car. I have no doubt my little girl would have died if she had been with us.

I sustained concussion and my left leg was badly hurt. After hospital treatment the pain was still so terrible I couldn't walk. I had to pack the gaping wounds on my leg every day and every night pull the bandages off. I tended to drag the leg behind me.

'Walk properly,' the doctor said. 'You've got to get the circulation going or you will lose the leg.' I had to walk a mile every day in excruciating pain. At the end of the walk, the bandages were soaked with blood.

The customers at our restaurants and the people whom we saw socially thought Mario was wonderful. They all told me how witty and funny and charming he was and how he often bought drinks for everyone and was immensely popular. They told me I was very fortunate to have such a husband. It was the same sort of thing people used to say about my daddy.

And one day I realized that my life in Birmingham was not much different from my life in Dublin. The man in my life now was an addictive personality, but rather than being an alcoholic he was addicted to women. And he abused me, not as my father had, by abandonment and neglect, but verbally and physically.

Mario continued pressing me to marry him. He said that unless we were married, the welfare people would take away my two daughters. He said the girls would be called bastards when they began to attend school.

I was trapped in my own prison. I had a terror of being homeless, of being rejected and abandoned. I had a horror of going back to the world from which I had run away. Out there I had no rights. I did not want to be an outcast, a nobody. My desire to protect my children outweighed my judgement about Mario. We were married.

I wore black.

Even though Mario was seeing other women, he continued to demand sex at home. I again became pregnant.

Mario's friend, the one who had called him that night to tell him I was smoking, continued to persecute me. She was angry because she suspected that her husband spent his nights with an English girl. She must have told Mario numerous lies. She said I smoked non-stop, that I put on lipstick as soon as he left the house in the evenings, and that I was on the telephone all the time. He always took her side. Usually he beat me. And that gave her even greater leverage in my life. She would not let me watch television and she would not let me use the washing machine.

I kept telling Mario that she was lying. One night when she was there he dressed, went out, then sneaked back into the house and heard her tirades in Greek, her insults, her threats. He lashed into her and told her never to speak to me again in that fashion.

This gave me strength. The next night Mario left the house. He had been gone only a few minutes when she made a comment about my children being bastards.

'I'll bastard you,' I screamed. I picked up a mop from a bucket in the corner and said, 'I'm going to break your fucking head for the years of hell you've put me through.'

I chased her through the house and I beat the hell out of her with that mop. When she was so tired she could run no more she fell to the floor and I poured the dirty water from the mop bucket over her.

'You've hurt me many times. I know it's because your husband is cheating on you. But look at you. You're so ugly, no wonder he is never home. Let me tell you this. If you ever threaten me, insult me, or lie about me again, I'll kill you.' And I waved the wet mop across her face.

Then I turned on both the television and the washing machine and stared at her, just daring her to say a word. She was terrified.

My work at the fish and chip shop never slowed. Part of it involved picking up 50-pound bags of potatoes, hoisting them high in the air, and dumping them into a machine that peeled and sliced them. During pregnancy I was still hoisting these heavy bags. The only advantage was that when I finished work, home and bed were only a few steps away. One day I cleaned the linoleum and put down newspapers so I could walk around without leaving tracks on the floor.

Late the same night I awakened with a severe pain in my stomach. I quietly got out of bed and went to the bathroom, across the newspaper-strewn floor, where I sat crouched, my arms wrapped around myself, teeth gritted in pain. Suddenly blood gushed from my body all over the newspapers. The floor was covered with blood and I was terrified that Mario would see what a horrible mess I had made. He would be very angry. I discharged something from my body that night. I thought it was a kidney. I knew nothing of my body. In many ways I was still terribly naïve.

I cleaned up the floor and the next morning I did not tell Mario what had happened. He left to buy a cooker for the shop and told me to get all the potatoes done before he returned that afternoon. I was very weak and knew I should go to the doctor. But Mario had been adamant about the potatoes and it was late that afternoon before I went to the hospital. I was carrying Helen as I walked through a cold lashing rain up the hill towards the hospital.

I was also carrying a canvas bag. And inside the bag, wrapped in newspaper from the floor, was whatever it was that I had discharged from my body the previous night.

I sat in the waiting room enjoying the rest and the quiet. The room was rather small, with a glassed reception area on one side and a table in the centre covered with carefully stacked magazines. In front of the glassed-in area was a bell that patients rang to get the attention of the staff.

After a while, the woman next to me pulled on my sleeve and said, 'Dear, you look very pale. What's wrong?'

'I don't know,' I said to her. 'But I think I lost my kidney last night.'

Her eyes widened and she leaned away in astonishment. 'Your kidney?'

'Yes. Would you like to see it?'

Before she could answer, I reached into the canvas bag, put the newspaper-wrapped package on my lap, and began unwrapping it. The woman looked on in disbelief. Then she got an awful shock. 'Oh, oh, oh,' she said with her hand clasped to her mouth. 'Dear, that's no kidney,' she said. 'That's a baby.' She jumped up and started pounding on the little bell, insisting to the nurse that a doctor come out immediately. The doctor took one look at the contents of the unfolded newspaper and admitted me into the hospital. He was furious. 'Why didn't your husband call us?' he said.

'He doesn't know.'

The doctor looked at me in astonishment. 'He doesn't know? But you said this happened in the middle of the night. You had a miscarriage in the middle of the night and your husband doesn't know?'

'I didn't want to wake him up. He would have been very angry when he saw how I messed up the clean floor.'

A few days later I returned home and went back to work. Mario not only continued to beat me, the beatings grew worse. He smacked my head against the wardrobe so many times that he smashed the wood. I was often black and blue.

As my children grew older, they saw what was going

on. One night I was in bed cuddling Helen and Androula when Mario came in from one of his lock-repairing trips. He did not like the way I looked at him so he smashed me in the nose and splattered blood all over the room. That was the first time he broke my nose. After it was broken a second time I had to have an operation to enable me to breathe properly.

Helen, who has grown up to be a talented singer, began singing as a child. She and I would be in the kitchen singing pop songs and laughing and dancing. Then we would hear Mario at the door and in an instant our moods became very sombre. Helen would begin singing the Greek songs that Mario preferred.

Many times I tried to leave my husband. The first time I ran away, I returned to Ireland with Helen and Androula, rented a tiny room, and got a job at a fish and chip shop. But Mario found me about two weeks later. He also discovered that my father was an alcoholic and not the owner of a sweet factory, that my mother was dead, and that my name was not Tina Hamilton. When he confronted me with all this, I told him about my past, including my being gang raped when I lived on the street.

For a while, Mario was sweet and kind to me. I told him that my mother had told me to look after my daddy and that I very much wanted to give him a home, the home he had never given me. And Mario, who could be sweet and kind, allowed me to bring my father to England to live with us.

My father was growing old. It was not long before his drinking created enormous problems and Mario said he had to go. I don't really blame him for that. Daddy was loud and abusive when he drank, he still talked of his failed promise and how he could have been a famous boxer. For the first time in my life I saw my father as he really was. Yet I could not lose my fondness of him and began calling him 'Pop'. I found him a little council house where he was to live for years, visiting the pubs with great regularity.

Two years later, when she was fifteen, Philomena came to live with us. After a while, she began to emerge from the horror of growing up in an orphanage. Gradually she began to want to stay out at night with people her own age. Mario did not like this. One night when she came in late, he confronted her. 'You will stop staying out late and acting like a whore,' he said. 'You'll do as you're told if you live here.' He slapped her and knocked her halfway across the kitchen.

'Don't hit my sister,' I screamed.

Mario flung me against the wall. 'Stay out of this or I'll smash you and your sister.'

Marco, the Alsatian, began to growl at all the noise and furore. The shouting so excited the dog that it bit Philomena. Mario thought this was funny. He laughed, picked up a kettle of boiling water from the stove, and poured it over the bite.

'This will kill the germs,' he said.

Philomena screamed and almost fainted.

I rushed her to the hospital. I think the doctor knew the burn had been deliberately inflicted. But my sister and I were terrified of Mario and we insisted it had been an accident. Philomena and I had no home other than with Mario. And deep in my heart I wondered whether all of this was my fault. Perhaps I was expecting too much from my marriage. I knew that I had my own idiosyncrasies: the scars from those years in Dublin. The nightmares that had begun after my mammy died were still plaguing me. I was very much aware that I was different and that I was difficult to live with. And I could not help but think that perhaps I deserved the beatings and the mistreatment. After all, my mother was a saint and she had been mistreated by her husband.

I ran away from Mario again. Of course I took my children with me. I could never abandon them. Each time Mario came after me, not so much to have me return as to reclaim his children.

Ten months later, Philomena moved out of the house and into a flat with another girl. Then she moved to Surrey and took a job at British Olivetti. Mario's beatings had taken a terrible toll on her.

My life in Birmingham revolved around my work. I worked from very early each morning to late every night at the two restaurants. I never seemed to stop working. After the restaurants closed, Mario would bring in his friends and give them food and everyone would smoke marijuana. But if I gave stale bread to the poor, he would complain. When I saw homeless people shuffling past the restaurant and called them in and gave them big plates of food, he beat me.

'We are in business to make money. And we can't make money if you are giving away food.' He was right about that. I understood.

It was during this time in my life, at a time of great misery and pain, that I had the dream about Vietnam. I don't know why I dreamed of Vietnam. Perhaps it was because the country was so much in the news at the time. In my dream, naked Vietnamese children were running down a dirt road fleeing from a napalm bombing. The ground under the children was cracked and coming apart and the children were reaching out to me. One of the girls had a look in her eyes that implored me to pick her up and protect her and take her to safety. Above the escaping children was a brilliant white light that contained the word 'Vietnam'.

At the time, I did not even know where Vietnam was. I didn't know anything about the people there. But after that dream I knew that it was my destiny to go to Vietnam and work with children.

The next day I told Mario about my dream and said that one day I would go to Vietnam. He snorted in disgust. 'Are you crazy? You can't even go up the fucking road. You'll never go to Vietnam.'

The talk of Vietnam made Mario very angry and gave him an excuse to beat me, not that he really needed an excuse. Often after he beat me Mario wanted to make love. It was inevitable that I again became pregnant. A few months later I was talking about Vietnam and Mario said he was tired of hearing about it. He kicked me in the stomach and I had to go to hospital. I lost the baby. A few months later I became pregnant again and this time I gave birth to Nicolas.

In 1974 Mario took all of us to Cyprus. We left Helen there with her grandmother because Mario wanted his daughter to learn to speak Greek. Not long afterwards, Turkey invaded Cyprus. Mario would not go back for Helen. He was afraid he would be drafted if he returned. But I was not going to let my daughter remain in the middle of a war zone. The Foreign Office said Cyprus was too dangerous and that I could not go there. But I disregarded this advice and flew to Cyprus, where I found Helen in a village near the fighting.

Obtaining exit papers was very difficult. So for a while she and I moved into a refugee camp where I helped Greek Cypriot refugees. One day I drove to Nicosia to enquire about the papers and while I was there fighting broke out anew. I had to flee the city. I tried to get back before dark. But I miscalculated and was out long after curfew. To compound my troubles, I took a wrong turn. When I stopped to turn the car around I heard gun shots.

Before I could make a run for it, soldiers materialized and dragged me out of the car.

'Irlandaise,' I shouted. *'Irlandaise.'*

The soldiers searched the car. They even pulled out the seats. Then they searched me. One of the soldiers pointed a gun at my head and said, 'You agent. You agent.'

'Irlandaise,' I said. I cradled my arms and rocked them back and forth. 'Baby. Baby. *Irlandaise.*'

I did not like the way the soldiers were staring at me. Suddenly memories of the gang rape flooded back and I became terribly frightened. Then one of the soldiers noticed that I was wearing a Greek cross.

'Why you wear cross?' one asked.

'My husband is Greek.' I spoke a few words of Greek to them and then, in a broken combination of Greek and English, tried to explain about Helen. The soldiers relaxed and told me I could continue my journey.

'You're lucky,' one officer said. 'Last night we shot an agent here. If you had run we would have killed you.'

A few days later Helen and I flew out on an RAF refugee flight.

Because my visit was successful about a dozen people in Birmingham asked if I would take money into Cyprus to enable their friends and relatives to get out of the country. I agreed, and a few weeks later left England with a small fortune in cash in my suitcase.

I was away from Mario. I was helping people. I was energized. My entire personality changed. I felt free and open and joyous.

The officials aboard the boat must have suspected that many passengers were carrying cash. An announcement came over the public address system to say that all money over a certain amount had to be turned in.

'Did you hear that on the tannoy?' I asked an English woman whom I had met on the boat. 'I can't turn in my money. I'm carrying a fortune. What should I do?'

I did not look like a person who carries around a fortune. She may have thought I was joking. She pointed to two men who were travelling first class. 'Those men are diplomats,' she said. 'They have immunity from being searched. They will take it in for you.'

I went straight over to them. 'Excuse me,' I said. 'I understand you fellows are diplomats. Is that correct?'

The two men looked at me in surprise. One of them nodded.

'And what country would you be from?' I asked.

After a long pause one of the men said in a soft voice, 'We are from Libya.'

'That's lovely,' I said. 'My name is Christina. You don't know me. But I'm here to help people so they can go to England. I'm carrying a lot of money to give to people who have lost their homes and their bank accounts and who have nothing. Now I just heard on the tannoy that I have to hand it in. Would you take it through Customs for me?'

The two men stared at me. I wondered if they had lost the ability to speak. 'I'm not doing anything bad. It's only money. You can have a look if you like.'

They looked at each other, then back at me. At last one of them slowly nodded. I passed him the briefcase. 'Promise me now, you'll give it back.'

He smiled. 'It will be returned to you,' he said. He was a real gentleman.

When I walked down the gangplank into Cyprus I was more than a little bit anxious. My baggage had been searched for money. Other people had had money confiscated. 'I hope those bleeders haven't run off with my money,' I said to myself. But there at the bottom of the gangplank was a big black limousine with a little flag on the front wing. People were looking at the car in a very respectful fashion. Then the rear window whirred down and there was a face I recognized. The man passed my briefcase through the window.

'Thank you, me darling,' I said to him. 'May Jesus, Mary, and Holy Saint Joseph of Cupertino take care of you.' I howled with laughter. They appeared to be trying not to laugh also.

I leaned closer. 'And I hope your lovely head of black hair will take a long time turning grey,' I said to the senior of the two. 'God bless you, me darlings. I'll never forget you as long as I live.' We shook hands.

'And where did you say you were from?' I asked.

'Libya,' said one of them. This time he did not lower his voice. 'We are visiting the Libyan embassy here.'

'Now that's lovely. I've never met anyone from Libya. Can I come by and have a cup of tea at your place? I've never been to an embassy.'

The senior diplomat laughed. I think he was beginning to enjoy himself. 'Yes. Come have tea with us.'

Later that day, after I had made arrangements to pass the money to its rightful owners, I went to the embassy where my new friends treated me with dignity and respect.

'You seem like gentlemen to me,' I said. 'I have talked to people who tell me the Libyans have been chopping people's heads off. But I don't believe it.'

We all laughed uproariously.

'Now you don't have any money with you, do you? I hear you blokes are very rich people. And I need more money to help these refugees get to England.'

One of the diplomats was laughing so hard he could

not speak. The other wiped tears from his face, reached into his pocket, and gave me a hundred dollars. I gave the money to an Englishwoman who was trying to get home.

The second trip to Cyprus was a wonderful interlude in my life. I felt light and free and happy. But when I returned home, the abuse from Mario resumed.

The fear I had of being beaten and the anxiety I felt about my life grew until there were many times I felt as if I had no control over anything. My fear of men and my fear of being raped increased. I dreamt of being pushed into a coffin. I had no-one to talk to. I was afraid Mario or his family would lock me up and I would lose my children. At night I never took my clothes off. Even in bed I wore long clothes. I locked the door and slept curled into a ball with my arms crossed over my breasts.

I began writing letters to my mam. They were long letters telling her what was happening to me and how I was feeling. I asked if she could help me find a way out of my marriage without anything happening to my children. I told her there were things inside me I didn't understand.

I thought my life in England had hit bottom and that things could not become any worse. Then one day I had the strangest feeling come over me. I was sitting on a high stool behind the counter of the shop when suddenly my head seemed light and my body started to tremble. My hair stood up on my arms. I thought I was going to die.

'Mario,' I said. 'Something is wrong with me.'

He merely laughed and waved me away.

I felt as if I were falling deeper and deeper into a black tunnel. I opened my eyes to stop the spinning but it wouldn't stop. Then I thought I had gone blind.

My whole being, my mind and body, were twisting and falling down a long black tunnel and an evil red wave washed over me, over my face and chest and body, nearly drowning me.

'Mario, I can't see. I'm blind,' I cried out.

'What is the matter with you?' he growled.

'Something strange is happening to me. I'm going into a black tunnel.' I remember singing 'O Salutaris' and 'Sweet Heart of Jesus', the songs I had sung in the church when I was eight years old, the songs of my childhood in the Liberties. I began saying an act of contrition.

Mario rushed me to the hospital where, as we waited, I continued praying aloud and singing hymns in Latin. Mario was laughing in embarrassment. Then a doctor examined me and said, 'This woman is physically and mentally exhausted. She needs a long rest, a long, long rest.'

15

It was more than fatigue that sent me to hospital, it was a depression of frightening depths. I came home from hospital terribly afraid. My body trembled constantly. I picked at my hair and face and I was afraid that I was going to die, afraid that I was having a brain haemorrhage, afraid that my heart was going to stop.

I went to another doctor who said I had an anxiety neurosis. It got so bad that I couldn't walk down the street without looking over my shoulder, panicking at the thought someone would attack. Stepping into a bath was like stepping into a coffin. I ran when I saw priests and nuns. I never seemed able to breathe normally. I knew that I was breaking down.

I went to a psychiatrist who said I was suffering from a nervous collapse. He admitted me to a psychiatric hospital and there I stayed for six weeks. There was no counselling during that time, only heavy medication.

After I came home, the nightmares were with me almost every night and they were stronger and more fearsome. One night after a particularly vivid and frightening dream, I got up to walk around the house and clear my head. I walked into the breakfast room and found Mario and a friend of mine making love on the settee. I went pale and started trembling so hard that I had to hold on to the door. I could not let my anger take control. Shaking, I returned to our bedroom where I held a pillow to my breasts and rocked back and forth, sobbing.

All I could see in my mind's eye was Mario downstairs having sex with another woman. He was having sex in our breakfast room. I pushed myself from the bed and went downstairs with tears streaming down my face. I made enough noise that Mario and my friend heard me coming down the stairs. When I arrived they were sitting there talking very calmly. I told Mario what I had seen. I confronted him with his infidelity and I reminded him of his promises to me in the past.

He threw me against the wall and said, 'You bloody Irish bitch. You are stupid. You imagine things.'

The futility of my existence weighed heavily on me. A few days later I ran away again. Again Mario found me. Sometimes I wonder if I wanted to be caught. But, on the other hand, Mario knew everyone I knew; there was no hiding place. This time when Mario caught me, not only did he beat me, he did something that horrifies me even today when I think of it. He pushed me on to our bed and tied the Alsatian to it. I couldn't move a muscle. The dog sat there tense, anxious saliva dripping from its mouth, just waiting for me to move. If I had, I believe it would have savaged me. I was there half a day.

I made a half-hearted effort to commit suicide by taking an overdose of pills. I didn't want to die; I only wanted somebody to help me. Again I was admitted to a mental hospital.

Mario came to visit me and was so solicitous. He gave flowers to the nurses and gold fountain pens to the doctors and said to everyone on the staff, 'Please look after her.' They thought he was a most wonderful man. Mario told them how much he loved me and that he couldn't understand why I ran away or why I had tried to commit suicide. He told the doctors he was taking me away from Birmingham. He said he wanted to take me to Australia where we could start a new life together. The doctors all thought a new life was the answer, so they discharged me.

Shortly after I came home an extraordinary thing happened. Mario wrote to the President of the United States asking if someone in America could perform a lobotomy on me. Of course there was no reply. But then he wrote to someone in Moscow. A Russian official responded and said they would do a lobotomy, but first they needed my medical records. Mario was immensely proud of that letter. He kept it for as long as I knew him. He would wave it in the air and say, 'The Russians have agreed to do a lobotomy on you. The President of America may not have answered, but the Russians did.'

'What is a lobotomy?' I asked.

'They take a little piece out of your brain and you will forget everything. You will stand when you are told and sit when you are told.'

It was not long after that I made a sincere effort to kill myself. I really wanted to die. I didn't want to feel any more or think any more. I only wanted to sleep. I bought a bottle of gin but it was such horrible stuff that I couldn't drink it. I poured out half the gin and mixed it with lemonade. Into that I dumped dozens of sleeping pills and other medications. I managed to get the whole lot down and then I staggered down to the train station. In case the gin and pills did not work I planned to throw myself in front of the London express.

The combination of alcohol and drugs knocked me out and I collapsed on the platform. When I awakened I was in the intensive care unit of a local hospital. Soon I was transferred to a mental institution. And there I was diagnosed as schizophrenic, sociopathic, psychotic, and depressed; they called me everything in the book.

I told the doctors about my childhood. I told them I was frightened of the dark and about my horrible nightmares. When they asked me about sex I was reminded of my relative turning the handle of the bedroom door and I could see his enormous body looming over me in the dark and I could smell the beer on his breath and I could feel him dropping down beside me.

When I asked the doctors, 'Why did me mam leave me?' most of them never knew about the sexual abuse I suffered less than a year after my mother died. I told them about the gang rape but I don't think they heard me.

They appeared to conclude I would never respond to psychotherapy. Instead they prescribed electro-convulsive therapy. I had ECT on a variety of occasions in one month. I remember they gave me Valium before I was taken upstairs and then I was given an injection of anaesthetic. To relax my body so that the convulsions would not cause spinal damage they gave me a form of curare called tubocurarine. In addition to being a muscle relaxant, it also caused both short- and long-term memory loss.

'I don't want that fucking electricity in my body,' I shouted at them. 'Get that needle away from me.' I had to fight even though I suspected that the more I shouted and the more I fought, the more convinced they were that I was crazy.

They always won. No matter how much I fought, it always ended with them taking me upstairs to a ward with a row of beds along each wall.

'I don't need it. I don't want it,' I insisted.

I heard the sounds of the treatment room, a frying, sizzling noise as the electricity was turned on, and then the thump of a body as it was racked with *grand mal* seizures. An awful smell, I don't know what it was, came from that room. Today if I hear a dentist's drill or a low-pitched buzzing sound I grow weak with fear.

As I was wheeled in, I saw sprawled on beds the unconscious bodies of those who had already received the treatment. The attendants rolled the gurney up next to a box with black wires coming out of it, forced my mouth open, jammed a big rubber device between my teeth, taped the electrodes to my temple, inserted an airway in my throat, then released me and stepped back. A massive electrical jolt surged through my body. I convulsed. Only my heels and the back of my head touched the bed. And then I was unconscious for a long time.

The treatments were so frequent and so intense that I wandered around the wards like a zombie. My eyes were blank and I mumbled to myself. As the treatments lessened, I stood in a corner and watched the other patients. I felt that if I ever became one of them I would be truly insane. I knew that I was sick, but I was sick with pain. I was confused. But I was not mad. All I wanted was for someone to love me and not hurt me or beat me. I wanted to be treated with dignity and respect. I wanted a family and food and a fireplace. I thought if somebody loved me and I could go home to them with a happy heart that all would be well. I worried constantly about my children and there were times when I wondered if they would be better off without me. Maybe I am a bad person, I thought. Maybe the devil is in me as the nuns said. So I withdrew from everyone and everything. I didn't trust anyone at the hospital. I ran away several times. But each time I was caught and each time there was more electro-convulsive therapy.

When finally it was all over I wanted to know what the doctors in Birmingham had thought was wrong with me. Those years when I was in and out of mental institutions gave me an insatiable desire to know everything I could know about myself, to come to grips with all that had happened to me in Ireland and England, and to make an effort to move on with my life. I began a long fight to see my medical records. I wanted them for two reasons: first, I knew I would eventually write a book, and I felt those years of therapy should be a part of the story. Second, I had to know what the doctors said about me so I could clean it all out of my thinking.

Eventually I obtained the records, and what I found there made me very angry. One of those doctors, under whose care I had been placed on several occasions, never knew who I was. For example, I had told him how much I loved my sister Philomena. I told him how Philomena called me 'Mam' and how I had taken care of her for years. But he saw in that a hint of lesbianism and wrote that while he had searched for evidence of incestuous behaviour between me and my sister, there was no evidence of it. He wrote that I was frigid. But the comment that angered me the most involved an epileptic man with whom I had become friends. He was a sweet and gentle man, and I would sit on the edge of his bed and we would talk for hours. I saw nothing wrong with sitting on the edge of his bed. But the doctor wrote in his report that I was a 'a *femme fatale*'. I didn't know what a *femme fatale* was; I had to look it up. I was furious. How could I be both frigid and a *femme fatale*?

Based on what I told the doctor about my father, he wrote that daddy was a schizophrenic and that I had inherited the disorder. His reason for saying that was that daddy had talked to my dead mother. The

English don't even talk to each other so they couldn't understand how we in Ireland talk to the dead.

Today I have all the records of my stays in mental institutions. When I return home from Vietnam I sometimes go through them. In my family we call them the 'batty papers'.

My problem had never been anything more than an extraordinarily severe case of depression. Eventually the doctors realized this and recommended simply that I leave my husband. 'Throw a stone behind you and don't look back,' one of them told me.

And that is what I did.

16

So it was then that I made the most difficult decision of my life: I left my children behind and ran away. I knew he would not follow me if I did not take the children. So in 1976 with only £20 and a few changes of clothes I left my children and my home of fourteen years. I had arrived in Birmingham as a frightened and scarred girl of eighteen; I left at thirty-two, still frightened and yet more scarred.

When I left Ireland I did not think there could be a greater pain than leaving behind a son. But I was wrong. Helen, my oldest daughter, had often counselled me to leave her father. But when I finally left I could not tell her what I was doing. More than anything else, I wanted to tell my children that every waking moment of every day would be directed towards making enough money to buy a house, hire a solicitor, divorce their father, and regain custody of them. I could not tell them because I was afraid they would have told Mario where I was and what I was doing. And I was not strong enough to fight him. Not yet.

I went south, to Surrey, where my sisters Kathy and Philomena were living. As often happens to someone after a massive and tumultuous change in their life I became seriously ill. Doctors discovered a tumour in my stomach. While in hospital, I thought I might die. I called Birmingham to talk to my children. Mario hung up on me. Later I found out that when he hung up he turned to the children and said, 'Your mother just rang up from a strip-tease club in London. But she didn't want to talk to you.' I called often, but he never let me talk to the children and most of the time he never told them I had called.

After leaving the hospital, I interviewed for a job at British Olivetti where Kathy worked. I told my prospective boss that I had left my husband and that he might come looking for me.

'Do you mind if I use another name?' I asked him.

The kind man allowed me to work there under the name Christina Nicola. I lived in a council house and began making plans to divorce Mario.

It was at British Olivetti that Kathy introduced me to Simon Noble, the assistant export-import manager of a large photographic company in London. His job often took him to Olivetti. Simon became a turning point in my life. He was the first truly kind and gentle man I had ever known. I will always remember him as the man who turned my life around.

Simon and I met for lunch one day and one of the first things I said to him was, 'I'm going to Vietnam one day, you know. I must go there to work with the children. I don't know when it will be. But one day I will go.'

'Why Vietnam?' he asked.

'Because of a dream I had,' I said. And I told him all about the dream and the white light that said 'Vietnam'.

'There's no war there now,' he said. 'So does it really matter?'

'Oh yes. I must go there. Vietnam is part of my life, part of my destiny. And when the time is right, I will go.'

Simon understood. He did not make fun of me or ridicule me. I told him everything about Ireland and Birmingham. He knew there were three things I felt compelled to do: I had to get a divorce and regain custody of my children; I had to have therapy in order to work through all the unresolved issues in my life; and, someday, I had to go to Vietnam.

Eventually my divorce was finalized; but before there could be a custody hearing, Helen called Kathy and asked her where I lived. 'I want to be with my mummy,' she said. 'I don't believe she is dead. I want to meet her in London.' Helen was then twelve years old.

When Helen and I were reunited, I immediately asked for an interim custody hearing. Mario was furious. He hired a very expensive solicitor who stood up in court and started talking about all the psychiatric hospitals I had been in, the electro-convulsive therapy, and how I walked out on my family. He said I was an anti-religious person and that I had had no contact with my family since I abandoned them. Then he proceeded to tell the court how Mario was a fine, respectable, financially able businessman who was also a wonderful father.

With a legal-aid barrister representing me, I stood up and said to the judge, 'I can't afford the kind of solicitor he can afford. But instead I speak the truth.'

I told the judge what had happened to me when I was married to Mario; of all the times I had tried to call the children and how he either hung up or told them I was working in a strip-tease club. 'I have not seen a psychiatrist since I left that man,' I told the judge. 'I have not taken one tranquillizer. Today I have a good job at Olivetti. And I have a home in Surrey for my children. I want all of my children with me.'

The judge awarded me temporary custody of Helen. Not long afterwards Nicolas called and I went through the same thing with him. Lastly, Androula joined us in the house in Surrey, and at the final custody hearing the judge awarded me permanent custody of my three children.

'Do you want to share custody with your former husband?' he asked.

'I want the children to be free to see him if they want,' I said. 'I don't want them torn apart. As long as there is no physical or mental torture, he can see them. But I want him kept away from my house.'

When I told Helen about Simon her eyes brightened and she hugged me. 'Does he shout at you?' she asked. 'Does he get angry? Will I be able to be me with him?' She quickly sensed his gentleness and they got along well together.

Simon was nearly six feet tall, had a medium build, and soft blue eyes. He had a full beard and dressed with style. He read a great deal. I've never seen anyone read as much as he did. He was the son of Sir Fraser Alexander Noble, ex-vice-chancellor of Leicester University.

As you might imagine, I was quite a shock to Simon's parents. I was Irish, Catholic, divorced with three children, and I had no education. Simon's father was very worldly and I felt that he liked me. But I did not feel the same about his mother.

It was after Simon lost his job and moved in with me that I realized the incredible difference in our backgrounds. Simon was on the 'phone one day to me and was overheard criticizing his boss. He was sacked. I told him to go back and tell his boss that the company could not sack him. A few days later he walked in, one hand in his pocket, very suave he was, and he smiled and said, 'I did it. I did it. I told them they were real shits and they couldn't sack me.'

It was almost irrelevant that he did not return to his job. The important thing was that for the first time Simon had confronted people in authority. Then he moved in with me and we had long talks about what he wanted to do with his life.

'Simon, your background, your upbringing, has made you too far removed from the real world,' I told him. 'You should get a job as a porter in a hospital, and then maybe work with children for a while. You have to meet, know and understand real people. Then you should study for a position caring for people. You are so good and kind. You would be wonderful in a career like that.'

That's when his mother stepped in. The idea of her son working as a porter offended her.

Kathy, Helen and I decided to have a tea for Lady Noble so she could get to know me and my family a bit better and to see how much Simon and I loved each other. We prepared duckling *à l'orange,* tea cakes and all sorts of fancy foods. I was nervous because I knew in my heart that Simon's mother would not accept me. Simon knew me well enough to be anxious about what I might say. So I promised to make a special effort not to embarrass him.

That day the telephone rang and a rather imperious voice asked, 'Is this the residence of Simon Noble?'

As I mentioned, I am a child of the Liberties. And when I heard that British voice the Irish in me asserted itself and all my good intentions were forgotten.

'Yeah,' I said roughly. 'And I'm Christina.'

The long pause told me that she knew her fears were justified. 'This is Lady Noble. May I speak to Simon?'

So Simon's mother and two of his uncles came to tea. They were very formal, very distant, and they directed their conversation solely towards Simon. They barely nibbled all the delicacies we had prepared. Kathy was upset that they would not eat her tea cakes.

She, too, is a child of the Liberties. She picked up a tea cake, shoved it under Lady Noble's patrician nose, and said, 'Oh, come on. Get in there and get this down your gullet.'

Kathy then jammed an entire cream cake in her mouth. It was spread all over her face. 'Now that's what I call grub,' she mumbled.

Simon's family looked at the food as if it were cooked with cyanide. They cut tiny little pieces of cake and nibbled on them for a long time. I could eat in a second what they took half an hour to eat. How can people enjoy food if they take such tiny bites?

After tea Simon's mother turned to him and said, 'I think you and I should go for a little walk.'

He never told me what was discussed. But I knew we were chalk and cheese and that she did not want us together. Nor did she want him to work as a hospital porter. Simon was an adult but his parents treated him as if he were a little boy.

It may have been the first time in his life that he had done so, but Simon went against his parents' wishes and we were married. He sent his parents a telegram telling them our happy news and they sent him a box of half-dead flowers from Jersey.

Simon and I enjoyed our life. There was no violence in him and our life was good. We did all the fun things that newly-weds do. I remember once we went to a motor race at Thruxton. If Simon's parents were not so stuffy he might have been a racing driver.

Then came another turning point in my life. One night a car pulled up to our house and Mario, accompanied by a man and woman, forced their way inside. Simon ran into the kitchen to 'phone the police.

Mario was there to take Nicolas away. The big thug with Mario threw me against a wall as Mario and the woman tried to push Nicolas outside into the car.

'Mummy, don't let them take me,' he screamed.

I saw red. Even though I have medical records that prove I am not insane, I believe I became insane for a few moments that night. I slammed a door shut on the big thug's arm and hurt him badly.

'Run, Nicolas,' I shouted. He pulled away and ran to the other side of the room.

Mario was looking at me in a most evil fashion. He thought that he could still intimidate me and that I would meekly agree to whatever he wanted. He was rather surprised when I stuck my finger in his face, and said, 'If you ever again put your hands on my son, I'll fucking kill you.'

The woman ran up behind me and tried to pull me away. She yanked my hair. I turned and kicked her harder than Mario used to kick me.

'Nobody touches my children,' I screamed at Mario. I was so angry I was trembling. I would have fought had there been a dozen of them. Two were nothing. 'Any of you touch my children again and I'll destroy you,' I said.

Mario looked at me for a long moment. Then he and his friends left and that was the end of it. It was finally over. That was the last effort from Mario. Now my children and I could begin to rebuild our lives.

I have never criticized Mario or spoken ill of him to my children. I told them that nothing is ever one-sided and that they must not judge their father.

'Oh, mummy,' Helen said to me one day in exasperation. 'When will you stop protecting him? He did terrible things to you.'

She told me that they had seen and heard the beatings he had given me. Even so young, they knew about his women.

In spite of Mario being finally out of my life, there remained much for me to work out. And I wanted to do it for me, not because someone was forcing me to do it. I talked to Simon about this. I told him that almost everyone has one or two terribly traumatic things in their life, things they need to talk with someone about. But my whole life had been a litany of pain. There was no beginning and no end. Pain had always been in my life. I wanted to work through the pain and find the sunshine.

I began what were to be long years of therapy. In the beginning, I had a therapist named Madeline. I worried that she would be judgemental. I was afraid if she knew my psychiatric background she would think I was a nutcase. But I was with her for four years. And she was wonderful. I told her about Vietnam and she understood.

Then I found a hypnotherapist in Surrey, a wise and patient doctor and a wonderfully sweet man by the name of Sean O'Connell. I was shy with him in the beginning. But he saw much good in me and he brought it out.

'You are a very special lady,' he used to tell me. And he would say, 'You always bring the sunshine when you come in.'

For about seven years he walked with me through the valley of the shadow and he was with me when I came out on the other side. We are always told to rebuild our lives. But sometimes the spare parts are not there. I had to break the cycle. I had to find the spare parts and put them together and make sense of it all.

Simon had to deal with all I was going through as I relived my childhood, my teens and my first marriage. It was nothing but pain, like a big pot of spaghetti from which I had to take out each strand, one by one. Of course that had an effect on Simon.

When my nightmares visited, I would awaken in the middle of the night screaming in fear. Simon was always there to reassure me. He spent years doing that. I wondered if he would abandon me, but he was always there. Through Simon I learned that I had rights, that I did count, that I wasn't stupid.

I learned from Simon there was peace and tranquillity in the world. He never got angry or judgemental about anything or anybody. He always kept an open mind. He knew how to turn aside my anger and my eruptions. When I came home from the therapist and I was terribly confused, he always reassured me.

'That can never happen again,' he said. 'You were small and vulnerable when all that happened. You never dealt with your mother's death. Therapy is making you stronger and stronger.'

Simon was my rock. He never changed. One day I began haemorrhaging from my uterus so badly that I had to have a blood transfusion. One pint of blood was the wrong type and had to be removed quickly. It spilled all over my bed. I looked down and all I could think of was that moment when my mother vomited blood all over the bed as she died.

'Don't let me die,' I screamed. 'Don't let me die.'

Simon was there. And he held me. And throughout the years of therapy, which was a pain-filled hell for both of us, he remained.

And then came another turning point: the end of my relationship with Simon. He finished a course at university and was hired as a probation officer, a job in which he was to be rapidly promoted. From me he had acquired a sense of strength and self-confidence.

He found a new life away from his parents. From him I learned there were gentle and kind and loving men in this world. In a way, Simon was my dad. Although he was six years younger than me, he was the father I never had. He never shouted at me. He never abused my weakness during therapy. At a time when I was coming to grips with all that had happened in my life, and when I would scream and cry and awaken in cold sweats, he was there.

The years of therapy were very difficult for Simon. And when we were both stronger, we went our separate ways. Simon found someone else and I found myself. I don't mean to sound cavalier, it's just that I know now it was a transition relationship for both of us. Our parting was inevitable. It was very painful but it was inevitable.

Afterwards, I was whole. I was me. I was lighter. I could connect with people. And the desire to fulfil my dream, to go to Vietnam, continued to grow. But it was not yet time. My children were growing up and I had to be with them. But Vietnam remained very much part of my life. And I often wondered how I would know when the time had come.

During those years in Surrey when my children were growing up, I had to take many jobs in order to support my children and pay for my therapy. For years Simon made no money at all. After I left British Olivetti I did nursing auxiliary work, I was a care assistant in an old folk's home, and finally I started a catering business. Over a period of several years the catering business became successful. I knew nothing about catering. The first business lunch that I catered was for twelve people at a company in Woking, and I transported the food on the bus. I picked up a big blue bread container at a bakery that was perfect for carrying the food. Into this went three salads, three types of quiche, asparagus, a honey-baked ham and a big gâteau.

I started operating a little restaurant at Chobham Airport. It was mainly patronized by aircraft crews. 'Will you come in and sit down and eat your soup before you get up in that big aeroplane,' I would say to them. I used to sing in the restaurant. The customers loved it. One morning I came in very early to prepare meals for the crew and passengers on a corporate aircraft. But they forgot their food and began to taxi out for take-off. I ran out on the tarmac and blocked the aeroplane. When the captain opened the window, I was furious. 'Don't you ever drive off again without picking up the food I prepared for you,' I shouted up at him. 'I came out here at half past five in the bloody snow. I have no experience in driving that stupid van. Now you open that door and come down here and pick up this food. And don't you ever do that again.'

I didn't know it, but the air traffic controllers in the tower were rolling on the floor. One of them told me he wished he had a camera to take pictures of me chasing that aeroplane.

My catering business grew in spite of my efforts to keep it small. I only wanted a little business to pay my bills and take care of my children. I wanted a business that was dependable. But it grew too much and that scared me. The biggest and most successful party I catered for was the St George's Tennis Club in Surrey.

I was asked to tender for a banquet the club was having. Many big companies put in bids. I looked around the waiting room and saw their representatives with their glossy brochures. I had nothing. I was sitting there like I was waiting at the dentist's to have my teeth taken out.

When it came time for me to make my presentation, I said, 'Look, I'm going to be perfectly honest with you. I hate bullshit. Bullshit takes up too much time. Brochures I don't have. All I've got are recommendations. But I promise you at the end of the night you'll shake my hand and everybody will be happy. You'll have to trust me. Here are the menus. If these don't please you, tell me what you want and I'll do it.'

Four days later the phone rang and I was told, 'You've got the contract.'

The dinner was for almost two hundred people. I had no staff. It was me, a little fridge-freezer and a four-ring cooker. 'OK,' I told the man on the telephone. 'Write down all the details and forget all about it. Leave everything to me. And can you send me a deposit?'

I used the deposit to buy a roll of red material. I had a woman make ten aprons and ten bow ties. Then I went down to the local council estate and found seven girls and three men and trained them very quickly. Be polite but not familiar and remember that the customer is always right, I told them. I dressed them in white shirts, black trousers, red aprons and red bow ties.

I had a girl make twenty-five gâteaus which I put into a rented freezer. For two days and nights I stayed up cooking turkeys and making salads. I don't know how I did it. But at the end of the dinner, they gave me a big bouquet of flowers and a big bottle of whisky. That night after the dinner, every time I moved, someone was shaking my hand and congratulating me and promising me more catering business. The people at the tennis club asked the staff to join the party and dance. It went off like a dream. All the food that was left, they gave to the staff. I paid everyone off and the staff fell asleep on the floor of my flat. The left-over food I took around to poor people. This dinner proved to me that anything is possible. But it also frightened me. I did not want a big business.

Even though it seemed I worked all the time during those years, I always made time for my children. We had a good life. I have always thought, as does every mother, that my three children were good children. But one day

I looked at them from a distance and I realized they were better than good, they were extraordinary young people. They were strong young adults who could deal with the world.

There have been times in my life when I have got down on my knees and lifted my eyes and opened my hands to God and begged and cried and demanded why I have suffered this way. The whole world suffers. I'm not the only one. But for me it never seemed to stop.

Today I do believe, and maybe it's because I need to justify the suffering, that it has prepared me to take care of the suffering and the sick. In my soul, in my guts, I believe in God. I believe God has taken me to where I am today. He spent all those years preparing me.

One day after my therapy was over, after the nightmares had stopped and I was able to look back over the first three and a half decades of my life, I sat down and wrote a poem about my father. I no longer felt guilty and I no longer felt responsible. It was the first time I was able to think clearly about what my father had been.

His bloodshot eyes, twisted lip,
The dead stare of blank wall reflect in grey
The shadows of his past, stagnant in alcohol.
He moans and groans,
No kind and gentle tones.
In the stillness of darkness, burning great shooting blazing images.
On one chair but empty room together alone, dancing in the gloom.
My heart he tore,
My love he wore.
He could hurt without hurting, freeze without freezing.
But he could never thaw the pain to gentle rain.

Oh, that foolish man, he never grows.
But I needed him, God knows.
And where is time now, old man?
You have no time since you left me in my mother's womb,
The clawing black cloud, stark naked moon.
I have left you in your tomb.
Whiskey soda sour, bitter sweet taste no more.
Alas, old man, your little girl has now closed the door.

I knew when I finished the poem that I had forgiven my father. Some have told me that I let him off too lightly, that I never recognized all the anger I felt towards him. Perhaps, but I was content.

Our roles reversed, as they can do when a child grows up. Pop was still living in Birmingham in his little council house, still visiting the pub as he would do all his life. I visited him several times each month. He grumbled about my wanting to sleep with the light on, but he had finally softened. I think deep in his heart he felt a great deal of pain about those years in Ireland.

In early 1989 I sensed that my life was coming into another period. I thought of little but Vietnam. In my mind's eye I could see that little girl in the dream reaching out to me. I tried everything to bring the vision to some sort of resolution. Once I even called up the Red Cross and said, 'I've had a dream. It was a vision telling me that I have to go to Vietnam and help the children. Can you help me get to Vietnam?'

'We'll call you,' I was told. But they never did.

Then I began seeing a man. Of course I told him of my dreams and my destiny to go to Vietnam. One day to my surprise he called and said he had been offered a job in Vietnam. He flew away and several weeks later he called me from Ho Chi Minh City. 'If you really want to work with children, there is plenty of opportunity here,' he said. 'The streets are overrun with destitute children. They are everywhere. And they need help.'

The time had come.

I accepted no more orders for my catering business. During the next four months I completed all my obligations and then I closed the business, packed a suitcase, and, in the autumn of 1989, with only a few hundred pounds in my pockets I went to Heathrow with Helen and Androula and Nicolas.

This was no summer holiday. I was going half-way around the world. Although I had dreamed of this moment for almost twenty years, I was frightened. Maybe it had been nothing more than a dream. Maybe this was only a silly lark. I did not know what would happen in Vietnam, nor what I would find there. I did not know what I would do once I arrived. All of my insecurities came rushing back and almost overwhelmed me.

I cried and kissed my children goodbye and I climbed up those long long steps to board the aircraft. As we took off, I looked out of the window and whispered a tearful goodbye to the green fields of England.

One way or another my destiny was about to be fulfilled.

Vietnam

17

'What are your names?' I asked the two little girls as they sat on my lap that day in the park soon after I arrived in Ho Chi Minh City. Like most street children, they understood enough English so that, when accompanied by a lot of sign language and a lot of love on my part, they knew what I was asking. Huong and Hang were their names.

We went back and forth on my name until we arrived at 'Mama Tina'.

'I will fight for you,' I whispered to them. I did not realize at that moment how soon I would have to make good on my promise.

I looked around. Soon it would be dark. I had to do something for these two little girls. But what? I picked them both up. The tent-top style blouse I was wearing was full and voluminous. Huong snuggled up under the blouse on my right side and Hang on my left. Each little girl sat astride my hips with her legs around me. I put my arms under them and hoisted them higher, making sure their legs were hidden by my blouse. Although they were feather light they were a bit difficult to keep in place. I headed for the Rex.

The Rex Hotel was then off-limits to Vietnamese. It was one of the smartest hotels in Ho Chi Minh City and strictly for foreigners. Security people were everywhere, especially in the lobby. I saw them staring at me as I carefully walked up the front steps. Obviously I was carrying something under my blouse. I was enormous. And I was all bent and stooped from trying to keep Huong and Hang riding on my hips and their legs tucked under my blouse.

The security men at the front door stared, but said nothing. I turned right immediately I walked in, hoping to make the elevators around the corner. The receptionist, a middle-aged woman, looked up just as Huong's leg slipped out from under my blouse. I smiled at her.

Hang's leg fell down.

My smile broadened.

I bounced and jostled the children, trying to tuck their legs back up under my blouse, and at the same time smiling madly. Minor officials in Vietnam are like minor officials everywhere, except more so. For a moment I was afraid that the official in the receptionist would overcome the mother. I pursed my lips and said 'Shhhhhhh' – the sound mothers all over the world make when they want their children to be quiet. The receptionist turned her attention back to her work. But I saw her quick smile.

The first elevator was open and I rushed in, pushed the button with an elbow and emerged hastily when we arrived at the third floor. Expatriates in Ho Chi Minh City, most of whom had lived at the Rex when they first came to Vietnam, called this floor Legionnaires Walk because so many people had fallen sick from the air conditioning. It was directly under the floor known as Salmonella Heights.

Huong and Hang were fascinated by my small hotel room. They wandered about looking at everything and looking at me for permission to touch the bed, the mirror, and the clothes I had lying about. The first thing I had to do for these two little girls was give them a bath. They were filthy. I laughed with recognition as

I filled the bath with hot soapy water. For Catholics, a wash is the first answer, no matter what the problem. The girls stared at the bath and they stared at me. To them it seemed enormous.

I draped a towel around Huong and undressed her under the towel. A child must have her dignity. She was still wrapped in the towel as I picked her up and slowly lowered her into the tub. Only then did I remove the towel. Then I did the same with Hang. The two little girls sat in the tub, soapy water up to their necks, smiling and giggling and splashing and playing as only young children can play. They were having the time of their lives. After I shampooed their hair and scrubbed them, I was amazed at the transformation. Their black hair glistened and their little faces were covered with sunrise smiles. They were even more beautiful than I had thought.

When I took them from the tub and dried them, I looked at their dirty and tattered clothing and knew I could not put those rags back on them. They needed dresses, proper dresses for little girls, dresses with lace and ribbons. I put the girls in bed and covered them so only their little faces were visible. Their dark eyes stared at me from over the top of the sheets when I pulled at my blouse and skirt and made motions to indicate I was going out to buy clothes. They seemed to understand.

I cleared the front steps of the hotel in a single bound as I leaped into the street, turned right, ran a few steps to the corner and turned right again on Le Loi. By now darkness was coming on and I was in a great hurry to beat the sundown and buy dresses for the girls.

My friend My Loc, whom I had met a few days earlier, had a small shop nearby. I ran through the side streets to her store, raced through the open door and said, 'Where can I buy some dresses for little girls?'

As usual customers were driving their motorbikes through the open door into the store. The fumes were almost choking me. 'Fumes bad for your chest,' I said coughing and pounding my chest. 'Jesus, this will kill you.'

My Loc smiled and offered me a bowl of food. I looked at the bowl. I thought it was dog meat. I pointed to the bowl and then pointed to My Loc's big German Shepherd. Tiu, his name was. My Loc shook her head in dismay. 'No, we no eat dog,' she said. 'Tiu is a friend.'

I turned down the food. 'I don't have time to eat. I want to buy dresses,' I told her. 'I want to buy beautiful dresses for two little girls.' I was bouncing from one foot to the other. My Loc smiled and nodded. 'Tomorrow I will go with you,' she said.

'No. Now.'

She was surprised at my impatience.

'Now,' I insisted.

She nodded for a cousin to take over the shop. Then she led me out and into the narrow street. It was now almost dark and little fires were glowing as people cooked their dinner in charcoal pots. We ran, down the narrow alley, cut across narrow streets, dodged people crowded around jammed stalls selling everything from sun-glasses to belts to shoes. The sight of a blonde Westerner aroused their competitive instincts. They blocked our way as they held up their goods and implored me to buy. I ignored them as I raced on behind My Loc.

We jumped gutters fouled with human waste. And we leaped over or dashed around people who were sleeping on the street. Rats were beginning to stir from the sewers and poke their quivering noses outside as they began their nightly hunt for food. In front of me was a man who had dropped his pants and was defecating off the edge of the kerb.

Occasionally My Loc stopped at a stall where girls' dresses were sold, but I could tell at a glance that what I sought was not there. On we ran into the gathering darkness. And then we were in an enormous warehouse-like building filled with untold dozens of individual stalls where everything from household wares to clothing was sold. It was a rabbit warren of confusing turns and corners and alleyways. There appeared to be hundreds of people in that jammed building. It was an anthill of activity.

What I wanted was in my mind's eye and I was aware that the second I saw the dresses, I would know they were right. But I must hurry. Huong and Hang were alone in the room and there was so much I wanted to do for them, so many things I wanted to show them.

We rounded a corner and there they were. Hanging from hangers about five feet over my head were several rows of little girls' dresses, exactly as I had pictured them. Lace border, full skirt, little rosettes on the front, ruffles, puff sleeves and satin belt. They were replicas of my Confirmation dress. I bought one in pink and one in yellow. And then I bought white socks and knickers and white shoes with straps. I did not wait for the clothes to be wrapped, I folded them over my arm and ran from the building.

' 'Bye, My Loc,' I shouted as I raced towards the hotel, back through those twisting, dark, oozing, pungent streets that were trying to claim Huong and Hang.

When I threw open the door of my room, Huong and Hang were still in bed, obviously comfortable, playing with a box of tissues. They looked at me with wide eyes. I held up the dresses in exultation. Then I dressed them in their little knickers and socks and shoes and those lovely dresses. I fixed their hair and stood them in front of a mirror where they stared for long minutes. They pulled at their frocks, looked down at their shoes – possibly the first they had ever worn – and then their eyes returned to the mirror; it was as if they could not believe what they were seeing. I watched them as they looked at each other, then into the mirror, and again at each other. Again they pulled at the frilly dresses in disbelief. They giggled.

The next day I bought them several outfits each of shorts and teeshirts. And I smiled to myself as I washed the outfits and hung them up to dry.

For several days afterwards Huong and Hang stayed in the hotel. But I knew that could not last. I showed the little girls a video of Mickey Mouse, which frightened them. I bought them dolls and toys and a copy book and pencils. We spent wonderful hours together. They were like younger sisters, but I was also their mam. Slowly their senses came alive and they changed from street children who felt nothing into little girls who wanted to play with dolls, who wanted to dress up.

After a few days I began sending Huong and Hang out of the hotel when night came on. They came back each morning and we played and they dressed up and I held their hands as we walked around the city.

I then began taking Huong and Hang and a group of street children to the Bach Dang ice-cream parlour on Le Loi Street every Saturday morning. I sat there with a dozen or so children and we ate ice-cream and, with the help of many gestures and a combination of English and Vietnamese, talked about life on the street.

In the aftermath of the war, there were hundreds, perhaps thousands, of Amer-Asian children on the streets of Ho Chi Minh City. I had heard stories of how they were rounded up in large numbers and taken away to camps where they disappeared. When I arrived in Vietnam, all the Amer-Asian children who had survived were grown. However, the attitudes that were manifest towards them were still very much in evidence where *bui doi* were concerned. There were many instances when the government rounded up street children and took them away to God only knows where. That policy still existed in 1989. And one Saturday morning I came face to face with the policy and with the police.

That morning I was merrily walking down the street with half a dozen children in tow. As I neared the ice-cream parlour, the children grew suddenly very tense. Their bodies stiffened and I saw them grow as alert and wary and frightened as wild animals. They hung back. When I asked what was the matter, one of the children circled the forefinger and thumb of each hand and held them up to her eyes. They wanted me to see what was happening. Several children clenched their fists and banged their wrists together as if they were being manacled.

They pointed down the street. A truck was parked across from the ice-cream parlour. The children who were there waiting for me suddenly scattered like a covey of birds. Their faces were contorted with fear.

I ran into the ice-cream parlour. Suddenly I was surrounded by frightened crying children and facing a dozen or so stern-faced men. They were in civilian clothes but it was obvious they were authorities of some sort. I motioned for all the children to stand behind me. Then I raised a fist towards the men.

'Leave these children alone or I'll fucking kill you,' I warned. I don't think they understood me, but from my expression, my gestures, and my tone of voice, they certainly got the message. The children clustered around me, pulling at my clothes, holding on to me and whimpering in fear. Their presence gave me strength. One of the men reached out to jerk a child away.

I leaped at him like an angry tiger and shoved his arm away. 'Take your hands off her,' I shouted.

I was really angry now. I faced the group of men, held up my hands, and beckoned them forward. 'Come on. I'll take on every one of you. I'll kill you all.'

They appeared bemused. One of them began talking to the woman who ran the ice-cream parlour. I turned to the children. 'Don't cry, me darlings,' I said. 'No-one is going to hurt you.' I touched and caressed and reassured them, all the while keeping a wary eye on the men.

The woman who ran the ice-cream parlour spoke a few words of English. She came up to me and said, 'Not good what you do. Dangerous.'

'Dangerous? It's dangerous for the children. That's who it is dangerous for. Those men are not going to put these children into trucks and haul them away. They are children. Not animals. These men are kidnappers. They want to take the children away.'

'Police. Police,' the woman said. She was very frightened. 'No kidnappers. Police.'

I looked at the circle of men and sensed that I was in deep trouble. One of the men, obviously the leader, nodded. 'Police,' he echoed sternly.

I had to protect the children. Because of my own childhood I knew what it was like to be a victim of authority. I shook my head and said, 'No. You are kidnappers who are here to take these children to Cambodia.'

'Police,' repeated the leader. He was exasperated.

'Show me your identity card if you are police.' The men appeared nonplussed. I pressed my momentary advantage. 'If you are not police, you are kidnappers.'

The men talked. They were going from exasperated to angry. The leader issued orders. I do not know what he said, but most of the men backed away, then fanned out and surrounded the ice-cream parlour, penning us inside. Several others walked out. About half an hour later they returned and stalked up to me waving little cards. They appeared very angry. No-one in Vietnam ever asks a policeman to prove his identity or to show a badge. I was a foreigner interfering with the laws of a highly authoritarian country.

After waving their identity cards at me, one of the men stepped forward. He had not been with the original group. He spoke to me in English.

'These men are police,' he said. 'You do not interfere with them.' His voice was flat. But I knew he was very determined.

'OK, so you are not kidnappers,' I said. 'The children will go with you. But not in the truck. They will walk with me.'

He stared for a long moment. His face was impassive. But his eyes flashed black sparks of anger. He looked over his shoulder and I thought he was going to order his men to haul the children away. But then he shouted orders to his men. He looked at me and nodded. I motioned for the children to stay close and tried to explain that I would walk with them and we would be safe. We slowly exited the ice-cream parlour and walked down the street surrounded by the stern-faced police.

By then quite a crowd had gathered. They looked on in curiosity as a blonde Western woman marched down the street with more than a dozen street children in tow. Huong was on my shoulder and Hang was clutching my hand. All the children were crying and looking around in fear and apprehension. They knew about the camps.

At one level I knew I was in trouble. But I did not think of that. I thought only as a mother. And I thought of that day when I was taken to Dublin Castle and the magistrates split my family apart. That Saturday morning in Ho Chi Minh City, I was a mother protecting her children, that was all.

The man in charge at the police station, I suppose he was the chief, sat behind a desk and listened as one of the policemen told him what had happened. The chief looked at me with stern eyes and waved me forward. Through the interpreter he said, 'You come to our country. You are a guest here. You ignore our laws.' He pointed at the policemen. 'These are police. They must do their job.'

'No, no, I did not ignore your laws,' I said apologetically. 'I did not know these men were policemen. I'm a mother, a mam. I have three children. I thought these men were kidnappers taking the children to Cambodia. Maybe they want to take these wonderful children and force them to become pickpockets. I don't know what they wanted. I respect your laws.'

Then I put the Irish on the man. I cried, threw my arms wide, and wailed, 'I'm a mam. I see babies in trouble and I am only a mam. All babies are the same. All children are the same. Irish babies. Vietnamese babies. All the same. I feel for them all like a mam.'

The poor man did not know quite what to do. I think he thought that I was not aiming to be defiant. He knew I was genuinely concerned for the children and was only taking care of them. I was acting as any mam would act if her child were threatened. But in the end he said I had to leave the children at the police station, Huong and Hang included, and that whatever happened to them was none of my business.

I heard the children crying as the police escorted me from the building. 'Mama Tina. Not go. Mama Tina.' Oh, how they cried as the police held them back. It broke my heart. But I could do nothing.

I waited outside for hours. That afternoon the children who could prove they had parents living in Ho Chi Minh City were released, Huong and Hang among them. Their parents came shuffling down the street and collected the two little girls. The family stood in a little knot as the two girls pointed at me and talked in a very animated fashion. Then the father solemnly looked at me for what seemed an eternity. He flattened his right hand, made a motion like an aeroplane taking off, and looked at me imploringly. 'You take,' he said. 'America.' I sighed and shook my head that I could not.

As I walked away, the children who had not been claimed were driven past in a police truck. I heard their cries as they passed and I knew they were being taken to a camp. I wondered if I would ever see them again.

I returned to the Rex where I locked myself in my room, kicked the floor, and threw pillows at the walls.

'Why do children have to suffer so much?' I screamed. 'What is wrong with this world?'

I cried for the children who had been taken away. I cried for my childhood and the years I spent on the streets of Dublin. I cried for children everywhere.

18

Huong and Hang told other children about their experiences with me, and more and more street children began coming to the Rex every morning asking for 'Mama Tina'. The security people at the Rex were terribly annoyed when street children began congregating in front of the hotel every morning before sunrise. No matter how early I went out, children in ever-growing numbers were waiting. And when they saw me, they jumped up and down and waved and laughed and shouted 'Mama Tina, Mama Tina'.

I cried the first few times it happened. To see those solemn little faces, many old before their time, suddenly break into a sunshine smile and to hear their sweet voices shouting my name filled me with joy. Even today, when I walk the streets of Ho Chi Minh City and see a grubby little street child look up, recognize me, and shout 'Mama Tina', my heart leaps.

Each day I played with the children for hours. In the park across the street from the Rex we played Blind Man's Bluff and Hide and Seek, and the laughter of the children filled the air.

Holiday-makers and business people would stroll from the Rex and shake their heads in dismay. They all thought I was a bit dotty. 'You're wasting your time,' they said to me when I told them I wanted to work with the street children. Some of them complained to each other about me. I embarrassed them.

It was very difficult bringing enough food and drink out of the hotel for the children, so instead I began bringing the children into the hotel. The first time it happened the staff were too shocked to say anything. The expats pulled away in disgust. I knew what they were thinking: they were in the poshest hotel in Ho Chi Minh City and they didn't expect to share it with a woman surrounded by a dozen or so dirty and scruffy little urchins in ragged clothes. Many of the children were hacking and coughing. Some had open sores or wounds. Their noses were snotty, their eyes were runny, and they always seemed to be scratching lice and fleas.

But to me they were beautiful. Whenever I caught the shocked eye of a guest I would smile and say, 'They're beautiful, aren't they? Beautiful children.'

Then I gathered the children around me and we jammed into the elevator and I punched the button for the fifth floor where the Rex's roof-top restaurant, one of the most famous restaurants in the city, was located.

At the time the restaurant featured an enormous metal elephant standing in one corner where it overlooked the busy corner of Nguyen Hue and Le Loi. A crown was the logo of the Rex and crowns decorated everything. An elephant and crowns, the symbols of imperialism, were everywhere, and here was I with a mob of street kids.

We caused bedlam. The guests atop the hotel were sitting on balconies in the sunshine making casual expat conversation as they sipped on whatever they were sipping on. They were dressed in all their elegant finery. And here was a fighting, hell-raising, shouting, pushing mob of street kids being led right through the middle of their little tea party.

I counted the children. There were ten of them. Then I turned to a waiter who appeared to be paralysed. 'Give me ten orange juices,' I said to him. I raised my finger. 'These are special guests of mine. So don't give me any of your old recycled straws. Give us new straws, me darling.'

He brought the tray of juices and passed them around to the wide-eyed children. 'Put it on my bill, sweetheart,' I told him. He stared at me. 'You're a kind man,' I said to him. 'That you are. Now be on your way and we'll be enjoying our juice.'

The kids were leaping around and laughing, playing as children should play. None of them had ever been inside a restaurant before and their behaviour was not the best.

In the days to come I brought children to the top of the Rex many times. I took them past the restaurant, past the elegant topiary, past the little pools filled with koi carp – the pride of the Rex – and around the corner to the swimming pool. I had to watch the children closely as we passed the shallow pools filled with koi. The first time the children saw the fish, a couple of them tried to jump into the pool and scoop them out. Then one day several children smuggled a grizzled old street cat up to the roof and tossed him in the pool with the fish. My God, what chaos.

When the children saw the swimming pool their squeals of excitement could be heard all over the place. Several jumped into the pool fully clothed. The real reason I wanted the children here was not to go swimming, but for the showers. Between the pool and a new wing of the hotel were several showers and wash basins. I ushered the little girls into one shower and the boys into another, then had them undress and pass their clothes out to me. I took their clothes to the foot bath and scrubbed them clean while the children played and whooped and shouted in the showers. Then I hung the tattered little rags on racks where they dried quickly in the hot sun.

In late 1989, the Russians were still in Ho Chi Minh City in great numbers. Many of them stayed at the Rex. Perhaps because they were from a cold climate they were the only ones around the pool in the mornings. They watched in amazement as the kids threw cans, bottles, and each other into the pool. The windows from the restaurant kitchen overlooked the pool and many times I looked up and saw a dozen faces staring out of the windows and laughing at the expressions on the Russians' faces. The Vietnamese are not overly fond of the Russians. (I was overweight at the time, and when the children came to know me better, several of them teased me with the nickname 'Madame Soviet'.)

The Russians inevitably complained about the children and the man in charge of the pool told me to control them or he would throw them out.

'These are your children,' I said to him. 'These are Vietnamese children. Your own blood. They need food and they need baths. You would throw them out and let the Russians stay? What sort of a man are you?'

'You American?'

'No, Irish.' Then I had an idea. 'Let the children stay and I will teach you English,' I said to him. 'Every day when they are in the pool you and I will have an English lesson. Soon you speak very good English. All of your friends will be impressed with how well you speak English.'

His smile of approval told me that my tactic was a success. The children could stay. It was the Russians who retreated. After a few more days, when they heard my crowd coming around the corner they gathered their towels and left. I smiled: Ireland, one. Russia, zero.

Over the next few weeks the size of my brood grew until I had to rotate the groups. There were too many to take to the top of the Rex at one time. Sometimes there were also mothers from the street, sick mothers with missing limbs or mothers with children on their breasts. It was becoming more and more difficult for me to shower so many children and clean their clothes. And I realized that this was not what my dream was about. I had not come half-way around the world to administer to a few children around a swimming pool. There were thousands of street children in Ho Chi Minh City and I had to find a way to reach them. Besides, my bringing children to the Rex was not only a terrible shock to the guests but a continual trial to the hotel staff. It lasted this long only because I was a guest myself and because, when necessary, I could 'put the Irish' on the poor staff and managers. In addition to this growing frustration, I felt a growing sense of desperation. My finances were dwindling rapidly. The day was coming when I would have to leave the Rex.

19

Before my story continues, and before I tell you more about those momentous days at the end of 1989, let me tell you about the street children, who they are, what they do, and how the Vietnam government has changed its attitude towards them.

Home and family are fundamental to most people. But if a child's home is filled with neglect and violence and pain and indifference, then sometimes he takes the enormous step of leaving his family. The child is then free not only from the family but from all the restraints and rules and conventions that society places on him. The child is challenging society's most basic values. And the structure of government, that is, the police, welfare, and social organizations, is geared towards pressurizing the child to repent.

From our cosy homes and comfortable families, we like to think that street children yearn to return home. We forget, or perhaps we do not know, that many homes are not like ours. Most street children do not want to give up the freedom and independence that goes with being on the street. To them, home is not love and security and warmth and food; to them home is fear and pain and beatings and repression.

There are various types of street children here in Ho Chi Minh City: the child who has either left home or who has no home and who sleeps on the street, the child who sleeps on the street with his family, and the child who lives on the street during the day but who goes home at night.

Children who sleep on the street are extremely vulnerable to being robbed or beaten. There is always the danger of being arrested. And there is the danger of being sexually abused by foreigners. These children have a great need for shelter. They need to be out of the weather and they need to be protected from those who would prey upon them.

I estimate that more than seventy per cent of the street children here are either vendors or scavengers. The vendors sell cigarettes, maps, and all sorts of trinkets. The scavengers pick up and then sell everything from beer cans to pieces of metal left in the street after a motorbike collision. My point is that, although there are pickpockets, pimps, and thieves, most of the street children in Ho Chi Minh City are not criminals.

Two other things about street children are particularly noteworthy. First, there is very little drug use. That is probably one of the few benefits of having been isolated from the world since 1975 by the American embargo. Second, more than half of the street children are literate. Most of them speak some English. And virtually all of them are fascinated by the West.

Vietnam, as do most countries that have large numbers of street children, finds them an embarrassment. And for a long time there was a policy of rounding them up, removing them from the streets, and institutionalizing them. It was like that when I first arrived. When I confronted the police at the ice-cream parlour that Saturday morning in 1989 there was only one policy regarding street children and it involved rounding them up and sending them away to camps.

Since then there has been a significant shift in policy.

Today the authorities are caught between the long-established 'round-up' policy and an increasing public desire to help and rehabilitate the children. Placing innocent children in camps merely turns them into criminals. So while the old policies still remain in place, there is now a greater priority placed on caring for the children.

I like to think that I have had some small part in that wonderful evolution.

20

Christmas was coming, and all I could think of was the Christmas after my mother had died. I remember how I sat in a freezing flat with my brother and sisters and told them the story of Bethlehem and tried to explain why there would be no Father Christmas and why, if Jesus was poor and hungry, it was OK if we were poor and hungry too. While the little ones and I huddled in the cold and dark flat, my daddy was out making the rounds of the pubs.

I was surprised that so many people in this communist country recognized Christmas. Someone told me that, because of the years of French colonialism, Vietnam, particularly Ho Chi Minh City, has many Catholics. That explained it. We Catholics do like to celebrate Christmas.

A few Christmas lights were appearing in the shops. Occasionally I saw people carrying Christmas trees on the backs of motorbikes. They were all smiling and I could see they were looking forward to Christmas with great anticipation. I remembered how in Dublin I used to watch everyone enjoy the bounty of Christmas while we had nothing. I remembered the noise and celebration of others from which we were totally isolated.

One day I was with a group of children walking down Le Loi. We stopped in front of a shop where Christmas lights were flickering and peered longingly into a window where Father Christmas sat. I turned and looked at the street and saw people carrying gift and cake boxes. I looked at the expressions of longing on the faces of the children gathered around me. Their pain and their isolation and their need to have Christmas shouted at me. When I looked at them, it was me I saw, me on the streets of Dublin. I wondered if anyone would open the door for these children. And I wondered if they already thought it was too late, that nothing mattered any more.

There was only one thing to do: I had to have a Christmas party for the street children, a joyous, gift-filled, food-filled, song-filled Christmas they would never forget.

When I told My Loc that I wanted to have a grand and glorious party for the children, she stared at me. 'You serious?' she asked.

'Of course I'm serious. Now where can I buy hats and those little whistles that unroll? And where can I get gifts and wrapping paper? And I want somebody to play a guitar.'

'Why you want to do this? Why you care?'

'They are beautiful children. They must have a Christmas party.'

She smiled at me in the way Vietnamese have of smiling at foreigners. I was not getting through.

'Look,' I told her, 'in 1971 – eighteen years ago – I had a dream about Vietnam and these children. I fought that dream when I first came here. But Huong and Hang are proof that God wants me to stay here. He used them to make me see that I must stay. I don't know if you believe in God. But He wants me to do this, so there it is.'

My Loc was beginning to think I was a dotty Irish woman.

I went down the corridors of the Rex Hotel knocking

on every door. 'I'm having a party for the street children. Could you give me some money?' I repeated countless times. Some said a direct no, most said they were too busy, but a few gave me donations. After I had canvassed the Rex I went to other hotels and I did the same thing. I stopped anyone on the street who looked like a foreigner and asked them to help. I raised the equivalent of several hundred dollars. Then I went to the manager of the Saigon Floating Hotel. This is a famous hotel that was once anchored on the Great Barrier Reef off the coast of Australia. It was towed up here and anchored in the Saigon River where it instantly become the most fashionable hotel in the city. Patrick, the manager, gave me another two hundred dollars.

With the exception of Patrick's generosity, however, I was saddened at the response. I thought Christmas was the one time of the year when adults wanted to help all children. But on the whole they thought I was a nuisance. However, I had enough money for a party. It would not be as grand as I had hoped, but it would be a party.

I went to the manager of what then was a very large restaurant on the ground floor of the Rex Hotel. He had on his dicky bow and his little black suit and I could tell by the way he looked at me that he was a proper manager.

'All right, me darling,' I said to him, 'I want to book your restaurant on Christmas Day. A private party I'm having for about one hundred and fifty, maybe two hundred guests.'

He nodded in appreciation. The poor man assumed that since I was a Westerner that my guests would be Westerners. As he was around the corner from the lobby, he had never seen my crowd of children coming in. Him and his little dicky bow thought a big party of rich Westerners was coming to celebrate Christmas Day.

'Now it's a plain menu we'll be having,' I said to him. 'My guests like to eat very simply. So we'll have chicken and rice and a big glass of orange juice. Can you do that?'

He nodded. He was obviously a bit puzzled, but of course he could do that. The thought of booking the entire restaurant had the man trembling in excitement.

'My guests will arrive about three o'clock,' I told him. 'Before we eat, presents will be taken from under a Christmas tree and given to the chil . . . to my guests. There will also be a guitar player. This will be a grand occasion. Do you understand?'

The man could not stop nodding. He was very pleased. This was an extremely prestigious event for his restaurant.

For the next few days I never stopped. I bought clothes for babies. I bought tins of condensed milk, packets of biscuits, and big boxes of sweets, all of which were wrapped in Christmas paper. Some of the Vietnamese people who were helping me grew impatient and wanted to take the presents to the party and pass them out unwrapped. The very idea appalled me. 'Children must see wrapping paper,' I explained. 'They must have something to unwrap. This is very important to them.'

It took two days and two nights to complete all the wrapping. I spent 23 December 1989, my entire forty-fifth birthday, wrapping presents. I told Tinh, a Vietnamese man who had begun helping me with the children, that it was the most joyous birthday I'd ever had.

On Christmas Day I put a green rosette on my blouse and green tinsel around my head. I had to show a bit of the Irish. Then I waited anxiously for the children. I knew if they straggled in one by one, that the police would take them away and the party would end before it could begin. So I had told them to gather a block away and arrive all together at three o'clock precisely.

At two o'clock I stood in the dining room and uttered a silent prayer that the children would not become anxious and arrive before the allotted time. I was also a bit worried as to the size of the dining room. It could only accommodate one hundred and fifty children and I was afraid there could be many more. I had appointed several leaders to count heads and make sure that no more than one hundred and fifty came to the restaurant.

I looked at the manager and his staff. The manager had everyone dressed properly. The women wore black skirts with red bows in their black hair. The men wore little red dicky bows and black suits. Funnily enough, it was the same way I had dressed my staff when I ran my catering service in Surrey.

'You look very smart,' I said to the manager.

At 3 p.m. I was pacing up and down, excited and nervous, as I checked the boxes of sweets and biscuits, and the little bottles of milk with nipples on them for the babies.

'Dear God,' I prayed, 'this is important for the street children. You'd know all about that. You were in a stable yourself. So make sure this goes all right.'

A few seconds after three o'clock the children appeared out of nowhere. One minute there was nothing; the next, dozens of big eyes were peering out of dirty faces through the windows and into the room. They had been concerned about the police and were determined their Christmas would not be spoiled. How they came to the hotel, I don't know. It was probably through back alleys and short-cuts no-one else in the city knew. Now they began banging on the big glass doors.

The manager was terribly annoyed. He motioned for some of his staff to shoo the children away.

'No, wait, those are my guests,' I shouted from across the room.

The manager stared in disbelief as the children flooded through the door. A few mothers, limping with illness, and with babies on their breasts, came too. But mostly it was children. They were scruffy and dirty and dressed in rags. Their noses were snotty. They had fleas and lice and runny eyes and open sores. They were shouting and laughing and pushing and banging chairs and talking and pulling each other away from the tables. Everyone was trying to get a seat so he would not be left out.

The manager, poor man, was transfixed. So was his staff. After a few minutes the manager shook away his paralysis and came bustling forward. 'No, no, no. This not good. No street children in here. No *bui doi.*'

'These are my guests, my beautiful guests,' I said to him. 'And these are your children, they are not foreigners. This is your flesh and blood. Isn't it better to have Vietnamese here on Christmas Day than foreigners? You've had trouble all your life with foreigners. It is good that Vietnamese children are here.' I waited a moment. He was not getting the message. I leaned closer and said to him, 'I have paid you. So make sure my guests are shown a good time.'

He backed away a step and looked at me. I could almost hear the gears grinding in his head. He was still not quite sure what to do.

I turned to the staff. Their eyes were locked on the manager and I knew they were waiting for an order. I had to act fast. So I roamed down the line of waiters and waitresses. 'You lot,' I ordered, 'now don't be standing there. Go get the orange juice. The children are ready to be served.'

I motioned them towards the kitchen. Then I ran into the kitchen myself and picked up a jug of juice. I had to keep the staff moving. I had to establish some momentum before the manager came to his senses.

The staff began bringing orange juice and plates of food out and serving them in a very hurried fashion, pushing them across the tables. They were offended that street children had taken over their restaurant.

'Don't do it that way,' I ordered. I stopped them and showed them how the food should be served. 'Do it proper,' I said. 'And give every child a smile and a squeeze. This is Christmas.'

One waiter was particularly mean. I watched him snap at the children and push them around. I came up behind him, grabbed his arm, spun him around, and shook my finger in his face. 'You will treat them with dignity,' I said in a very sweet Christmas voice. 'Because if you don't, me darling, I'll break your fucking neck. Do you understand me?'

He did.

I put on a hat with a big feather in it and began running about blowing a whistle, the sort that rolls and unrolls. Other whistles were on the tables and soon the children were standing on chairs and blowing the whistles and laughing.

Then I was back in the kitchen. 'Serve them faster,' I ordered. 'They need their juice.'

The staff were amazed that I was interfering with their duties, but they said nothing. I pushed them around and got the job done.

And then something glorious happened. It began when I put my arms around a particularly dirty and scruffy child who had been pushed off a chair and was sitting on the floor crying his little heart out. I kneeled, pulled him to me, and kissed him. I held him until he stopped crying and then I gave him a whistle and put him in a chair. I looked up and saw a transformation taking place in the eyes of several waitresses who were watching. It was a universal look of love, the same look that people everywhere give children. And suddenly everything in the room slowed. The children were being served slowly and with dignity. The staff were laughing and talking to the children. Suddenly it was OK. Suddenly the staff saw the street children as human beings. Suddenly we had our Christmas party.

In that moment it was all worthwhile. I realized that if one person at that party had changed his mind about how he perceived these children, if one person no longer saw them as *bui doi* but as children with the same tears and the same longing and the same feeling as any children, then the miracle of Christmas had taken place.

'Thank you, God,' I whispered.

After everyone had eaten, I stood at the front of the room and sang 'Jingle Bells' and 'I'm Dreaming of a White Christmas'. Of course, the children didn't understand most of the words. But they understood the feeling. I tap danced and sang and the kids roared with laughter. I apologized to them for not knowing any Vietnamese songs.

After the guitar player had played and the singing was over and the gifts had been distributed, the party began to wind down. I said to the manager and the staff, 'Let's all hold hands and sing another one. Let's sing "We are the World". After all, we are all the same.'

The manager announced in Vietnamese that we were going to sing one more song and that the children should listen closely as I told them the words in English. Slowly I repeated the words. Then I had the children stand up and link hands. The manager and the staff all held hands with the children. And then we began singing. They forgot most of the words and the only place where they sang loud and clear and as one was at the words, *We are the world. We are the children.*

I looked out over their little scabby bodies and dripping noses and heads raw from lice, but all I saw were the smiles on their faces and the light in their eyes.

We are the world. We are the children.

They sang it over and over and over that afternoon.

Then it was time for the party to end. I looked out and there were dozens of faces in the windows, the faces of children who had heard about the party but who could not get in. I knew about being on the outside looking in and I was determined these children would not suffer that. I opened my purse. I did not have enough money remaining to feed them in the hotel. But I did have enough to take them to the ice-cream parlour.

So I went outside and told the children we were going to have ice-cream for Christmas. I threw my hands high in the air to rally them around me, clenched my fist and said, 'Let's go. We are the world.' The children who had followed me out of the hotel thought that was a cue. They began singing. *We are the world. We are the children.*

People on the street were perplexed. There was a blonde, middle-aged Westerner leading more than a hundred singing street children down one of the busiest thoroughfares in Ho Chi Minh City. Many people stared in bewilderment. Some smiled. Some even applauded. Our voices were raised in a song that could be heard for blocks.

At the ice-cream parlour I noticed some of the children were huddling together and whispering among themselves. Then a little boy who sold maps on the street came forward. Very slowly he handed me a map. When he handed me the map the children looked at each other, and at a signal, said in English, 'Happy birthday, Mama Tina.'

For a moment I could not speak.

I was later told that the map was the last one the little boy had. The other children had convinced him to give it to me. They said they would repay him a little at the time. The map cost two thousand dong, about a shilling, but to that little boy it might as well have been a hundred pounds.

I clasped the map to my bosom and tried to control my voice as I talked to the children. 'Thank you. Thank you. Thank you. This is the most beautiful thing I've ever been given in my life. Nothing has ever been given to me with so much love. I know what this map means to you and I want you to know it means as much to me. This is what Christmas is all about. This is the most glorious Christmas I've ever known.'

I wiped away my tears, managed a laugh, held up both arms, and said, 'All right, me darlings. Let's sing one for the road.'

And their little voices, sweet as a heavenly choir, came back: *We are the world. We are the children.*

21

That Christmas was a turning point. Even though the day had not erased the memory of that Christmas following my mother's death, it had made it OK. Far more important was what the party had done to others. For a few hours there had been no divisions of race, age or wealth, there had been only fun. And those children now had a good memory of Christmas. Children need good memories.

A few days after the party, the Deputy Chief Prosecutor in Ho Chi Minh City asked if I would speak at one of the local language institutes. He was an administrator at the school and he wanted me to talk about my life and about my work with street children. Of course I agreed. It was very important to me that the Vietnamese authorities, especially in the area of law enforcement, became knowledgeable about the street children.

When I arrived at the school I talked first with the faculty and the administration. I told them about my dream, about Huong and Hang, and about my plans for working with street children. Then the prosecutor asked if I would talk with the students.

For a while I talked to the students in very general terms. When I asked them, 'What do you think of street children? How do you see them?' the students looked at me and at the administrators who had come into the classroom. They were reluctant to speak.

'Don't be afraid,' I said to them. 'Only by telling me what you feel can I understand and help.' I pointed to the Prosecutor, Mr Bong, and said, 'Mr Bong here is interested in helping the children. That's why he asked me here tonight. He is interested in having a better understanding of their way of life.'

The students began to loosen up.

'Street children are dirty,' one said.

'They are not educated,' said another.

The comments, all negative, poured forth.

'They are pickpockets and thieves.'

'They have no place in society. They should all be taken to the camps.'

'I don't like them. No-one likes them. They are dangerous.'

'They have no future. They are very stupid.'

I waited and said nothing until all the students had spoken.

'I understand why you say this and I understand why you see them as you do,' I said. 'But have you ever talked to them?'

No-one in the class had ever talked to a street child.

'Have any of the street children ever picked your pocket or hurt you?'

Again, no student had been a victim nor did any of them know of anyone who had been the victim of a street child.

'Let's change the subject,' I said. 'Rather than talking about the street children, let's talk about me. What do you think of me? What is your feeling about me?'

They looked at each other in confusion.

'You seem to be a nice lady,' one student said. Several others nodded in agreement.

'Do you think I'm stupid?'

They shook their heads.

'Do you think I'm dirty or a thief? Do you think I have no future? Do you think I will pick your pocket?' The students' faces showed bewilderment.

'I want to devote my life to working with the street children here in Ho Chi Minh City, so do you think I have nothing to offer to your society?'

Vietnamese students are very courteous. By this time they were all shaking their heads.

'Well, suppose I told you that I was once a street child. Suppose I told you that I have lived their life, that I was dirty, miserable, sick, hungry, sad, and in desperate need of a friend. Suppose I told you I had absolutely nothing and that other children wouldn't play with me. Suppose I told you that I was once all the things these street children are.'

They shook their heads in disbelief.

The importance of having these students, the future leaders of their country, understand about the street children overcame me. 'I now have three children of my own. My children are educated. Now I am trying to help street children because I understand their life. I was everything they are. All I needed was a chance. All I needed was for someone to love me, to believe in me, and to give me a chance. All I needed was one friend, one person who did not reject me.'

'You are a foreigner, a Westerner,' one student said. 'That's different.'

'Yes, I'm a foreigner to you. But first I'm a human being. The only difference between us is the difference we construct. Once you understand the children and love them, I promise that you will find they are no different from you. Of course, they are not as fortunate as you. If they steal, it is because they are hungry. If they go up an alley at night it is because they need a safe place to sleep. If they seem aggressive, it is because when they go up that alley they don't know if they will come out.'

I could see from the faces of the students that they had never considered this. Even more important, I could see from the faces of Mr Bong and the other administrators that *they* had never considered this. Although I was speaking to the students, it was Mr Bong whom I wanted to reach most urgently.

'Try to get to know the street children,' I said. 'See them as they are. Learn about them. Maybe you can help them. Maybe one day they will sit where you are sitting with the same rights you have.'

I looked at Mr Bong and I shrugged. 'I am a foreigner,' I said, 'and a white woman. I think it is better if Mr Bong talks to you. I don't have the right to stand here and lecture you. I am nobody. I just happen to love children from whatever corner of the earth they come from. I believe children have rights, that they have a right to freedom and choice and justice. Otherwise, what is the point? It is better to die in the womb than to live a life of suffering and nothing.'

Then Mr Bong talked to the class in Vietnamese and told the students it was their responsibility to learn more about the street children and that, after all, the street children were Vietnamese. 'These are our children,' he said.

I knew then that I had the Deputy Chief Prosecutor of Ho Chi Minh City as a friend. I did not know if he would be a supporter, but I knew he had looked into my heart and had not turned away.

A third thing that grew out of the Christmas party involved Huong and Hang. Every day after their parents had sent the little girls out begging, they came to me. The father would make the aeroplane motion with his hands and stare at me imploringly. I could not of course take his children but I did manage to locate the girls' uncle and aunt who agreed to accept not only Huong and Hang, but, if some financial assistance were provided, the parents also. I begged and scrounged enough money to buy the father a cyclo and put him in business. So Huong and Hang found a home and, at my insistence, were sent to school. Today they live outside Ho Chi Minh City and are no longer street children.

I could go no further with Huong and Hang. The children who were responsible for my staying in Vietnam had found a home of their own. For months afterwards I visited them and took them dolls and made sure they were not back on the streets. But there were many other children to help.

As much as I dislike formal organizations and bureaucracy, I realized that I had to become organized. But I had no money, no office, and I spoke only a few words of Vietnamese. How was I to realize my dream of helping street children on a large-scale permanent basis?

One day I went for a long walk in order to decide what to do. I still didn't know the city very well and was heading nowhere in particular. I had prayed and I knew that God would direct me to a place where the answer could be found. I walked around the downtown area, by the waterfront, and then back up Dong Khoi past the Caravelle and the Continental hotels and out beyond the business district.

After a while, I don't know how long it was, I looked up and found myself in front of a Catholic church. It was a beautiful red-brick church built during the French colonial period with imported bricks. There is a small island of green in front of the church and in the middle is a statue of the Virgin Mary.

I sighed. This must be a mistake. I don't like churches, particularly Catholic churches. But I had asked God for direction so I must be here for a reason. I went inside, to the front pew, and I knelt and prayed. 'God, you know I don't like coming into these places. But I've come to explain to you, to show you how much I have to do this. It doesn't matter how many people I talk to. You are the only one who knows how hard I have fought. My dream, everything that has happened in my life, there was a reason for these things. They have been my education. Now please tell me what to do.'

I kneeled there for more than an hour. But nothing came to me. I was soaking wet from perspiration. Then, almost as an act of desperation, I left the pew and walked up to the altar where I prayed aloud: 'God, I have seen so much pain and suffering here in Vietnam. It's hurting me a lot, God. That pain and suffering is inside me now. I could leave this place and cut it all away. I could do that and I could justify it. But I can't turn my back.'

In my confusion I cried out, 'God, you have to help me find a way. I don't know what to do.'

For long minutes I stood there waiting. I heard nothing. God was not telling me what to do. I turned and walked slowly from the church and stood on the street. I did not know where to go or what to do. My heart was heavy. I had talked to God but received no answer. In my despair and pain and confusion I started walking. I walked as I had walked so long ago in Dublin, my hands in my pockets, my head down, my shoulders hunched. I walked for hours.

It was on that walk that I came upon the orphanage.

22

After leaving the church I walked past the Reunification Palace. Drawn by something – I do not know what – I went across the wide expanse of Dien Bien Phu Street and its throngs of bicycles and cyclos and motorbikes. I walked a few blocks, ignoring the hustle and bustle of what is one of the busiest streets in Ho Chi Minh City. I did not know and still less cared where I was going. Then I turned and walked up Le Qui Don. Suddenly I stopped. I looked up and saw a sign for Tu Xuong Street. I turned and walked down the street. All my senses were suddenly alive and I knew that the reason I had come to this quiet part of town was about to manifest itself.

A few doors down the street I stopped and listened. What was that noise? I walked a few more steps, stopped in front of a green gate, and listened again. I heard children. Many of them. They were crying. I looked up and over the gate a sign said Ba Muoi Tam Tu Xuong, or 38 Tu Xuong Street.

A security guard was at the gate. He stared at me impassively. I tried to talk to him but he did not speak English and my Vietnamese was not good enough to get my meaning across. He called to a young girl within the compound. 'Hello,' she said. 'Hello. Hello. Hello.' I thought that was the extent of her English, but then she stopped and asked, 'You American?'

'No. Irish.'

She smiled. But I could see she did not know what that meant. And I thought everyone knew of us.

Another young girl came out and stared. At that time there were not many Western women in Ho Chi Minh City. They all presumed I was Russian.

'Can I come in and see the children?' I asked.

The security guard and the two girls turned and looked over their shoulders. They stiffened in deference at the sight of the person approaching. It was a woman with black wavy hair pulled back and tied in a bun. She walked very upright and her face was stern. She was wearing traditional black trousers with a loose white blouse. On her feet were sandals. She was obviously in charge of the compound.

This was Madame Nguyen Thi Man, one of the most self-possessed and poised people I've ever met.

With help from one of the employees who spoke a little English and through a lot of gestures and slow speech and repetition, Madame Man and I communicated. She understood that I wanted to come in and visit the children. She looked at me, unblinking.

'Where are you from?' she asked as we walked slowly across the compound.

'I'm from Ireland but I have lived in England for many years.'

She escorted me inside the building. It was dark and dismal, and inside were lots of children crying and screaming. It was obviously an orphanage of sorts. In one room there were a few rusty iron cots. Children, sometimes two or three in a bed, appeared very sick. Their heads hung off the beds and their eyes were glazed with pain. Many had open wounds. Many wore bandages that clearly had not been changed for days. A terrible odour of urine and faeces permeated the air. The nurses appeared to have been plucked from the dark ages. They were barefooted and wore old-fashioned little hats.

Madame Man escorted me upstairs. The top floor was divided into wards where handicapped and disfigured children were housed. I looked at Madame Man with a question in my eyes. What could cause such horribly mutilated children?

'Agent Orange,' she said.

I looked around in horror as I realized for the first time the pervasive and long-lasting effects of the war with the United States. Later I was to find that Vietnam has the highest rate of skin cancer and the highest rate of unusual forms of cancer of any country in the world.

I knew then that Vietnam had not won the war. No-one ever wins a war. And while the history books will record the war with America as a great victory for the Vietnamese, it is perhaps the most Pyrrhic victory in history.

After a while I gathered the courage to go from child to child. Instinctively I picked up many of the children. I felt I wanted to love them all.

Madame Man, by not speaking, gave me implicit permission to continue. I went to each and every one, picking them up, caressing them, kissing them, loving them. I wanted to hold every child in that orphanage. Children need holding and loving. Within minutes the toddlers were reaching up and tugging at my slacks. Their little hands were coming from all directions. As I looked at their faces and their imploring hands, a sudden shiver went down my spine. Those little hands were the ones I had seen in my dream.

God had not only sent me the dream; He had led me to the place where the dream could come true. From that moment on I had no doubt that I was where God wanted me to be and that I was doing what God wanted me to do. That knowledge gave me more confidence and more assurance than I have ever known. Now it did not matter what barriers might be put in front of me. They would merely be a test of my faith. This orphanage would become my heart, my home, my base of operations.

In one shining moment, standing in the midst of that place of horror, I knew I was doing what God wanted me to do. I sat on the floor and gathered an armful of children and pulled them into my lap.

At last I was home.

At last I could begin my work.

I cried for a long time.

Then Madame Man and I walked downstairs. As I prepared to leave, I looked around that bleak and desolate ward where there were so many needs. I pulled out all the money in my purse, the equivalent of about one hundred dollars, and gave it to Madame Man.

'Take it,' I said. 'Take it and use it for the children.'

She accepted the money but said nothing. Now I was becoming excited. If this was where I was going to work, I had to start now.

Madame Man and I stepped outside and I noticed in the rear of the compound an empty broken-down wreck of a building. I pointed to the building and said to Madame Man, 'Would you let me build a centre for the children there, in that building?'

She said nothing. I was going to have to prove myself to this woman.

'It will be for the children,' I said. 'For the sick, the poor, for the street children.'

Then Madame Man spoke. In a slow and magisterial voice she said, 'You are a rich lady from the West?'

'No. I am a poor lady from the West. But I was an orphan. I lived on the street. I understand the way of life of the poor. Will you trust me? Will you let me build a medical and social centre here? Say "yes" and I will do everything I can do to help the children of your country.'

'Why do you want to do this?'

I told her about my dream. I told her about Ireland. I think she understood.

When I left I said, 'You will see me again. I promise.'

A small smile tugged at her lips. She knew I would be back. Vietnamese people are not as spontaneous or as demonstrative as we Irish. I knew it was the wrong thing to do, but I could not help reaching out, hugging her, and kissing her on the cheek. She was undoubtedly surprised. And I like to think she was pleased.

I bounced out of the compound on to Tu Xuong Street and was overcome with sudden exhaustion, physical, mental, and spiritual. I felt utterly drained. And then I realized that I had wandered the streets for hours before I found myself in front of the orphanage and that I had no idea how to find my way back to the Rex. I waved down a cyclo and sank into the seat. When I arrived at the hotel I remembered I had given all of my money to Madame Man. I had to run upstairs and dig out a few dong to pay the cyclo driver. I was almost broke. Within a few days I would have to leave the Rex. If I could not support myself, what could I do for the children?

I sat in my room for a long time wondering how to go about my new-found work at the orphanage. I knew this business had to be official. I had to have the sanction of the Vietnamese government. That meant a trip to Hanoi to get permission to work with children. I also had to put my plan and my goals on paper. I would have to prepare a report of what I had seen and what I wanted to do.

I laboriously wrote everything down on hotel stationery. And then I used a borrowed typewriter to type it all up. This took several days. I began making the rounds asking for donations, at first with great energy and a light heart. People would not fail to support such a worthy project. The project manager for BP Oil turned me down. He said what I wanted to do was impossible. I couldn't count the number of Japanese businessmen who dismissed my idea out of hand. They did not want to think about children. Many foreign businessmen were in Ho Chi Minh City to buy rice. The Mexicans, Taiwanese, Germans, all turned me down. The feeling seemed to be universal in the business community that there were so many poor and abandoned children that what I wanted to do was negligible. Whatever I did would be an insignificant drop in the ocean. Everyone was so negative.

Whenever I had a meeting with foreign businessmen they all wanted to meet at the Floating Hotel. The dining room there is the finest in the city. Every time I had a meal there I took a plastic bag with me and ordered the largest pizza or the biggest dish on the menu. I knew I could eat only a part of it. The remainder went into my bag and I gave it to the children. If a waiter came to clear the table, I pushed his hand away. 'Leave that. I'm taking it,' I said.

This was very embarrassing to the expatriates who hung out in the dining room. After all, this was Vietnam and things are the way they are. People don't like to be reminded of poverty and disease and hunger.

After several weeks I was exhausted and depressed. My visa was about to expire. I was broke. I wondered how God could show me so clearly what I was to do and then put so many obstacles in my way. I wondered if I had been right to assume that I was doing what God wanted me to do. If God were interested in this business, it should have gone a lot smoother.

My only good memory of those early days is the time I spent on the street with the children. I spent hours every day and night with the children. I sang with them. I danced with them. I walked and played with them. The people in Ho Chi Minh City began to look on me as an Irish oddball, the woman who spends all her time with those wretched and dirty little children.

I had about reached the end of my rope when I went to see a chap named Jeremy Martin at Enterprise Oil. I told Jeremy about the Medical and Social Centre I envisaged. He was very polite and he listened but I could see he was not convinced.

'Come with me,' I said. I stood up and seized his hand. 'I want you to come with me and see what I am talking about. I want you to see the children.'

'No, no. I understand,' he said.

But I insisted. And so he came with me to the orphanage where I picked up a little boy and put him in Jeremy's arms. 'This little boy has no father,' I told him. The boy stared at Jeremy with dark haunted eyes.

I started to tell Jeremy again how needy the street children of Ho Chi Minh City were and how a Medical and Social Centre would help them. As I was talking the little boy reached up and put his arms around Jeremy's neck and snuggled close.

Jeremy cleared his throat. 'Let me talk to the accountant,' he whispered.

He walked out wiping his eyes.

'Thank you, God,' I said.

A few days later Les Blair and Tom Newman, executives of Enterprise Oil, came to the orphanage and listened as Madame Man told them her needs. A week later the officials of Enterprise Oil invited me down to An Phu, an area on the south side of

Ho Chi Minh City where many expatriates live and work. I presented my report and explained yet again what I wanted to do.

They asked me why a Medical and Social Centre? I said the medical side would take care of the physical needs of the street children while the social centre would care for those who were not physically sick, but who were orphans or who had been abandoned. It had to be both.

These men were tough business people and they asked tough questions. Never was I more aware of my lack of education than I was in talking with them. It should not have been so, but in my heart I felt if they rejected my idea, it was me they were rejecting. I was torn between the fear of being rejected again and the knowledge that my dream had brought me here and that I was doing what God wanted me to do.

'Are you a nurse?' one of them asked.

'No.'

'Why do you want to do this?'

I told them about the dream. And I gave them a bit of the Irish. Les Blair is Scottish. He knew what I was doing and he smiled. I decided then that being Scottish is almost as good as being Irish.

When it was all over, the manager said to me, 'We'll come and have a look.' Madame Man was contacted and approved the visit. The executives came to the orphanage, looked around, and agreed that something needed to be done. But of course they said they wanted to go away and discuss the issue further among themselves.

They were very thorough and very businesslike and I knew that my idea had to make good business sense to them or they simply would not give me the funding. Two weeks of silence later Les Blair called and said,

'Christina, we've made a decision. Meet me at the Rex and we'll talk.'

I was terribly worried. His voice told me nothing. 'Can't you give me a bit of a hint, Les?'

'See you at the Rex.'

'OK. See you there.'

We sat in the sunshine and made small talk. I drank coffee and Les had a beer. I looked around at the pools where my street children had tried to scoop out the fish. They were still and calm now, in contrast with my turbulent feelings.

Les could see how anxious I was. I wondered when he would get to the point. He wanted to talk about a thousand other things. Suddenly he smiled and said, 'Christina, we are donating ten thousand dollars.'

I looked at him and then I jumped up in the air and shouted with pure happiness. I applauded Les. I kissed him on the cheek and said, 'Oh, God, thanks. This is fantastic. This is the beginning. This is the beginning.'

23

I was now out of money and had to move from the Rex into a small room in a house on Le Loi that was owned by an expatriate. He used the house as an office. One of the three vacant rooms was given to me rent free. The Vietnamese staff prepared their lunch in the house and I ate with them. It was my only meal each day. All the money I had received from Enterprise Oil was going into the renovation of the building at Madame Man's orphanage. Already I referred to it as 'the Centre'. I had no money of my own at this time and I became very thin and weak.

I couldn't write and ask my children for money. They were worried enough without my sending them letters asking for money. Once during those days I was so hungry that I walked into a hotel restaurant to ask for food. As I was waiting, I saw a European tourist take a few bites of his meal then get up and leave. I quickly made my way towards him, smiled, touched him on the arm, and said a few words. The poor bewildered man walked on, paid for his meal, and left. I sat down at his table and began eating. When a waiter walked up and questioned me, I pretended to be very angry.

'That was my husband,' I said. 'He had an appointment and had to leave. Now get away with you and let me finish my meal.'

Madame Man suggested several times that I go to Hanoi to get permission to work with the children.

But I used the excitement of bringing in architects and talking about plans for the old building as an excuse for delaying the trip. We had to decide whether we should knock the old building down and start over, or if we could renovate it. In the end, we kept the staircases and a few walls, but virtually everything else was rebuilt.

We finished what was now called the Children's Medical and Social Centre on 23 December 1990 – my forty-sixth birthday. But we could not open it because we had only the building. There was no equipment.

I needed more money to staff the centre with doctors, nurses and aides, to buy medicine and equipment, and to buy food and medicine for the children. I needed money to start a school and to begin various social programmes for children. The needs were endless. But the most pressing need of all was for medical equipment. To equip the Centre and turn it into a true paediatric clinic would cost a fortune. The money-raising had to continue.

Once again I began making the rounds of foreign businessmen in Ho Chi Minh City. Neil Rigden was an English consultant who had been sent to South-east Asia to take charge of drilling operations for Enterprise Oil. I took him to the Centre, told him what I was doing, and asked if he would help. He gave me a cheque for nine thousand dollars.

Neil Rigden had been in Singapore before he came to Vietnam, and he knew of a priest there with a very wealthy diocese. He gave me the priest's name and phone number and I was off to Singapore. I knew the Catholic Church was very good at taking money from people who had it. I was about to find out how good it was at giving money to people who needed it.

I borrowed money for the airline ticket. When I arrived in Singapore I called Father Simon, told him who I was and what I was trying to do. He said he would take me to lunch the next day and we would discuss it further. I also called on a number of Neil Rigden's friends in the oil business. From them I extracted promises to send donations amounting to about three thousand dollars. I knew the money would arrive soon in Vietnam. I was excited. This trip was proving promising. But I hoped the big money was going to come from Father Simon.

Father Simon looked the part of the priest who leads a flock of millionaires. He arrived in a big Mercedes that glittered in the sunshine. He wore a gold watch and fancy leather shoes. His nails were manicured. He was smooth and polished and his voice was soft. This man had the resources to turn the Children's Medical and Social Centre into a fully operational reality.

I was wearing what I usually wear – blue jeans, tee-shirt and sandals. The *maître d'* turned us away from the first restaurant, because of my attire. Father Simon smiled and suggested a nearby cafeteria. It was a very grand cafeteria.

Until its recent lifting, most countries honoured the trade embargo against Vietnam that had been in place since 1975 and, as a result, the country shows the terrible cumulative effects of isolation. Many of the basics most people take for granted, such as fresh milk, were almost impossible to find in Ho Chi Minh City when I first arrived. Everywhere I looked in Singapore was opulence and abundance. The cafeteria where we sat had more food than I'd ever seen in one place. In fact, there was enough food on Father Simon's plate alone to feed many children. But he did not seem too interested in it. His eyes roamed around the restaurant as I talked.

I was exhausted. My months of working at the Centre and of raising money had worn me out. But I tried to make polite conversation with Father Simon. He could do so much for me. In an effort to seize his attention, I told him about the Catholics in Vietnam.

He smiled. 'They say they are Catholic, but they are not. They are pretending.'

I did not know what he meant, but I came to the point. I told him about me, about the Centre, and then said, 'Father, can you help me?' I suggested that he visit the Centre and see the work that was being done.

He nodded and said that he was having a meeting that night with some of his parishioners and he would let me know before I returned the next day to Vietnam.

I was running late the next day. There were more oil company people to talk to and I had to buy two big teddybears for the children. It was time for me to catch my flight back to Vietnam and I had not heard from Father Simon. I waited and waited. I was biting my fingernails. Father Simon was going to help. I knew it. I just knew it. Then, at the very last minute when I was about to dash to the airport, a messenger arrived. He had two parcels from Father Simon, one big, one small. The small parcel felt like a stack of money.

'Oh, thank you, God. He's given me the money,' I thought to myself. But I didn't want to open the packages then. I wanted to wait until I was in the Centre and could open them in front of Madame Man and the staff and the children. I wanted them to see the cash when I pulled it out of the envelope.

I was riding the fish flight from Singapore to Ho Chi Minh City, a twice-weekly flight that carried both passengers and cargo. Most of the cargo is fish.

At the airport I was joking with one of the men handling the big pallets of frozen fish. He lifted out a big salmon and gave it to me.

'Take that with you,' he said with a laugh.

I roared. When I stood the fish on its head, the tail came to about my shoulder. It must have weighed sixty pounds. I wrapped a piece of plastic around the middle of the fish and picked it up. As I was going through customs one of my sandals broke. I put the shoe in my pocket. I had one shoe on and one shoe off. The fish was under one arm while the teddies (one was a panda) were under the other. In a sturdy plastic bag I was carrying bottles of fresh milk and other items impossible to buy in Ho Chi Minh City.

Once on the plane, I stood the frozen salmon on its head and stacked it in the space in front of me. It was beginning to defrost a wee bit. I noticed the water dripping off and said aloud, 'Oh God, don't let this bloody fish melt in the aeroplane.'

After an hour the fish was growing rather limp. A great puddle of fish water covered the floor around my feet. But the people aboard were good sports and everyone was laughing about being on the fish flight. They seemed highly amused by my fish and assorted teddybears.

We landed at Tan Son Nhat and, accompanied by cheers from my fellow passengers, I raced towards the terminal. The plastic wrap around the salmon covered only its middle so the tail and head flopped about. The bag containing the milk was stretching and about to break so I jettisoned a bottle and gave it to an English fellow.

'Do you want some milk?' I said to him. 'It would be lovely in a cup of tea.'

He looked at me and said nothing. He stared at the bottle of milk as if it might be poisoned. You know how the English are.

'Go on,' I said to him. 'Take it. I'm sure you're gasping for a cup of tea with milk.'

'Thank you very much,' he said carefully.

'My pleasure, me darling. Maybe one day you'll give me something for the children.'

Of course Customs were very curious about my hand luggage. They looked at the limp fish with some trepidation.

'No need to worry about him,' I said. 'Just don't put him in that old fashioned X-ray machine of yours or you'll radiate him. He's from Alaska, you know. And he's dead as a doornail. He won't hurt you.'

So, with one shoe still in my pocket, the bag containing milk and other goodies threatening to tear open at any minute, and with a dead fish rapidly defrosting under one arm, I fled from the airport. My first stop was Enterprise Oil. I gave my salmon to the people in the office.

Then I raced to the Centre, sat down with Madame Man and some of the children, and told them about the money that would be coming from the oil people in Singapore. I told them about Father Simon and I held up the two packages and began to open them. The children were very excited.

The large package contained a picture of Jesus' footprints in the sand.

'Ohhh, that's lovely,' I said. 'But I can't feed that to the children.'

The money had to be in the smaller package. I opened it slowly. Inside were several hundred small oblong cards, replicas of the large picture. There was also a note from Father Simon. I pulled it out and read it aloud: 'You are doing wonderful work. God has chosen you to do his will. But you look tired and must take better care of yourself. God bless you. We will pray for you.'

That was it.

I cried.

I gave away the picture of Jesus' footprints and tossed out the little cards. I lay down on a bed and cried and thought of the times when as a child in Ireland with no shoes and nothing in my belly I had gone to the Church for help. Then they gave me prayers to wear on my feet and prayers to eat. Now I needed money to buy food and medicine for the children of Vietnam and the church was again giving me prayers.

Nothing had changed. Nothing had changed.

24

Madame Man did not seem terribly surprised by the lack of support from the Catholic Church. She is a devout member of the communist party and the communists put no faith in the Church. She was much more concerned with the fact I had not gone to Hanoi. She said my concerns about medical equipment and hospital supplies had to take second place to obtaining government permission to work with children. She insisted that I make the trip up to Hanoi and explain to government officials what I wanted to do and how I wanted to do it. Madame Man was very influential in government circles. If she said I had to go to Hanoi, I had to go.

I had been afraid to make the trip. Every time I thought of going to Hanoi I heard the nuns at the industrial school asking, 'What if the communists stood you against a wall and threatened to shoot you? Would you renounce your faith?'

In 1990, when Westerners left Ho Chi Minh City for other parts of Vietnam, they had to have special government permission. This I obtained after a few days and eventually I climbed aboard an ancient Russian propeller aircraft, the only Westerner aboard the flight from Ho Chi Minh City to Hanoi. I was wearing white trousers and a green tee-shirt with a harp and the word 'Ireland' across the front. I wore a green kerchief around my neck. It never hurts to wear the green.

I noticed as I got aboard that the wheels of

the aeroplane were threadbare. Inside, there were no reserved seats. People sat wherever they could. As soon as the door shut there was a hissing noise and a thick fog flooded the cabin of the aeroplane. I panicked. 'Oh my God,' I thought. 'The nuns were right. The communists are gassing everyone just to get me.' I was so scared I almost twisted my colon. The crew never explained anything, but another passenger told me it was some sort of spray for insects.

No-one said anything about using seat belts. Some people stood in the aisles and talked from the time we took off until we landed. It was like a bus trip. Everyone was smoking. When a snack was passed around, I took one look and shook my head. 'That looks like dog,' I said. 'Is that dog?' The flight attendant smiled and shook her head. She did not understand.

At Hanoi airport, which was far out of town, I hired a cab. The road into town was a mass of enormous pot-holes but the driver never showed any signs of slowing down. He drove very fast and refused to give an inch to other road users. I thought we were bound to have a collision, but remarkably, we arrived in the city unscathed.

My appointment with the Ministry of Labour, Invalids and Social Affairs was the next morning. When I walked into the government office at 10 a.m., I was met by three men and one woman seated together along one side of a table in the centre of the room.

'We know you are interested in children and in opening what you call the Children's Medical and Social Centre,' said Mr Nghiem Xuan Tue, Deputy Director of the Department of International Relations in the Ministry of Labour, Invalids and Social Affairs. He was the senior official present. 'We would like for you to tell us why you want to do this. Why does a Westerner want to come here and work with children?'

Everyone held me in their gaze. We were in a conference room where formal meetings are held. The table at which I was invited to sit was oval and made of highly polished blond wood. Mr Tue was flanked by an interpreter and two assistants. I sat on the other side. In between us sat an exquisite vase of lacquered wood containing fresh flowers. Around the edges of the room were straight-backed chairs. The only thing on the walls of the room was a portrait of Ho Chi Minh, to whom the Vietnamese reverently refer as Uncle Ho.

'I know your country is very poor,' I began. 'The Americans have embargoed you for fifteen years. Your government needs money in every area. I am from Ireland. I have no money. But I love the children. That is the reason I want to do this. I have a passion for the children.'

'But why do you care?' asked Mr Tue. 'You are from the West.'

'Yes, that is true. But I was one of them once. I was a street child. I lived a life of poverty, pain, deprivation and abuse. Even though I am from the rich West, I know what it is to live the life these children are living. I want to help. I am asking you to believe me and to trust me.'

'But why Vietnam?'

I told them about my dream but I sensed they did not understand. 'Why does the bee sting?' I said. (I knew by then that the Vietnamese like parables and riddles.)

This was not a good answer so I quickly continued. 'It is very simple. The children are human beings. I'm a human being. It is normal to want to help. That's the truth. Either you believe me or you don't. But it is the truth. I'm a simple person. I'm just a mum.

There is nothing sophisticated about me. I have no social graces.'

Then we talked about the Medical Centre, about the furnishings, the staff, the supplies, everything I envisaged. They explained that they had to be careful not to infringe on the territory of the Ministry of Health.

We talked more. I put the Irish on them. I cried. I waved my arms. I talked incessantly. I could see Mr Tue's mouth opening and closing as he tried to jump in, but I kept talking. This was my one chance and I had to make it work. Finally the poor man just sat back and listened. I talked for more than an hour. I even got down on my knees. I gave it all I had. 'You must trust me,' I said. 'It's for the children.'

It was almost two hours before I finished. Mr Tue smiled, I think in relief, and said, 'We trust you.'

I laughed. 'Ah, you don't trust me, but you're willing to give me the benefit of the doubt. That's OK with me. I must tell you that it is necessary for me to raise money in the West, and to do that I must seek publicity. When I get publicity I promise you now that I will stay away from politics.' I shook my head and threw my arms wide. 'I don't understand politics. All I'm interested in is the children.'

They nodded and smiled. I shook hands all around and stood up to leave. I had walked out the door before I realized that in this country in love with bureaucracy, I needed proof of Hanoi's approval. I needed a piece of paper with signatures and a government seal.

So I rushed back into the room. They were startled and looked up in surprise. 'Can you put it on paper?' I asked.

They did not understand.

'I need a piece of paper. Nothing fancy, you know. Nothing very long. Just a little piece of paper saying

Christina Noble can work with the children of Ho Chi Minh City. No, make that the children of Vietnam. And could you put one of your lovely red stamps on it for me?'

They continued staring.

'I won't let you down.'

They put their heads together and whispered. After a moment Mr Tue nodded. 'You come back at 3 p.m. tomorrow,' he said.

'Tomorrow,' I said before I could think. 'That's going to cost me a few bob for another night in a hotel. I'm trying to save money.'

They laughed when the interpreter told them what I said. But the next day the piece of paper was ready. I held it up and turned to Mr Tue. 'This paper is very thin, you know. Terribly thin. Don't you have anything else?' He waved me out the door. I think he'd had enough of the Irish for a while.

I looked at the skimpy piece of paper in my hand and realized what a treasure I had. This was official permission from the government of Vietnam that said I could work with the children of this country. And it had the lovely red stamp on it.

Mr Tue is the conduit through which all the non-governmental organizations from around the world go when they want to work in Vietnam. Many of those organizations have thousands, some millions of dollars, to spend. It is relatively easy for a government official to grant such a group permission to spend money and to work in Vietnam. But I had nothing except my dream. For Mr Tue to give me permission to work in his country was an act of faith. I love the man. I send him reports every three months and see him about once a year. He has laughed many times about our first meeting and how much I talked. And he has told me that he will never let another Westerner do what I have done. I shall always be grateful to him.

I must say, too, that the government in Hanoi has always been very good to me. I have overstepped the mark several times, not deliberately, but because I did not understand the Vietnamese way of doing business. Each time they lectured me very sternly and let me continue my work.

I remember that not long after my trip to Hanoi I wanted to put on an exhibition of local artists with the proceeds going to the Centre. I went to see the manager at the Floating Hotel and he agreed to host the exhibition. We put together an exhibition of embroidery and paintings. I showed it all to Madame Man and told her what we were doing. The next thing I knew I was being summoned to Government House to have an urgent meeting with an official from Hanoi. I could tell from his face that this was serious.

'You are a guest in this country,' he began, 'and while we are grateful for your work with the children and for everything you do for our country, you must remember that. You cannot go above the head of Madame Man to do this exhibition. You must have government permission first.'

I was very contrite and apologetic and explained that there had been a misunderstanding. I simply had not known it was necessary to get permission for an exhibition. And all the money was going for the children. I thought having Hanoi's permission to work with the children covered this. But evidently it did not.

'Remember,' the official from Hanoi said, 'nobody else is privileged to work as you do in Vietnam. You must obey rules.'

'I made a mistake. I'm sorry. It's not because I meant to go over your head. It's because I'm an ignorant woman from Ireland. I don't understand these things.'

He handed me a thick pile of books. 'You must read Vietnam laws,' he said.

I shrugged. 'They will only confuse me. I like everything simple. Just tell me what I'm not supposed to do.'

He pointed at the books, his face stern. 'You must read these books.'

'I don't want to read them. I will be confused.'

'You read books.'

I took the books.

The exhibition was successful and we raised a few more dollars for the Centre. By then I was living in a room there. I had no money. My breakfast usually consisted of an egg sandwich. Sometimes that was all I had to eat until the next morning. I was too proud to have lunch at the Centre with the staff. It was something to do with my childhood. I do not know how to receive. I must hold my head up. I must have my dignity. I felt I would be losing face by accepting food at the Centre that I was not able to pay for. As a result, however, I was becoming weak and losing a great deal of weight. No longer did the children call me 'Madame Soviet'.

Day and night I was with the children. I kept a close eye on the work being done and I sought to establish new procedures for the staff. One day I went swimming in a nearby pool for a few hours' relaxation. It was very difficult for me to get into a bathing suit and swim in a public pool. But I did it. And I enjoyed myself. A few days later my stomach began swelling. Day by day my stomach bloated until I was in terrible pain. I thought it was a bad case of food poisoning. Then one morning I could not walk. I had resisted going to the main hospital in Ho Chi Minh City, the ten-storey white building at Cho Ray, because I was told if I went in I could not come out until released by a doctor. And I could not afford to spend days and days in hospital. But by now I had to have medical attention.

Most expatriates in Ho Chi Minh City have big chests of plasma, antibiotics medicines of all sorts, virtual hospitals in their homes. In many respects the expatriates are better equipped than the local hospitals. At the first sign of an illness that might grow into a major problem, they jump on a plane for Singapore and a modern hospital. But I had no medicine chest and I was too ill and impoverished to fly to Singapore.

I continued to grow worse. A doctor was summoned to my room. She performed many tests but seemed puzzled. After she studied the results of one test she asked if I had been swimming in a local pool. When I said that I had she told me that rats seeking drinking water sometimes fall into pools. Fear causes them to urinate. Sometimes they drown and their bodies stay in the pool for days. As a result I had contracted this horrible illness. Over the next two weeks I was given twenty-four injections, after which the doctor said, 'Vietnam is in your blood now. Quite literally.'

I thought for a long time about what she had said. She was right. To her words I could only add 'for ever'.

After the great swelling in my stomach subsided and I thought I was on the mend, the fevers began. The most awful fevers and chills and sweats which went on for weeks until I was so feeble I could not even get out of bed. I knew by the expression on Madame Man's face that I was very sick.

One of the aides was Lai, a Cambodian girl who had seen her father beheaded by the Khmer Rouge in the killing fields. One afternoon as she wiped my fevered brow, she whispered, 'Mama Tina is very sick. Mama

Tina must eat.' She offered me a bowl of soup. But I was too weak.

'Mama Tina worry too much about the children,' Lai said. 'Mama Tina need to worry about Mama Tina.'

'Go away. Leave me alone,' I said. When I am ill, I am like a wounded animal and must be alone. Either I will get well or I will die.

Lai was not to be persuaded. 'You sick. I take care of you,' she said.

'Go away.'

Reluctantly, Lai backed from the room. Afterwards my fever became worse and later that night I realized I was near death.

I slowly pulled my hands together in front of me and took a deep breath. My skin was clammy and my body was racked with chills and shakes. I said, 'God, if you are there, if you really exist, listen to me. I'm trying to help the children here. I'm trying to do good. I believe you sent me here. If what I am doing is good and if I am doing it for the right reasons, help me find a way to get well and to get medical equipment for the Centre. Do you understand me? Help me find a way to become strong again. I'm not asking you to do it, I'm asking you to help me find a way to do it myself. But if I'm asking for the wrong reason, if I'm not the person to do this work with the children, maybe it is better you let me die. Maybe it is better if I leave this country. So why have you let me get this far, God, if you're not going to let me go all the way?'

I was seized with such sadness that I cried. I made no noise. I cried silently as my mother had cried. Tears ran down my cheeks until my pillow was soaked. Then I realized that the moisture did not come entirely from tears. I had broken into drenching perspiration.

Then something extraordinary occurred. I knew that

night for the first time in my life that there is a God. I knew, I really knew, that He exists. I was no longer a little Catholic child asking for help, I was a woman reaching out to a greater force. It was then that I actually felt something leave my body. It rose up, hovered above me for a moment, and then left the room. It was up in the air and then away and I was left with a peace I had never known before, a kind of tranquillity I did not know existed.

I thought I was dead. I touched my arm and my skin was cool to the touch. It was not hot or clammy or sweaty. I looked around the room. Everything was the same. But I wondered whether if someone came in they would see me. I wondered if I put my foot down whether I would feel the floor. I slowly sat up and swung my legs around and dropped my feet to the floor. It felt cold. I stood up and walked to the balcony and looked over the compound. Dawn was breaking and in the soft morning light the security guard at the gate saw me. He waved and said, 'Good morning, Mama Tina,' and I knew I was alive. I waved and smiled and then laughed in relief and exultation. 'Hello,' I shouted. 'Hello.' I was alive. I was feeling so light. I went back into my room and lay down and thanked God for my recovery and then I fell into a deep and peaceful sleep and slept all that day and through the following night.

When I awoke the next morning, I dressed and went downstairs to seek out Madame Man.

She smiled and said, 'You look well and rested.'

'Madame Man,' I said to her. 'I am going to call the airport and get on the first available flight to London. I am going to the UK to raise money and to find medical equipment for the children.'

She nodded.

I left the next day.

25

Immediately after landing at Heathrow I went to Surrey where my children lived. They were over the moon to see me, although worried about how thin I had become. We sat around the fire and I told them of my life in Vietnam. We talked until early in the morning. I was too excited to go to sleep. So much was at stake for me. If I was unable to raise the money for medical equipment my dream would end in a renovated but empty building.

I pulled out the old computer I had used when I owned the little catering business, and all that night and the next day I spent going through the telephone book and looking up the addresses of medical and paediatric clinics, medical equipment manufacturers and hospitals, foundations and large companies. I knew nothing about fund-raising. I simply sat down and wrote letters to the sort of people I thought should be interested.

After posting the letters there was nothing I could do for a few days. So I drove up to Birmingham to see my daddy. I told him what I had come home for. He said it had been more than a year since we had seen each other and that since I was going to be very busy for the next few weeks, why didn't I stay the night so we could talk more. Of course I agreed. My daddy was eighty-two. He would not live for ever.

That afternoon he went out to the pub and he was in his cups when he came home. I had already gone to bed.

And, as always when I slept in his house, I left the lights on. When daddy came in, he growled about the lights, and turned them off. In the darkness I sensed what his face looked like. I had seen it so many times as a child.

'Pop, I can't sleep with the lights off.' I got up and turned the lights on.

'I feel your mother around,' he groaned. 'Maybe I'm going to join her. Do you feel your mother's presence?'

He turned the lights off.

I exploded. Years of suppressed anger towards my father, all the things I had felt but never said, suddenly erupted.

'Fuck you. Fuck you. Fuck you,' I screamed. 'I don't have to take this shit any more. Mother is not around. She is not in this room. She's been dead since I was ten years old. You can't make me feel guilty. It was your drinking that caused mam's death. Your drinking caused all the pain in this family. Do you have any idea of the hell you put us through? Do you have any remorse? Don't you care? Don't you wonder why I am middle-aged and can't sleep in the same house with you unless the lights are on? Don't you know I've been in nut houses because of you? I was afraid to walk, to talk, to mix with people. I couldn't remember who I was. And now you stand there shuffling and trying to make me feel bad. Are you trying to kill me? Mother gave us what you never gave us. She gave us strength and love.'

My daddy started crying. 'You are trying to poison me. You are trying to kill me,' he said.

I knew his tricks and I was not having it. I jumped from the bed and faced him. 'No. You poisoned yourself and you killed yourself with alcohol. I refuse to sit here and listen any more to your shit.'

I grabbed my clothes and began dressing. He stood in the middle of the floor crying.

'I'm leaving you, Pop. I drove up here from Surrey in fog and rain to protect you when you never protected me. But nothing is ever enough for you. What do you want me to do – die for you? Well, I'm not dying for you. I don't have to take this any more. I'm leaving. And I never want to see you again as long as I live. You can go to hell. You can go straight to hell, you fucking bastard.'

A few days elapsed and I was about to begin the long tedious process of knocking on doors all over London, following up on my letters, when I received a phone call. My daddy was seriously ill.

I dropped everything and raced to the hospital in Birmingham. My brother Andy said Pop came home drunk one night, fell, hit his head, and suffered a brain haemorrhage. The doctors expected him to die any day.

'All we can do is give him TLC,' one of the doctors said.

Pop was unconscious. His eyes were open but he couldn't talk. He was very grey and his face was drawn; around his eyes the skin was black. Those blue eyes, the most incredible blue eyes I've ever seen, were sunken and bloodshot. When I looked on his face it reminded me so much of my mother's face when she lay dying. All I could think of was that day so many years ago when daddy and I had gone to the Union and he had been given a dying pass for us to visit my mother.

I knew daddy was terrified of dying. He had always had a great fear of the devil and of burning in hell for an eternity. I sat by his bed for days and spent hours talking to him. I told him everything that was in my heart that I had never been able to tell him in the past.

'Don't be afraid to die, Pop. Don't be frightened. You have the sacraments. No-one really knows what happens after death. But there is nothing to be afraid of. You are in a state of grace. You'll go to heaven and you'll meet mammy there. Maybe you'll begin to live again, really live again. I don't know, Pop. Just tell mam we are OK and that we've made it one way or another. Tell her that she's never really left us. Because I wouldn't be here without her, Pop. Tell her that I love her. And I love you too, Pop.'

I knew my daddy could hear me. Even though he couldn't speak, I knew he could hear me. 'Don't be afraid, Pop. Don't be afraid. I will be with you until the end. The end will be the beginning for you.'

Before he died, there was something the little girl in me had to know. But both the little girl and the adult were afraid of the answer; I looked at his flattened nose, his cauliflower ears, his craggy face and I leaned closer.

'There's something I have to ask you, Pop,' I whispered. 'I have to do this.'

I took a deep breath. 'Did you ever love me, Pop? Did you really love me? If you did, try to move one finger. Let me see it. But if you didn't love me, if you never cared, wave two fingers.'

I fearfully slid my gaze down the outside of the covers to where his hands rested. I didn't know what he would do. His hands were large and gnarled from his years in the ring but they seemed so frail that day. I watched for a long time. I looked at his face and I knew he was trying with every ounce of his being to respond. After a long time one trembling forefinger lifted and quivered and for a moment was very steady. That was the only time daddy ever said he loved me. But it was enough.

'Oh, daddy, I've loved you all my life,' I cried out. 'I still believe in you. I never stopped believing that one day you would be the person that you really are when you are not drinking. Without the drink you are such a good man, a good, kind and decent man. There have been many times when I was very angry with you, Pop. But I understand that your life was very lonely and empty.'

I paused to gather my thoughts. The emotions were tumbling over and over in me. And I did not want to cry. Not now. There was so much I had to tell daddy.

'For all that has happened in our lives, Pop, we have grown. We are trying to do the best with what we've managed to salvage of ourselves. If mum was alive, she would have been proud of the fact we never became criminals, we never hurt other people.'

And then I told him of the pain inside me, the sadness I felt, the loneliness, and the difficulties I was experiencing in my life. I told him about Vietnam and the children there.

'Maybe, Pop, this is what God has made for me. Maybe this is my destiny. Vietnam is a communist country, you know. And I know the word communist frightens you. But they are not bad. It's not like the nuns used to teach us. There are thousands and millions of very poor families, children who are starving and diseased and who sleep on the streets.'

I shrugged and managed a laugh. 'They remind me of us, Pop. They struggle and they try to survive the way we did. There is hope in them. When they look at me there is a look in their faces that reminds me of me. I'm lucky, I can see into their hearts and their souls. I see their needs. I couldn't have done it if I hadn't suffered, if I hadn't lived their life. I think that God made all this happen for me. You think I don't like God and that I gave up on Him a long time ago. But I didn't give up on God, I just gave up on the religion part.'

My daddy and I came to terms with each other that day. I knew he loved me. And I felt very serene when

I told him I was soon going to return to my work.

Another reason I had to return, and one that I could not tell Pop, was that I had to go to court in a few days. My home in Surrey was one that Simon and I had shared. It was a house we had because of his job, but I desperately wanted to keep it, not so much for the children as they were grown and could take care of themselves, but as a symbol for me, a place where I could satisfy my need to smell cakes baking in the oven.

Late that night, my son Nicolas came to my room, awakened me, and said, 'Mum, I think something is wrong with granddad.'

Nicolas was covered with perspiration and he seemed very anxious. 'What's wrong? Are you sick, Nicolas?'

'I had a dream about granddad. He was talking to me. I think he's dead. I'm scared.'

I put my arms around him and held him tightly. 'Don't worry, son. Everything will be OK.'

But Nicolas remained very agitated and insisted something had happened to Pop. So I tried to call but could not get through to the hospital.

A few hours later, shortly after 5 a.m., I received a telephone call from Andy: Pop's stout Irish heart had finally stopped beating.

One of the first things I did was ring up Dr Sean O'Connell, the therapist who had been so tender and so caring with me during those troubled years.

'Dr O'Connell, do you think I am strong enough to handle the funeral?' I asked him. 'I'm afraid.'

'You have great strength, Christina,' he said. 'And you have good instincts. Do you want to go?'

'Yes.'

'Then go. You will be fine.'

Philomena flew over from her home in Canada for the funeral.

'Oh, mam,' was the first thing she said when I met her at Heathrow. I thought of our mother when I looked at Philomena. Like her, she looked Jewish. In fact, she was wearing a Star of David around her neck. She stayed at my little house in Surrey and drove up to Birmingham with me and my three children.

I rented a red car for the drive to Birmingham. Kathy was there. All my brothers were there. It was the first time the family had been together since my mother died when I was ten years old.

It was a wet foggy day, typical mid-winter weather in England. Cold and dreary. At the church, I could see my brothers Michael, Andrew and Johnny and some of my father's relatives sitting at the front. Kathy was there with them. Philomena walked down the aisle to join them. But I sat in the back of the church with my children. I didn't want to feel anything. I sat with my head bowed. I didn't want to see what was happening. I could sense my children's anxiety about me and I was trying to be strong for them. But with my family all together there in one place all I could think of were those terrible years in Ireland.

Maybe withdrawing is nature's way of protecting one's sanity. I couldn't allow myself to feel. I had no expression on my face as I looked around the church. When I saw the stations of the cross all I could think of was Ireland.

Then the service was over and they were wheeling the coffin down the aisle. My brothers and sisters were all behind the coffin. As they came up the aisle, Nicolas reached over to hold my hand. 'It's all right, mum,' he said. Androula leaned over and whispered, 'It's OK to cry.' Helen was crying. Nicolas was crying. Androula was crying. But I could not cry.

Except for Philomena, my brothers and sisters did not know I was in the church until they came down the aisle and saw me. Each of us was very much aware of the pain of the past. It was too much to let out. We couldn't afford to remember all that had happened to us and how we had paid for it. So we were almost like strangers with each other. There was a steel barrier around each of us, barricading the love.

Because of the fragmentation of our family, no-one had ever put their hands on us or their arms around us and told us it was OK. There was no love in our house in Dublin. My mother couldn't give us love because she was trying to live with ill health and six kids and poverty and drunkenness and trying to maintain her self-respect. My father was an alcoholic who was incapable of expressing love.

One of the church officials said that I should be in the black car that would lead the funeral procession to the cemetery.

'No,' I said. 'I will follow in my little red car.'

I couldn't have coped being in that hearse with my brothers and sisters. It was too much to ask.

When we came to the graveyard I did not speak to my brothers and sisters. And I did not follow them to the graveside. I saw the hole in the ground and turned back to my car where I waited until it was all over. The grave was close enough for me to watch the priest and see them lower my father into the cold dirt of England. It occurred to me that my mother and my father were buried in separate countries; they were as far apart in death as they had been in life. I thought of how it all began and how it was ending. I had to be very strong because there was so much work to do with the children in Vietnam.

After the funeral the family met at a pub. It is the Irish way. We have a wake for the dead. We meet in a pub and drink and tell stories about the dead person. I hated it. I hated the smell of the pub, the booze and black beer. This is what destroyed my father. I sat there and said nothing.

Johnny came over to me and said, 'You've gone very thin. You've lost a lot of weight. What's wrong?'

I couldn't tell him about my illness in Vietnam or how much pressure I was under to raise money for the clinic or about anything.

'It's better to be thin,' I said.

We all moved to Andy's house where we sat around and looked at each other. No-one would express emotion. No-one would say anything. Then Philomena leaned over and put her head on my shoulder.

'It's finally over now, isn't it?' I said to her.

She broke into tears. 'Mam, I know what you're feeling inside and I know how hard it is for you.'

She sobbed and sobbed. I put my arms around her and said, 'It's OK. It's all over now. It's all over.'

I had to leave. I stood up and said, 'I have to go now.'

My big brother Michael walked up to me and stared at me. He said nothing for a long time. We were both waiting. 'All right?' I said to him.

'All right,' he said.

Then he looked straight into my eyes and said, 'Well, he's dead. Now I can begin to live.' His manner was very calm and he spoke very slowly, but there was so much pain in his voice. Michael had become a very distinguished-looking man. But I saw a little boy in his face. All his life he had been haunted by my father. He had seen my father beat my mother and he had seen the family become fragmented and he carried a lot of guilt.

'Do you ever remember mam telling us she loved us?' he said. 'Do you ever remember being held in her arms? We had no love.' Michael was very angry. And I realized again how our childhood remains with us for ever. That is true for children the world over.

I reached out for Michael's hand. 'I love you,' I said.

He stood there, his face frozen in pain.

I turned and waved at everyone. 'Cheerio. I'm going now. Goodbye.'

I opened the door and was about to walk out when my little brother Johnny called me. Johnny still had the blond hair, fair skin, and big eyes that he had as a boy. Today he has a pub in Zurich called the Oliver Twist. Johnny put his arms around me and hugged me. Then he smiled and said, 'Sis, let's sing one for the road.'

Johnny and I stood there with our arms around each other. My head was on his shoulder because he had grown so much bigger than I. We held each other and sang 'Danny Boy'.

Half-way through the song my brother began crying. Tears rolled down his face. 'Sis,' he said. 'They'll never know. Nobody will ever know. No matter how much you tell them, they will never understand what we went through.'

I nodded.

'Sis, I love you.'

'I love you, Johnny.'

Several months later I returned to Vietnam. By then I had set up the Christina Noble Foundation in London. And I held a document proving the Foundation now had almost £100,000 in a London bank. And following behind me, in shipping crates aboard a boat, were eleven incubators, forty new cots with special hot-weather mattresses, ECG machines, sterilizers, and more medicines than I could possibly list.

In July 1991, less than two years after the day I first arrived in Vietnam, the Children's Medical and Social Centre in Ho Chi Minh City officially opened.

26

Sometimes it seems only yesterday that I was so dependent on Mario that it felt as if I had no life without him. But once I broke out of that marriage and pushed myself through those painful but liberating years of therapy, my life leaped away from all the old restraints. Now many people are dependent on me. And I, who was so weak that even my children considered me something of a mouse, am the strong one whom others lean upon. At the Centre, doctors and nurses and aides and the administrative staff all depend on me to raise the money to keep the place running and to pay their salaries; and the children depend on me to be strong enough to protect them from the world.

For a few months after the Centre opened, the overwhelming need for money lessened and I could devote my time to working with the children. That is how I see my role here in Vietnam. I am first, last, and always, a mum. I am a mum to every street child in Vietnam.

Working with children is a constantly evolving process. One of the first things I did was to build trust between the children and me. And I wanted them to understand that just because they were street children, it did not mean they were nobodies.

I never did like the term *bui doi*. I began calling the youngsters 'my sunshine children'. However, the term *bui doi* is so engrained in Vietnamese society that this is how the children refer to themselves. If they are going to use the term, I want them at least to be proud of it, and I have convinced them that *bui doi* are Number One. When I walk around the streets of Ho Chi Minh City, children will give me a thumbs-up and say, 'Hey, Mama Tina. *Bui doi* Number One.'

As the Centre began to gather momentum with a growing staff and well-established procedures, I realized I should branch out into what I saw as the social aspects of my work with the street children. For months I walked the streets of Ho Chi Minh City at every hour of the day, and I noticed that many of my sunshine children hung out around the clubs favoured by foreigners. They had discovered long ago that intoxicated foreigners are often receptive to buying stamps or coins or maps or souvenirs. I noticed that some of the foreigners seemed too friendly with the children. As the mother of three children I know when an adult is being genuinely friendly or loving or considerate towards a child. It is in the body language and the smile and the demeanour. I also know when an adult has something else in mind. This suspicion was turned into horrible reality when I heard some Westerners calling Vietnamese children 'fresh meat'. And as the children grew to trust me, they came to me with more and more stories about incidents involving foreigners.

It was time for me to look deeper into this. So I took to the streets late at night, the time when the clubs are at their busiest and when there are many children about. I was usually accompanied by two Vietnamese friends. They insisted on coming and were very protective. One is a young artist, a member of a wealthy Vietnamese family, and a man with a deep social conscience. His name is Trung and I have seen him weep at what he witnesses in the streets of

Ho Chi Minh City. In addition to his intensity and compassion he has advanced training in a deadly form of martial arts and he can overcome three or four men at once. I have seen him do this.

The other is Han, a middle-aged bear of a man who was once an army officer. He is quiet and soft-spoken, but when the need arises he has the most intimidating glare I have ever seen. If the glare does not suffice, the self-confident way he can walk into a crowd of late-night revellers causes them to drop silent.

When I go out at night Trung and Han stay very much in the background. They do not interfere even if I am having a confrontation with a foreigner. I have instructed them to do nothing but watch while I do what I must do. No matter what they see or hear, they are to remain invisible unless I signal them to come forward. I believe I can take care of most situations by myself. But Han and Trung are very alert and they can be by my side within seconds.

There is a rhythm to the nights in Ho Chi Minh City. Early in the evening there is an air of excitement and anticipation. About 10 or 11 p.m. there is a lull; it is as if the evening is gathering its breath and summoning its energy for the period around 1 or 2 a.m. when people leave the clubs and the streets seem to explode with energy. Watching the foreign men as they leave the clubs, one can sometimes sense in them a reaching-out for sexual excitement.

Early one evening a group of my sunshine children came to me and said an *anh* – the Vietnamese word for an Englishman – was giving beer to a young Vietnamese girl. They told me her name. She was ten years old but appeared to be no more than eight. I remembered her for two reasons: first, she had to earn money for her parents, and, second, she once told me she wanted to be a lawyer when she grew up.

I searched for some time before I found her. She was going into a hotel accompanied by a very tall man. I ran after them and caught them in the lobby, just about to enter the lift.

'Hey,' I shouted.

The man turned around and stared at me, not sure it was he who was being addressed.

'Why are you bringing this child here?' I demanded. 'She is only ten years old. You don't have the right to bring her here. She is a baby.'

The Englishman was astonished. 'And who might you be?' he said indignantly. He was so drunk that he swayed as he stood in front of me.

'My name is Christina Noble. And I work with the street children of Ho Chi Minh City. This child has been in my care.'

The Englishman smirked at me in a very patronizing fashion and remarked, 'An Irishwoman with a Mother Teresa complex.' It was clear from his tone of voice that he thought we Irish are the scum of the earth. He was one of those very proper public-school boys of whom England is so proud: about thirty, well-dressed, educated, and liking sex with little children.

'Would you do that in London with a ten-year-old English girl?' I asked.

'English children don't do this sort of thing,' he said.

'If you tried it in England you would be arrested.' My voice was beginning to rise.

'For God's sake, she's only a whore.' And he turned towards the lift.

That's when I lost my temper. I really lost it. I grabbed him by the arm, spun him around, and shook my finger in his face. I was so angry that my eyes were squeezed almost shut and spittle was flying from my mouth. 'The fact that she lives on the street does not make her a whore. She is a street child. A baby. A *baby.*'

'Please.' He pulled away as if my hands had soiled his shirt.

I grabbed his sleeve again. 'Listen to me. If you put your hands on her, I'll tear you apart.'

An aloof smile appeared on the Englishman's face. His eyebrows arched. I had committed what to an Englishman is the unpardonable sin – I had displayed emotion.

'And do you live on the street too? It would seem so to judge by your language.'

'And it would seem that you are a dick-head. Now take your hands off that child.'

I looked down at the wide-eyed little girl. 'This child doesn't understand,' I said. 'Can't you see how small she is?' The little girl was confused and frightened. She had been visibly upset by this exchange between us. I reached out for her.

'Fuck off,' the man said. He raised his hand, I don't know whether to hit me or to push me away.

'You put one hand on me and I'll kill you. No man is ever going to hit me again.' I stepped even closer. I remembered the years of abuse from Mario, all the beatings I suffered from him, all the times he had bashed in my head or broken my nose. I was ready to fly in this man's face. I almost hoped he would hit me. I wanted to strike back. By hitting him, I would be hitting back for street children and abused women everywhere. I would have destroyed that man. He looked into my eyes and he knew that.

He backed away and I took the opportunity to grab the girl's hand and pull her to me. Then we turned and walked rapidly from the lobby, after which I took her straight back to the Centre and gave her a long lecture about foreign men.

After this experience I began having meetings twice a week with large numbers of the children. I cautioned them about the intentions of some foreign men. Vietnamese women are always present to translate so there is full and unfettered two-way conversation. At one of the first meetings the children told me of a foreigner who had been soliciting girls to go to his hotel room. They knew the hotel where this man was a guest and they said he took different girls to his room every night.

For three nights I watched the hotel until early morning but never saw him. On the fourth night, about 1 a.m., a tall Asian man, I guessed that he was Singaporean, walked into the hotel holding on to a little girl in each hand. They looked to be no more than five or six years old. Babies, they were. I raced to the door and saw him walk the girls past the staff in the lobby, none of whom said a word. He got into the lift about the time I charged into the lobby. I kept one eye on the indicator over the door of the lift as I strode to the desk.

'My name is Christina Noble and I work with the street children of Ho Chi Minh City. I also run the Children's Medical and Social Centre.' I heard my Irish brogue becoming broader and broader. It happens when I become angry. The man at the desk stared at me in confusion.

'A foreigner just came in here with two children.' I looked over my shoulder and saw the lift indicator stop. 'They are on the third floor.'

The receptionist stared blankly. He could not imagine what I wanted.

'If you don't go up and bring those children down, I will ring the Chief of Police and the Deputy Chief Prosecutor, Mr Bong. I know them both. They are close friends.'

The people at the desk were shocked and began muttering to each other.

'Get me the manager,' I ordered. 'Send him here immediately.'

A few moments later the manager, a well-dressed and polished gentleman, came towards me rubbing his hands. Before he could speak, I told him what was going on. 'Two children are up on the third floor in a room with a foreigner. Vietnamese children. Babies. Your government has very strict laws to protect these children. I shall make a report to the Chief of Police if you don't do something right now.'

The manager sputtered in Vietnamese and wrung his hands and tried to make out he did not understand. I was having none of it.

'You speak English. I know you understand me. You go up there now and get those children or I will. I'll break the door down. Your government has said no children are to be taken into hotels by foreigners or other strangers.'

The manager shook his head. I went to the door and shouted for Trung to come inside. Trung explained the situation in Vietnamese, but the manager would not give in. The two chattered back and forth and I saw this could take ages. In the meantime those two little girls were upstairs.

'That's enough,' I interrupted. 'You either get those kids out of that room now, this minute, or I'm going up to break down the door. Then I'll call the police.'

The manager needed no translation. He picked up the telephone, turned his back to me, and began speaking very urgently. I don't know what he said but a few minutes later the man stepped out of the lift with the two little girls. They were soaking wet. He had been bathing them before he took them to bed.

'Why did you bring these little girls here?' I asked. 'They are children.'

He went very pale. Some foreigners think they can do these things with impunity in Ho Chi Minh City. Poverty – not just doing without clothes or goods, but a poverty that causes starvation – causes many young Vietnamese girls to drift into prostitution. What this man was doing was no different from what dozens of other men do in this city every night. But I intended to break that cycle.

Not in his wildest dreams did this man think anyone would care what he was doing. He appeared almost in shock. But he was calm.

'They are only street children,' he said.

'You are from Singapore?'

The man's eyes widened.

'If you found children on the street in Singapore, would you take them to a hotel and abuse them? Would you take your own children into a strange room and abuse them? Do you think that because they live on the street they can be treated like this?'

'In Singapore we don't have street children.' He was regaining confidence. 'You should mind your own business,' he said.

I snatched the children from him.

'You've been doing this on a regular basis. We have witnesses who have seen you. I'm telling you to leave little girls alone. If I ever find out you have touched another Vietnamese girl your photograph will be in every international newspaper in South-east Asia. I will personally contact the newspapers in Singapore and tell them what you were doing.'

He looked me up and down. 'Just who do you think you are?'

'I told you. My name is Christina Noble and I work with the children of this city.'

'You're nobody,' he blustered.

But he was a beaten man and he knew it. I pulled the two little girls to me and looked for a long time into the man's face. 'I want to remember your face,' I said to him.

Afterwards, Trung and Han reminded me that what I had done was very dangerous. I had no authority to go into a hotel and demand that a guest be sent to the lobby. I had no authority to ask questions of the manager and take the girls from a guest. I could have got into severe trouble again with the authorities. I knew that of course, but my instincts as a mum were stronger than my sense of the law.

In the weeks to come I discovered much more about how foreigners seek to take advantage of children here. Even though I grew up on the street, in many ways I had remained terribly naïve about the ways of the world. But I was learning.

I found, for instance, that Burmese children are kidnapped and forced to work in Thai brothels. Later, if they are tested HIV positive, they are given lethal injections.

I found that men from several Arab countries travel to Pakistan in order to buy children – boys and girls – and take them home. The girls are sold into prostitution. The boys who end up as prostitutes are lucky; the others are tied to the backs of camels during camel races. As the camels speed across the desert the boys become hysterical with fear and begin screaming. The screams make the camels run faster and faster. At the end of a race some of the boys are near death.

I found that Taiwanese men come to Vietnam to buy twelve- and thirteen-year-old virgins. Poverty is so terrible here that some families will sell their virgin daughters for anything up to $2000. The foreigners keep the girls prisoners for several weeks, abuse them daily, and then kick them out on to the street. After such an experience there is nothing for these girls except prostitution. They are damaged physically and emotionally for the rest of their lives.

Late one night I was down near the Saigon River talking to a group of sunshine children. I wanted them to come to the Centre for the night. A man came up and started talking to some of them. He was too far away for me to hear what he was saying. When I asked him what he wanted, he smiled lazily and said, 'Cocaine? You want to buy cocaine?'

I see red at the very mention of drugs. I grabbed that man by the throat and said, 'You bastard! Get the fuck out of here. Get away from these children.'

He shouted something in Vietnamese that I did not understand and cyclos started coming at me from all directions. I was surrounded. At that moment Trung and Han pushed their way through the crowd and pulled me out.

Another night I was riding around in my jeep looking for children in trouble when three kids ran out of the shadows and waved for me to stop. They started to tell me about a man they did not like when suddenly, out of the shadows, a big smiling Vietnamese man approached. He walked straight up to me and said, 'You want sex? You want sex with big man or little boy?'

I stepped out of the jeep. 'Now could you repeat that again, me darling?'

He did. I was reaching for his throat when Trung beat me to it. He threw the man across the sidewalk.

I found that some foreign men like to take children into the cinemas. The same thing goes on in the discos. Some of the discos here are so dark that you can see only by the flashing strobe lights. Men act in here as if they are in bedrooms. They commit sexual acts in public with boys and girls.

This crime is on the increase in Ho Chi Minh City. One reason is because the government of Thailand, historically the world centre for paedophilia, has begun to crack down on sex tourism. Until the last year or so, the target for most of the enforcement efforts was the children, the victims, rather than the perpetrators. But more and more this is changing. So the men who once went to Thailand, mostly English, Americans, Australians and Germans, are coming here. They come to Ho Chi Minh City not only to avoid the Bangkok police; they think that because the American embargo has, until recently, cut off Vietnam from the world there is less danger of contracting AIDS. What they don't know is that Thai men and Japanese men and Taiwanese men had the same idea long ago.

In spite of the fact that the government of Vietnam is taking strong steps to prevent Ho Chi Minh City going the way of Bangkok, you can go into the nightclubs and see foreign men openly looking for children. They stand around the places where the children sell trinkets and extend their forefingers from their clenched fist and then bang their fists together in a gesture that means, 'You and me, we go together.'

Sometimes a man will take a handful of girls or boys, rent a car and go to a seaside resort about two hours' drive from Ho Chi Minh City. In this beautiful remote setting, the man rents a hotel room for a few hours of debauchery with children.

Sometimes the evil that men do is very insidious.

One day I was driving around on my bike and from a distance I saw a foreigner with a group of children. This was another example where, on a purely intuitive level, I sensed something was wrong. As I drove closer I saw the man had a big fancy camera. He was paying the children in order to take their pictures. But before he photographed them he was making them strip off their rags and stand huddled in a puddle of water and stare up at him with beseeching eyes.

The first thing I did was pull the children out of the puddle and have them put their clothes on. Then I sent them on their way. Finally I turned to the foreigner.

'Who the fucking hell do you think you are?' I began in my subtle fashion. 'How dare you take the clothes off these children?'

The man then proceeded to give me his card, saying that he worked for a well-known European charity and that the goal of his organization was to generate financial support for Vietnamese children. He said to do that he was taking photographs which needed to engender sympathy and pathos.

'I have to take pictures like this or people will not respond,' he said. 'The kids agree to do it. It doesn't make them lose their dignity. It doesn't humiliate them.'

'If you believe that, you're stupid. These children are so poor that they will do this sort of thing for the money to survive. But you are stealing their dignity and humiliating them.'

He wasn't having any of it. He shook his head in denial and started to walk away. At that point I tried to snatch his camera but he was too big for me. I later investigated the photographer and found he had earlier been deported from the Philippines because he was suspected of paedophilia. And now he works for a famous European children's charity.

One of my goals is to set up havens for girls who have been abused by foreigners. I want to stop the practice of selling young virgins. I want to stop the practice of kidnapping young girls and selling them into prostitution in other countries. I want to give girls who have been abused an alternative to prostitution. But I can't stop it all. Those girls who have been abused and dumped in the streets, I can help rebuild their lives. The government has opened a house here for the rehabilitation of young prostitutes where they are taught skills and jobs. I am very proud of the fact that my foundation provided the furnishings for the house.

I am proud, too, that the Centre has become well known in Ho Chi Minh City as a place of refuge for children. If you come here, wave down a taxi, and give the driver the address of the Centre – Ba Muoi Tam Tu Xuong. Chances are the driver will turn around, smile in approval, and say, 'Ah, you go see Mama Tina. She good to children.'

27

One day Peter Williams, the British ambassador, came down from Hanoi. Peter is a tall stout man with grey hair and a reddish complexion. He is very distinguished but also a low-key fellow who enjoys a good laugh. Everyone calls him 'Ambassador' and I suppose I should also, but he has become a friend and I call him Peter. He likes me and he reckons I am a bit of a character. I know I can always go to him if I am in trouble.

'You know,' I said to him on one of his visits to the Centre, slipping into the Irish as I pointed at a group of children, 'the monsoon is coming and I've nothing to wash their nappies with. If you buy me a washer, World Vision will buy me a dryer.'

The ambassador was not going to have the United Kingdom made to look mean by a non-governmental organization such as World Vision; the Crown had to carry its share of the load.

'Christina, I'll buy you a washer,' he said.

So then I went to World Vision and said to them, 'If you buy me a dryer, the British ambassador will buy me a washer.'

'Sure, we'll buy you a dryer.'

'And will you have it shipped for me?' I asked.

'OK, we'll have it shipped for you.'

'God bless you. You're good people.'

I don't consider this sort of thing manipulative. I don't consider it politics. I consider it as nothing more than one street child using her wiles to help other street children.

I do the same thing with Vietnamese officials. In the park across the street from the Rex Hotel is a large statue of Ho Chi Minh. He is seated and he has his arm around a little girl and the two of them are reading from a book. It is one of the most popular attractions in the city. In meetings with government officials I pull out a picture of the statue and say, 'Uncle Ho loved children. Look at the expression on his face as he reads to the little girl. I am trying to do what Uncle Ho wanted. Uncle Ho and I are the same in our love of children.'

It works. It is a common meeting-ground with local officials, and it puts me squarely on the side of Vietnam's greatest hero.

The most difficult thing I have to do, and one that continues to cause me great heartache, is dealing with the bureaucracy that is growing up around my work. I am a mum. That is all I am and all I want to be. I want nothing other than to work with the children. But people in other countries can't send aid to a lone mother. They have to have an organization, a structure, and there must be very strict procedures for handling donations. That's why the administrative side of the Centre is handled by professionals.

Madame Man and I are co-directors at the Centre. She supervises the doctors and nurses and aides and takes responsibility for them. If something happened to me the Centre wouldn't collapse. And with Madame Man handling the operational side, I can go out on the street where I like to be. I can work with the children. I can be a mum.

At first I was reluctant to set up foundations elsewhere. But when people abroad give money, I have to answer for it. Donors must have letters of thanks; I have to tell them what I am doing with their money; these are the laws. So, in addition to a foundation in England, foundations were established in France, America and Australia. And I have plans to establish them in other countries too.

Inevitably, there have been problems. In one country, members of the foundation decided they were embarrassed by me – a former street child from Dublin – and they indicated that the foundation should have more class and polish.

'We have grown too large to remain a street-child operation,' one of them said to me.

I disagreed vehemently. 'This will always be a street-child operation. The street children will always be our main concern.'

I am a political novice, but I have around me a few people who are not. We quelled that little rebellion.

Then a group of French television people came out and did a documentary that, when it was broadcast, caused the most tremendous response of anything I had ever known. The French opened their hearts as a nation, and the documentary, since shown in many other European countries, has had a similar response elsewhere. After the documentary was shown in Germany, people started coming out here to see the Centre and to offer their help. They still appear, literally on my doorstep, asking what they can do to help. Sometimes they say, 'Your documentary made me think. Part of me was closed and you made it open up.'

I am flattered that these people should travel so far to see the Centre. They are good people and they have good intentions. But some of them are a wee bit misguided. I opened the door one day and there was a young woman telling me that she was going to build communes all over the world in my name.

'Get away with you,' I said. 'I'm working me fingers to the bone here and you talk of communes.'

Then there was the Canadian hairdresser who had been living in Tibet. He came down out of the mountains to buy food, found an old newspaper, and saw a story about the work here. So he packed up and somehow got to Vietnam. Turning up at the door he said he wanted to be a disciple. 'I've found you,' he said. 'We are going to work together.'

'Get out of here,' I said. 'I need tablets for septicaemia. I need paediatric nurses. I need money to build a school. I don't need disciples.'

I welcome people who want to tour the Centre. And I hope that once they see what we are doing they will lend real support. One day I showed round a group of people from England. One of the men walked around the room saying 'Hi' to every child. They thought he was introducing himself. And as he walked on, the children would point towards him and say 'Hi'.

I have almost no time for anything not connected with my work. I'm sure that's because so much of my early life was filled with suffering, and now, in middle age, the Children's Medical and Social Centre is the most successful thing I've ever done. The children of Ho Chi Minh City are my life.

I used to go to the Floating Hotel one day each week for the buffet. They have the most enormous and varied buffet of any restaurant in the city. You can eat all you want for a given price. I always took Han with me. We would load up our plates and then go to a table. I would eat a little and put the remainder into a bag I had under the table.

'Han,' I said on the first occasion. 'You are still hungry. Go back and fill up your plate.'

'No,' he said, rubbing his stomach, 'I full. I full.'

I shook my head. 'No you're not. You're still hungry. Now go fill your plate.'

So he filled his plate and returned to the table. When I thought no-one was looking, I took his plate and tipped the contents into the bag under the table. This would be a feast for the children. I pushed the plate back across the table. 'Han, you are still hungry. Go and fill your plate.'

One day the manager caught us. Luckily he was a nice man and very kind. 'You know, I don't think it is a good idea for you to do that.' I told him it wouldn't happen again, omitting to mention that it had been going on for months. I kept my word to him. The people at the Floating Hotel have always been very good to me. Now when I have reporters or visitors from abroad we go there and I tell them to heap their plates high. The bag is then slid round under the table and my companions take great pleasure in tipping the contents of the plates into it. I don't do it myself; not after I told the manager I wouldn't.

It has long disturbed me that most of the money and assistance for the Centre comes from abroad. I believe that the Vietnamese should be involved in the Centre. After all, it is Vietnamese children we care for. One way I found to bring my work to the attention of local people is to sing in local restaurants and bars and nightclubs. I still love to sing and dance. And I reckon sometimes it is as much for me as for the children when I get up on stage and sing the songs of Ireland. I used to sing at the Floating Hotel; and as long as I was singing and only occasionally making a quick reference to the children, it was OK. But being very intense and passionate about what I do, once I dropped down on my knees and started shouting about the rights of children and how we are all one world and one love and one child. Some of the guests complained, so the management asked me not to sing about children any more.

I have never been involved with the expatriate community in Ho Chi Minh City. Many of them live in large homes inside walled compounds protected with gates and patrolled by security guards. They probably see life outside as harsh and mean and violent. However, I have made friends with several Englishwomen on whom I am beginning to depend hugely for their support and generosity. Sometimes we go with a group of children to the seaside at Vung Tau. By the end of the day we look like giant red lobsters leading a shoal of shrimps along the golden sands. With the sun going down over the South China Sea it could be heaven.

28

We have come a long way in a short time. I'm talking less of the building and the equipment and the staff at the Centre than the attitude. To me the attitude we have towards children is far more important than buildings and equipment.

Let me give you an example. The nurses here at the Centre used to shovel food into the mouths of the babies. It was like an assembly line. Now they have been encouraged to feed each child slowly and carefully, they understand they must respect the dignity of the child.

I am very proud of what I have done here. As far as I know, it is the only Centre of its kind in Vietnam. In one sense, it is *all* I've ever done. But it is enough. There are times when I am walking down the street and one of my sunshine children shouts at me from a distance and I am so happy that I laugh and break into a skip and I shout for all the world to hear, 'My name is Christina Noble and I built a hospital and social centre for the children of Vietnam.'

The Centre continues to grow. We have four doctors, two medical students, six nurses, twelve nurses' aides, and any number of workers and handymen. The staff numbers about fifty. There is an Intensive Care Unit which almost daily receives children who are seriously malnourished or otherwise acutely ill. Some have been abandoned. After the worst is over they are moved to the residential care facility where special nutrition and treatment continues. At any given time we have about seventy-five children as patients. We also treat more than a thousand children each month on an out-patient basis. We have vaccinated hundreds of children for polio, diphtheria and other diseases. We treat them for intestinal and respiratory disorders. The root cause of many of their problems, however, is malnutrition.

It costs almost $10,000 each month to operate the Centre, the school, and the outdoor activities. Raising money is a constant and immense pressure. Many times it has been very dicey and very close but I have always met my payroll. I do that by leaving Vietnam several times a year and going on fund-raising trips to England or mainland Europe or Australia or America.

In addition to the clinic, I have opened a school. I call it the Sunshine School. It is situated next to the Centre and has about eighty students. Alongside it we have set up the Sunshine School Programme which assists children in schools elsewhere. We hope pupil numbers will grow to about 350 by the end of 1994. Medical care is given to all these children and a nurse gives hygiene, health and nutrition courses. There have already been success stories amongst our Sunshine School children: Minh Chau for instance. I met him on the streets when I first arrived in Ho Chi Minh City. We became special friends and he attended the Sunshine School; now he is a Buddhist monk working with children in the border province of Ca Mau.

In the spring of 1993 I went to Hanoi for a talk with Mr Tue, the government official who first gave me permission to work with children. I was delighted when he asked if I would open a new Centre in Hanoi. He said the government would provide me with a building near the edge of the city on the airport road.

He said there are 4.4 million handicapped people in Vietnam and that 1 million of them are children. About 400,000 children receive some sort of help from the government, but for the other 600,000 there is nothing. The size of the problem increases daily. As Vietnam changes into a market economy, hundreds, perhaps thousands of children, are pushed into the cities from the countryside.

There is so much more I want to do here. I want to bring in kindergarten teachers from England or America and have them work alongside Vietnamese teachers. I want specialists in physiotherapy and psychology to deal with handicapped children. I need someone to teach braille. I need a centre for the deaf and the blind; I must take the stigma away from those disorders. Just because a child is blind or deaf does not mean that he doesn't have a brain. I want to build a primary and secondary school. I want to build 'nests' around Ho Chi Minh City, places of shelter and safety that the street children can go to each night. They must have a secure place to sleep. Ideally, I would like to build ten nests around the city plus other nests in Hanoi, Vung Tau, Da Nang, Da Lap and several more down in the Mekong Delta. I want to build a much bigger Centre in Ho Chi Minh City, one big enough to hold 400 patients. It would have a special unit for sexually abused children with specialist staff. I want to build the facilities for teaching and training people to work with children. I want a beautiful school for the street children, a school with sports facilities, a music room, an art department, computer technology, domestic science, and training in life skills.

I want to bring American veterans, men who fought in Vietnam, back to this country to build the nests and homes and schools. Those veterans were so young when they were here before. Some of them were little more than children themselves. For some the pain of this country was so great, they have been damaged for life both physically and mentally. Only now are we beginning to discover the horrible things that happened here during the war. Agent Orange was one of the worst. We still have babies being born without limbs, blind, maimed, and with rare types of skin and blood cancer. Vietnam has the highest incidence of skin and blood cancer among children of any country in Asia. I would like former GIs, as rehabilitation, to return here. I offer them the chance to do something positive in this country and to close the gap between our worlds. We must heal each other. It would also show the Vietnamese children that America is more than guns and bombs.

I am receiving help now from many countries and many individuals. The French tend to send food and medicine for the children. The Germans send clothes. The Americans and British send toys and books.

Often I run 'English in the Park', an English-language session in the park across the street from the Floating Hotel. Someday I hope to have a qualified English language teacher to do this.

Every day when I come into the Centre I pause and look to my left. High on the wall is a painting done by one of my sunshine children. The painting keeps fresh in my mind the reason I am here. One day I asked the children, 'What do you want?' I told them to sit down and use their paints to depict for me the things they wanted most in the world. One little boy painted a heart, flowers, sunshine, and a schoolhouse. When I asked him to tell me about the painting, he said the heart represented love, that the sunshine and the flowers represented happiness, and the schoolhouse represented an education. What struck me most about this picture was that it proved once again what I have always believed: all children, no matter where they are from, need essentially the same things.

Occasionally I go to international conferences on children. In 1993 I went to such a conference in Paris. It was sponsored by my old friend, the Catholic Church. Many priests and nuns were there and their presence made me quite nervous. 'There was a time when I used to run from you lot,' I told one of them. The thing I remember most vividly about that conference is how real issues were skirted. There was a lot of talk about setting up bureaucracies and managing staff and administering funds. By the time it was my turn to speak I had heard enough.

'I don't have time to be polite about this,' I began. 'Everyone here is caught up in bureaucracy. We are about children, not about red tape. We can blame whoever we want. At the end of the day it is my fault and your fault and the church's fault. You welcome people with money, but if someone comes to you with a dirty nose and no shoes, you have him wait in the rear. I was one of those children pushed to the back and I know what I am talking about. Today, I am about children. What are you about?'

And then I got to the heart of the matter. 'Let me tell you about one of my sunshine children in Vietnam. She is twelve years old. She has polio. Her body is twisted. But she sells that twisted little body for the equivalent of a shilling. She doesn't do it for fun, she does it because she is hungry. When you are hungry you will do whatever it takes to get food. Those of us who are about children must respond to this directly and stop worrying about bureaucracy. We must remember the children.'

Afterwards, a radio reporter raced out with his recorder and played my little lecture on the radio.

Everyone acted as if what I said were revolutionary. But it's only common sense.

I try to keep very focused about my role here. One way I do that is by living very simply. Everything I own could be put into two suitcases. I live hand-to-mouth in a small apartment in a very rough part of Ho Chi Minh City. It is a five-minute walk from the Centre. Outside my door is a place where homeless people build shacks. Almost every time I leave my apartment I must walk through a group of prostitutes. It breaks my heart.

Living here is sometimes very hard for me. This place is brutal on Westerners. We are not used to the parasites often found in the food and always found in the water. I have an attack of amoebic dysentery at least once every three weeks. It incapacitates me, sometimes for several days. I have had various other tropical disorders. Every time I take a team of doctors and nurses down to Ben Tre province in the Mekong Delta to care for the village children, I become sick. It is the same when I travel up to Loc Ninh on the Cambodian border where a number of tribal groups live and where children are sometimes terribly brutalized.

I miss my own children very much. I miss sitting around the fire with them and hearing what is going on in their lives. Helen, my first child, looks very much like me. She is fair, blonde, exuberant, and has my stubborn streak. And, like me, she displayed a talent for music and dancing from an early age. Like my mother, I was determined that Helen should have voice training. So all the family chipped in with pennies to give her lessons. We lived on beans and toast for days at a time. Today she is under contract to Atlantic Records and has released two albums. She is enjoying a successful career in Europe and has just received her first gold album and an International Star award.

Helen loves her father and talks to him occasionally. She wants him to recognize her pain. She wants to talk to him about her childhood, about her Greek heritage, and the fact that choosing not to marry a Greek does not make her bad. But he has not changed. He has mellowed a bit as he has become older but not enough for his children to be free with him. And they desperately want that. They love him and he loves them. But whatever money he has sent them has always been conditional. He is a typical old-world Greek.

As for Androula, she is tall, dark, and has brown hair with auburn highlights. She was very insecure when she first came to live with me. I asked her 'Are you OK?' so many times that she told me to stop. Androula is a brilliant student, very determined, and has not only won a literary prize, but was once compared to the young Sylvia Plath. Much to our delight, some of her poems have been published. She is currently doing an MA in Social Work at London University, specializing in child abuse. She is quiet, serious, very studious and witty.

From the time Nicolas was born Mario pounded into him the belief that if a man shows emotions or cries he is weak. Nicolas is a very sensitive young man. As a child he frequently measured his nose with a piece of twine. He was afraid he would grow up with a long Greek nose. I told him it was OK to cry, that for a man to cry is a sign of strength and not of weakness, and that he should never be afraid to cry. Slowly he is coming to be his own man. He has studied business and finance and is now working in Edinburgh. But he is still very protective of me.

All my children had when they were growing up was each other, me, and a lot of love. We didn't have material things. But we eventually made a good life for ourselves. I know my mother would be proud of them. My life has been hard, but in compensation, God has given me three of the most beautiful children in the world. They give me the energy I need to go on with my work and with my life. Sometimes I think of my favourite pub in London and of a cheese sandwich and a shandy. I think of meeting friends there, going off with them and having a laugh. I cry from home-sickness. It's hard here, always the same food, the same heat, the same problems.

When reporters come here they see my work and invariably refer to me as a Mother Teresa. I don't know why they do that, it only proves that they don't really know me. I'm not at all like Mother Teresa. Mother Teresa will probably be made a saint one day. No-one will ever put a halo on me. I do all the things a saint wouldn't do. I belt out songs in clubs, songs about strong feelings and anger. I shout about the rights of children. I enjoy a double whisky now and then. I love dancing. I like to ride fast on the back of a Honda. Sometimes I will rent a cyclo, put the driver in the passenger seat and I pedal the cycle as fast as I can down the street. Once a policeman tried to catch me but I was pedalling too fast for him. He tooted his little whistle and waved his white stick and I kicked my foot out and laughed. All at once he bent over laughing. When I glanced back he pointed at me and shouted, 'You very funny lady.' I like lipstick and I like to dress up. Although I detest violence if I have to protect a child by giving someone a wallop, I'll do it. I'm more than a little bit wild. I'm Irish. Mother Teresa I am not.

For me, everything always comes back to being a mother. The child is the lifeline of the world. We can talk forever about the ozone layer and about the environment, but what good is a clean environment if the inhabitants of the world are thugs? A child learns from its elders. If a child is kicked from the womb on to the street, all it knows is segregation and selfishness. Children need love. They need to be listened to. They need to be understood and given a voice. We are the Herods of the modern world. We are murdering our children in a hypocritical and underhand way. Every child, be he black, white, yellow, rich or poor, is our responsibility as a human being.

When I first came to Vietnam I was afraid. I didn't want to feel any more pain. I knew that day in the park if I touched those two little girls that I was in this thing for the rest of my life. And I knew even then it was not going to be easy: I had no money, no education, no business connections and no famous mother or father. I had nothing. Who would take notice of me? How could I help children? I was afraid that putting my arms around them would give them false hopes. I was afraid I would be just another adult who raised their hopes and then dumped them. I was nobody. Who the hell would listen to me?

Of course, when I began here in Vietnam, people said what I wanted to do was impossible. 'You are only one person,' they said. But when I was a child, I needed only one person to understand my suffering and pain, one person to love me. One is very important. There are many ones, and they add up. Sometimes people sit in their homes and they are bored and they say, 'I don't know what to do.' I say to them, 'Go outside your home. Visit the orphanages; go and talk to people on the street, and every time you see someone who is poor or homeless, ask yourself, "If that was my brother or my father or my child, what would I do?"'

It is tempting and easy to think that the only answer to the many needs of humanity is money or food or housing. But these things by themselves will never end human misery and never answer human needs. More than anything else the world needs love. Love and understanding and listening and compassion. We must unite to do this for the children. We must put aside our differences to love the little ones. We must give children unconditional love. It doesn't matter if they are dirty, malnourished, and have every illness that flesh is heir to. What we all can do is look on them in a pure sense. We can see beyond the dirt and the snot and the disease and see them as children. If we give children unconditional love, then many of those other needs will follow.

If we could get people to see each other for what they are, as human beings, there would be no differences. If we could love each other, see each other, touch each other, the differences among people would disappear. But for that to happen we must give children the foundation to grow on. We must water the seeds and nourish the blossom. I believe that children are the purest things in this world of ours. They learn from us. So we adults must question ourselves. We must ask, each one of us, if we are really free of prejudice. We can't say, 'I'm not prejudiced, but I don't want my daughter to marry a black man.' And we can't say, 'I think we are all equal, but orientals live like sub-humans.'

Sometimes I try to be a bit more low-key, I try to be less evangelical, I try to be less angry. Usually I do not succeed. When my feelings threaten to overwhelm me, I take to the streets of Ho Chi Minh City. The streets are my safety-valve, the place where my anger is mollified and my pain dissipates. Ho Chi Minh City, like any large city, can be a tough town late at night. But these streets hold no fear for me. The children protect me, even down near the river which is one of the most dangerous parts of town. If I hear that a foreigner is taking children to a hotel down there, I do not hesitate. As I approach the river the street children come out of the darkness. They shake their fingers at me just the way I sometimes shake my fingers at them.

'Mama Tina, not good you here. Very dangerous for you,' they say. One of the older boys might make a stabbing motion towards my stomach and say, 'Dangerous here. Somebody do you.'

Eventually the children realize they cannot change my mind. Some unheard signal goes out and other children emerge from nowhere. One of them will say, 'Because you say *bui doi* Number One, we take care of you.' And they form a ring about me, a dozen or more children, sometimes almost twenty of them surround me as I press deeper and deeper into the heart of the darkness along the river.

If anyone approaches me the children grow very anxious. I suspect that some of them have their hands on their flick knives. I know if I ask them, they will deny having a knife. I shudder to think of what those children would do to anyone who threatened me. I am off limits to the criminals of Ho Chi Minh City.

One night when I was down by the river, some of the children ran to find Trung or Han and have them bring a motorbike to pick me up. Trung and Han and my landlady Madame Oanh were at my apartment wondering where I was. They were very nervous about my being out by myself. Madame Oanh jumped on to the back of Trung's motorbike while Han drove his own. They picked me up and lectured me more severely than ever before. By then it was almost 2 a.m. and as we drove through the streets our Hondas pulled close together in the dense and almost impenetrable flow of traffic that goes on all hours of the night in Ho Chi Minh City. I reached across and held Madame Oanh's hand.

'Shall we sing one for the road?' I asked her.

She smiled and nodded. I had been forgiven.

'Let's sing your song,' I said.

More than forty years ago Madame Oanh had a boyfriend whom she loved very much. They had a song that they frequently sang to each other. The boyfriend went to America and died there before he could return. Madame Oanh still has a piece of cracked and folded paper on which is written the words of their song. After we had been friends for a long time she told me her story and showed me the song. It was a song that I used to sing in Ireland.

When I suggest to Madame Oanh that we sing her song, her dark eyes always light up. On this occasion she held my hand tighter between the two motorbikes. Trung and Han were unsmiling. They were still cross with me. And I don't know what they thought about their two female passengers. I told them to stay together and not to let the bikes drift apart. So we drove through the late-night streets of Ho Chi Minh City, weaving as one through the traffic, while Madame Oanh and I held hands and sang:

> For ever, my darling, my heart will be true.
> Sweetheart for ever, I'll wait for you.
> We both made a promise that we'd never part.
> Let's steal a kiss, a kiss for ever, my sweetheart.

29

One morning I had breakfast with a friend at the Floating Hotel and afterwards, as I walked across the gangplank to the street, I noticed a young businesswoman in front of me. Her hair was cut in a very stylish manner, she was dressed in a smart suit, and she carried a briefcase.

'Get my car,' she ordered one of the attendants. Then she turned and her eyes sliced through me as if I did not exist. It is a look I have known since I was a child.

'Get my car,' I mimicked. 'Get my car. Jesus H. Christ.' As the young woman drove away in her Mercedes, I realized I am still a child of the Liberties, I am the same kid I was in Dublin.

The parallels between Ireland and Vietnam continue to amaze me. For years, outside powers have tried without success to dominate both countries. People of both countries have been reviled and ridiculed and patronized and underestimated but somehow they prevail.

Vietnam is something I can't explain. Vietnam has become part of my roots. When I leave the country, half of my heart remains. I can't go around with half a heart, so I must always come back to Vietnam. I am sure that before long I will work with children in Cambodia, Burma and Korea, but I will always return to Vietnam.

Recently I returned to Ireland to revisit the haunts of my childhood. I even drove to Clifden to see the industrial school. The convent is unchanged but the school is closed. It is still a grey and stark collection of buildings atop that cold and windswept hill. The wet wind from the Atlantic still lashes the old place. When I returned I came in through the back gate just as I did the first time I arrived so many years ago. The sight of a nun standing under the porch of one of the buildings caused my stomach to become weak and fluttery.

Afterwards I went to Dublin and visited Phoenix Park and the mollyers and the markets and even along the street by the quay where I was picked up that night so long ago. I walked in front of the Gresham and Shelbourne Hotels and peered in at the tourists and wondered what it would be like to go inside and have tea. I could have done that; I even said that I would. But I never did. The old ways are too strong.

When I was there I found myself reverting to the way I walked as a child: my hands jammed deep in my pockets, my shoulders rounded and stooped and my eyes filled with fear. In Dublin I am defensive. I feel a nobody. I cry very easily. If I live to be a hundred I will always cry when I return to Dublin.

I have such terrible conflict with Ireland. It is my country and I have a great love for it. But visiting the place reminds me of the injustice I suffered. I feel vulnerable and am overwhelmed with a sense of great loss.

Dr O'Connell taught me that we all have a shadow and we can never break loose entirely. But we can learn to live with it, to place the pain and anger in a little pot and put it to one side. Sometimes the top loosens and they escape. These feelings enable me to fight for the children. As long as there is breath in my body and strength in my back, I will never allow what happened to me to happen to other children.

The world of children is easier for me than the world of adults. With adults I am sometimes like a square peg in a round hole. But I can communicate with children, I can make them laugh, I know what children need. They need to be held by a father and a mother, they need someone to listen, they need to know the security of a cake baking in the oven when they come home.

Those who know me say that I am sometimes irrational in holding my course where it concerns the children. What they do not understand is that I am every child I see. I am every sick child. I am every abandoned child. I am every lost and defiant and angry child. I am every criminal child. And I am every child who wants nothing more than for someone simply to listen.

There are things in my work that I do not do as other people might do them. I don't work the way a large charity organization works; I do what works for me. Sometimes it is wrong and I get frustrated and know things would be different if I fitted more into the mould of what people expect. But I am what I am.

I realize there have been times when I hurt my cause. For instance, when I went to Singapore to talk to the priest with the wealthy parish I might have had different results had I not worn jeans and sandals. I have found that big organizations, be they church or society or foundation, want the people who come to them for aid to look as if they don't need it. I know when I go to the West to raise money for my sunshine children that it helps if I wear a nice dress and jewellery and high heels. But I am a child of the Liberties – a street child. And that is why I have done what I have done. I know that if I am worthy to take care of the children that God will find a way to help me continue my work.

It is my work with the children that brings me satisfaction, not the approval or the friendship of big people. Once I encountered a group of street children who are particularly tough. One of the boys carries a flick knife. Because I put up with no nonsense from the children, some of the tough guys run when they see me coming down the street. But on this day they did not run. Among them was a little boy named Lap who has a large tumour on his spinal column. The tumour is malignant and terminal; Lap will soon die.

I talked with the children for a while and then I asked them if they would visit the Catholic church with me. 'Let's say a prayer for Lap,' I said. They followed me. Along the way, some children I knew joined in and there was a crowd of perhaps two dozen of us when we arrived at church.

At first some of the children acted the way all children do. There was smirking, giggling, and a bit of acting-up. Then a choir began singing and the expression on the faces of the children was absolutely amazing. One of the toughest kids in the bunch had tears in his eyes. I smiled and nodded to let him know it was OK to cry. But he glared defiantly, angrily rubbed his hand and arm under his nose, folded his arms, and stared straight ahead.

We listened to the choir for a few minutes and then I took the children down to the altar and led them in a prayer for Lap. When we left the church, I held up Lap and kissed him and told him how much God loved him. I held Lap close to my heart. Then I noticed the little tough guy, whom I thought I had alienated, walking away. He returned a few minutes later carrying two ice-cream cones. One he gave to Lap, the other to me. I don't know where he found the money to buy them.

'Mama Tina, we love you,' he said.

I wish it were always that way. But it is not. And sometimes when the enormity of the task before me threatens to bow my back, and when I am almost overcome with desperation at the amount of money

I must raise to keep the Centre going, I take off for an evening to have a bit of fun. I start with a drink at the rooftop restaurant at the Rex Hotel. Sometimes my favourite waiter is there, the one who would not treat the children properly the day of the Christmas party. He dislikes me and tries to ignore me. I always smile, motion for him to come to my table, and then ask if he remembers me. He always apologizes and says he does not. But sure the little darling remembers me; after all, I threatened to break his neck if he didn't treat the children with more dignity. And just to make sure he doesn't forget how the world works, I order a big meal but take only a few bites. Then I tell him to bring me a bag so I can give the food to my children and I talk to him so he cannot walk away and I make him watch as I empty the plate into the bag. 'God bless you, me darling,' I say cheerfully. 'May the sun shine down on your beautiful brown eyes.'

And then I walk a few blocks to Maxims, a very famous night-club here in Ho Chi Minh City where I like to sing. Singing remains my salvation, my link with the world, the touch of Ireland in my soul. I sing the songs of Ireland, but I always end with a song that I have adopted as my own, a song I sing for the children. Before I begin the final song, I stand looking out over the crowd and wait until they are silent. Then I introduce myself to them.

'My name is Christina Noble and I work with the children of Ho Chi Minh City and the world. We have forgotten the child. We have forgotten that the child has rights. It is up to us to make sure children have a choice. As I sing this song for the children, I want you to really think about them.'

Maxims is on Dong Khoi Street down near the river and there are many street children in this neighbourhood at night. Maxims is at street level with enormous glass windows. And the PA system is piped on to the street. Whatever is taking place on the stage at Maxims can be heard for several blocks. The kids hear me singing and they begin drifting towards the club. They know that this last song is especially for them. They peep in the windows by the dozen. Many of them manage to sneak inside and stand in the corners.

I sometimes wonder what the audience, a truly international crowd, makes of this performance. It is evidently quite unlike anything they expected. Part of the way through the song I stop and make a plea on behalf of the children.

'I need your help. Vietnamese children are still suffering the effects of dioxin. Children in this city go from the womb on to the street. I'm only one woman. I need your help. We are many nations here tonight. But we are all one. Join hands and sing with me.'

I look up and the children are laughing. All around the room, in the windows, in the doors, in the corners, I can hear their wonderful laughter. They give me a thumbs-up and I can read their lips and I know what they are saying: 'Yeah, Mama Tina. *Bui doi* Number One. *Bui doi* Number One.'

CHRISTINA NOBLE CHILDREN'S FOUNDATION

Only through donations from people who care can we continue our work in helping the children of Vietnam and Mongolia. If you would like to make a donation or sponsor a child, you will find the address of your nearest Foundation office on the following pages.

GLOBAL OFFICES

AUSTRALIA
P.O. Box 9131
Scoresby
Victoria 3179

Bank Account Details: Christina Noble Children's Foundation, Commonwealth Bank
A/C No: 10706062
BSB No: 062 000

BELGIUM
De Villegasstraat 28
2600 Berchem
Antwerpen
ph: 3232185709
fax: 3227610041
email: belgium@cncf.org

FRANCE
Association Christina Noble
83 Boulevard de la Republique
92100 Boulogne
France
ph: 33 1 4608 1847
fax: 33 1 4233 4498
email: acnf@club-internet.fr
or france@cncf.org

Association Loi De 1901

GERMANY
c/o Mossbauer GmbH
Weissenburger
Strasse 10 Munchen 81667
ph: 49 89 489 2890
fax: 49 89 489 28950
email: n/a

HOLLAND
Weteringstraat 27
1017 SL
Amsterdam
ph: 31206276577
fax: 31204222731
email: holland@cncf.org

Bank Account Details
Postbank gironummber 449
Kamer van Koophandel
Stichringenregister
Number: S213312

HONG KONG
House 2/3 Consort Rise
Pok Fu lam
Hong Kong
ph:852 2817 8646
fax: 852 2818 6124
email: hongkong@cncf.org

Bank Account Details:
Hong Kong Bank
A/C no: 500-316153-838
Charity File No: 91/4639

IRELAND
Postal Address:
44 Grafton Street
Dublin 2
Office Address:
14 South Anne Street
Dublin 2
Phone: + 353 1 671 5729
email: ireland@cncf.org

Bank Account Details:
Allied Irish Bank
Sort Code: 93-12-33
A/C No: 41516084
Charity Registration Number:
Chy 12636

MONGOLIA
P.O. Box 74
Post Office 48
Ulaanbaatar
ph: (976-11) 323060.
325945, 327446
fax: (976-11) 323060
email: mongolia@cncf.org

Bank Account Details:
Trade & Development Bank
A/C No: 212834 86
Registered Charity Number:
1036025

NEW ZEALANDa
c/o Green & McCahill
374 Church Street
Penrose
Auckland
ph: 64 9 579 5005
fax: 64 9 579 2783
email: erin@gmltd.co.nz

UNITED KINGDOM
1st Floor
114-146 Buckingham Palace
Road
London SW1W 9TR
ph: 44 20 7233 1413
fax: 44 20 7233 1424
email: uk@cncf.org

Bank Account Details:
Natwest Bank Plc
Sort code: 60-24-20
A/C no: 03722090
Registered Charity Number:
1007484

USA
email: usa@cncf.org

Bank Account Details
Allied Irish Bank
New York Branch
405 11022
Routing Number: 026008853
A/C No: 010017961

VIETNAM
P.O. Box 386
Saigon Post Office Centre
Ho Chi Minh City
ph: 84 8 932 6484
fax: 84 8 932 7276
email: vietnam@cncf.org

Bank Account Details:
Christina Noble Children's
Foundation
Hong Kong and Shanghai Banking
Corporation
75 Pham Hong Thai Street, District 1,
Ho Chi Minh City, Vietnam
A/C No: 001-018548-021
Registered Charity Number: 038/UD
Committee for Non-Governmental
Affairs/Vietnam

INTERNET HOMEPAGE ADDRESS:
http://www.cncf.org

CNCF GLOBAL E-MAIL ADDRESS:
cncfinternational@cncf.org

Information: info@cncf.org

MAMA TINA
by Christina Noble
with Gretta Curran Browne

The inspiring sequel to *Bridge Across My Sorrows.*

When she told the story of her early life as a Dublin street-child in her bestselling autobiography *Bridge Across My Sorrows* Christina Noble had no idea that it would prove an inspiration for so many others who had suffered childhood pain and rejection.

In 1989, driven by a dream and by the memory of her own past, she travelled 6,000 miles to Vietnam, a country of great beauty where war has left a terrible legacy. Against extraordinary odds she opened the Christina Noble Children's Foundation, a haven of food, beds, medical aid and schooling where the street children of Saigon can find safety and new beginnings under the protection of 'Mama Tina'.

In this vivid and moving book Christina's compelling story continues with the amazing tale of what she and her Foundation have achieved. She takes us from the streets of Saigon to the Children's Prisons of Mongolia. A staunch campaigner for children's rights, for her there are no frontiers, only a world filled with children reaching out.

'*Mama Tina* tells the intensely moving stories of some of the children she has helped, and also reflects, with renewed insight, on her own life'
Harpers & Queen

'Most of us feel impotent in the face of Third World poverty, but Christina Noble proves it's possible to help if we choose to'
Woman's Journal

0 552 14632 3